The Brooklyn Murders

Nadakkavu, Kozhikode, Kerala, 673011
www.insightpublica.com
e-mail: insightpublica@gmail.com

Title: **The Brooklyn Murders**
Author: **G. D. H. Cole**
First Insight Edition: August 2024
Copyright © Reserved
All rights reserved.
Printed and Published by
InsightinPublica Printers & Publishers Pvt. Ltd.
ISBN 978-93-5517-966-1
₹500

The Brooklyn Murders

G. D. H. Cole

G. D. H. Cole

(25 September 1889 - 14 January 1959)

George Douglas Howard Cole was an English political theorist, economist, and historian. As a believer in common ownership of the means of production, he theorised guild socialism. He belonged to the Fabian Society and was an advocate for the co-operative movement.

Contents

Chapter I
A Family Celebration

At seventy Sir Vernon Brooklyn was still the outstanding figure in the theatrical world. It was, indeed, ten years since he had made his farewell appearance on the stage; and with a consistency rare among the members of his profession, he had persisted in making his first farewell also his last. He had also for some time past resigned to younger men the actual direction of his vast theatrical enterprises, which included five great West End theatres and a steady stream of touring companies in the provinces and overseas. Both as actor and as manager, he was wont to say, his work was over; but as Chairman of the Brooklyn Dramatic Corporation, which conducted all its work under his name, he was almost as much as ever in the eye of the public.

Like most men who have risen by their own efforts, aided by fortune and by a public which takes a pleasure in idolatry, to positions of wide authority, Sir Vernon had developed, perhaps to excess, the habit of getting his own way. Thus, although his niece and house-keeper, Joan Cowper, and his near relatives and friends had done their best to dissuade him from coming to London, he had ignored their protests, and insisted on celebrating his seventieth birthday in the London house, formerly the scene of his triumphs, which he now seldom visited. Sir Vernon now spent most of his time at the great country house in Sussex which he had bought ten years before from Lord Fittleworth. There he entertained largely, and there was no reason why he should not have taken the advice of his relatives and his doctor, and gathered his friends around him to celebrate what he was pleased to call his "second majority." But Sir Vernon had made up his mind, and it was therefore in the old house just off Piccadilly that his guests assembled for dinner on Midsummer Day, June 25th.

Like Sir Vernon's country place, the old house had a history. He had bought it, and the grounds with their magnificent garden frontage on Piccadilly, looking over the Green Park, from Lord Liskeard, when that nobleman had successfully gambled away the fortune which had made him, at one time, the richest man in England who had no connection with trade. Sir Vernon had turned his purchase to good use. Facing Piccadilly, but standing well back in its garden from the street, he had built the great Piccadilly Theatre, the perfect playhouse in which, despite its size and large seating capacity, every member of the audience could both see and hear. The theatre covered a lot of ground; but, when it was built, there still remained not only the old mansion fronting upon its side-street—a cul de sac used by its visitors alone—but also, between it and the theatre, a pleasant expanse of garden. For some years Sir Vernon had lived in the house; and there he had also worked, converting the greater part of the ground floor into a palatial set of offices for the Brooklyn Dramatic Corporation. On his retirement from active work, he had kept in his own hands only the first floor, which he fitted as a flat to house him on his visits to town. On the second floor he had installed his nephew, John Prinsep, who had succeeded him as managing director of the Corporation. The third floor was given over to the servants who attended to the whole house. It was in this house that Sir Vernon was celebrating his birthday, and his guests were to dine with him in the great Board Room of the Corporation on the ground floor—formerly the banqueting hall of generations of Liskeards, in which many a political plot had been hatched, and many a diner carried helpless from under the table in the bad days of the Prince Regent.

Between the house and the tall back of the theatre lay the garden, in which a past Lord Liskeard with classical tastes had erected a model Grecian temple and a quantity of indifferent antique statuary, the fruits of his sojourn at the Embassy of Constantinople.

In this garden, before dinner was served, a number of Sir Vernon's guests had already gathered. The old man had been persuaded, despite the brilliant midsummer weather, to remain in the house; but Joan Cowper and John Prinsep were there to do the honours on his behalf. As Harry Lucas came into the garden, John Prinsep was laughingly, as he said, "showing off the points" of a dilapidated Hercules who, club, lion-skin and all, was slowly mouldering under the trees at one end of the lawn. The stone club had come loose, and Prinsep had taken it from the statue, and was playfully threatening to do classical execution with it upon the persons of his guests. Seeing Lucas, he put the club back into the broken hand of the statue, and came across the lawn to bid him welcome.

"You're the last to arrive, Mr. Lucas," said he. "You see it's quite a family affair this evening."

It was quite a family affair. Of the eight persons now on the lawn, six were members of the Brooklyn family by birth or marriage; Lucas was Sir Vernon's oldest friend and collaborator; and young Ellery, the remaining member of the party, was Lucas's ward, and was usually to be found, when he had his will, somewhere in the neighbourhood of Joan Cowper. As Sir Vernon had fully made up his mind that Joan was to marry Prinsep, and there was supposed to be some sort of engagement between them, Ellery's attentions were not welcome to Prinsep, and there was no love lost between the two men.

But there was no sign of this in Prinsep's manner this evening. He seemed to be in unusually good spirits, rather in contrast to his usual humour. For Prinsep was not generally regarded as good company. Since he had succeeded Sir Vernon in the business control of the Brooklyn Corporation, of which he was managing director, he had grown more and more preoccupied with affairs, and had developed a brusque manner which may have served him well in dealing with visitors who wanted something for nothing, but was distinctly out of place in the social interchange of his leisure hours. Prinsep had, indeed, his pleasures. He was reputed a heavy drinker, whose magnificent natural constitution prevented him from showing any of the signs of dissipation. Many of Prinsep's acquaintances—who were as many as his friends were few—had seen him drink more than enough to put an ordinary man under the table; but none had ever seen him the worse for drink, and he was never better at a bargain than when the other man had taken some glasses less than he, but still a glass too much. Men said that he took his pleasures sadly: certainly they had never been allowed to interfere with his power of work; and often, after a hard evening, he would go to his study and labour far into the night. But, for this occasion, his sullenness seemed to have left him, and his rather harsh laugh rang out repeatedly over the garden.

Lucas had never liked Prinsep; and he soon found himself one of a group that included Joan and Ellery and Mary Woodman, a cousin of the Brooklyns who lived with Joan and helped her to keep Sir Vernon's house. Presently Joan drew him aside.

"Uncle Harry," she said, "there's something I want to tell you."

Lucas was, in fact, no relation of the Brooklyns; but from their childhood Joan and George Brooklyn had known him as "Uncle Harry," and had made him their confidant in many of their early troubles. The habit had stuck; and now Joan had a very serious trouble to tell him.

"You must do what you can to help me," she said. "I've told Uncle Vernon again to-day that on no account will I ever marry John, and he absolutely refuses to listen to me. He says it's all settled, and his will's made on that understanding, and that we're engaged, and a whole lot more. I must make him realise that I won't; but you know what he is. I want you to speak to him for me."

Lucas thought a moment before replying. Then, "My dear," he said, "I'm very sorry about it, and you know I will do what I can; but is this quite the time? We should only be accused, with some truth, of spoiling Sir Vernon's birthday. Let it alone for a few days, and then I'll try talking to him. But it won't be easy, at any time."

"Yes, uncle; but there's a special reason why it must be done to-night. Uncle Vernon tells me that he is going to announce the terms of his will, and that he will speak of what he calls John's and my 'engagement.' I really can't allow that to happen. I don't really mind about the will, or John getting the money; but it must not be publicly given out that John is to have me as well. Uncle Vernon has no right to leave me as part of his 'net personalty' to John or anybody else."

Lucas sighed. He foresaw an awkward interview; for Sir Vernon was not an easy man to deal with, and latterly every year had made him more difficult. But he saw that he was in for it, and, with a reassuring word to Joan, passed into the house in search of his host.

As Joan turned back to rejoin the others, Robert Ellery stepped quickly to her side. Slim and slightly built, he offered a strong contrast to Prinsep's tall, sturdy figure. Joan's two lovers were very different types. Ellery was not strictly handsome; but he had an invincible air of being on good terms with the world which, with a ready smile and a clear complexion, were fully as effective as the most approved type of manly beauty. Still under thirty, he was just beginning to make himself a name. A play of his had recently been produced with success by the Brooklyn Corporation: one of his detective novels had made something of a hit, and his personal popularity was helping him to win rapid recognition for his undoubted talent as a writer. Moreover, his guardian, Lucas, was a big figure in the dramatic and literary world, knew everybody who was worth knowing, and had a high opinion of the ability of his ward.

It was obvious that Ellery was in love with Joan. Few men had less power of concealing what was in them, and everybody in the Brooklyn circle, except Sir Vernon himself, was well aware that Ellery thought the world of Joan, and more than suspected that she thought the world of him. Of course, the theory could not be mentioned in Prinsep's presence; but, when he was not there, the situation was freely discussed. George Brooklyn and his wife always maintained that, even if Joan did not marry Ellery, she would certainly not marry Prinsep. Carter Woodman, Sir Vernon's lawyer as well as his cousin, held firmly to the opposite opinion, and often hinted that Sir Vernon's will would settle the question in Prinsep's favour; but then, as George said, Woodman was a lawyer and his mind naturally ran on the marriage settlements rather than the marriage itself.

The Brooklyns were neither particularly united nor particularly quarrelsome, in their own family circles. They had their bickerings and their mutual dislikes to about the average extent; but more than the normal amount of family solidarity had manifested itself in their dealings with the outer world. Two "outsiders," Lucas and Ellery, were indeed recognised almost as members of the family; and, on the other hand, one black sheep, Sir Vernon's brother Walter, had been driven forth and refused further recognition. For the rest, they stuck together, and accepted for the most part unquestioningly Sir

Vernon's often tyrannical, but usually benevolent, authority. If Joan had been a real Brooklyn, George would hardly have been so confident that she would not marry Prinsep.

But Joan was not really a Brooklyn at all. She was the step-daughter of Walter, who had for a time retrieved his fallen fortunes, fallen through his own fault, by marrying the rich widow of Cowper, the "coffee king." The widow had then obligingly died, and Walter Brooklyn had lost no time in spending her money, including the large sum left in trust for Joan by her mother. But it was not this, so much as Walter's manner of life, that had caused Joan, at twenty-one, to say that she would live with him no longer. Sir Vernon, to whom she was strongly attached, had then offered her a home, and for five years she had been in fact mistress of his house, and hostess at his lavish entertainment of his theatrical friends. From the first Sir Vernon had set his heart on her marrying his nephew, John Prinsep, who was ten years her senior. But Joan was a young woman with a will of her own; and for five years she had resisted the combined pressure of Sir Vernon and of John Prinsep himself, without any success in persuading either Sir Vernon to give up the idea, or Prinsep of the hopelessness of his suit. Prinsep persisted in believing that she would "come round," though of late her growing friendship with Ellery had made him more anxious to secure her consent to a definite engagement.

Ordinarily, Prinsep had a way of scowling when he saw Joan and Ellery together; but to-night he seemed without a care as he came up to Joan and invited her to lead the way indoors. Dinner was already served; and Sir Vernon with Lucas was waiting for them all to come in.

There, in the great Board Room of the Corporation, they offered, one by one, their congratulations to the old man. An enemy had once said of Sir Vernon Brooklyn that he was the finest stage gentleman in Europe—both on and off the stage.

The saying was unjust, but there was enough of truth in it to sting. Sir Vernon was a little apt to act off the stage; and the habit had perhaps grown on him since his retirement. To-night, with his fine silver hair and keen, well-cut features, he was very much the gentleman, dispensing noble hospitality with just too marked a sense of its magnificence. But it was Sir Vernon's day, and his guests were there to do his will, to draw him out into reminiscence, to enhance his sense of having made the most of life's chances, and of being sure to leave behind him those who would carry on the great tradition. The talk turned to the building of the Piccadilly Theatre. The old man told them how, from the first days of his success, he had made up his mind to build himself the finest theatre in London. From the first he had his eye on the site of Liskeard House; and it had taken him twenty years to persuade the Liskeards, impoverished as they were, to sell it for such a purpose. At last he had secured the site, and then again his foresight had been rewarded. Not for nothing had he paid for George Brooklyn's training as an architect, based on the lad's own bent, and given him the opportunity to study playhouse architecture in every quarter of the globe. The Piccadilly Theatre was not only George Brooklyn's masterpiece: it was, structurally, acoustically, visually, for comfort, in short in every way, the finest theatre in the world. It was also the best paying theatre. And, the old man said, if in his day he had been the finest actor, so was George's wife still the finest actress, if only she would not waste on domesticity the gift that was meant for mankind. For Mrs. George Brooklyn, as Isabelle Raven, had been the star of the Piccadilly Theatre until she had married its designer and quitted the stage, sorely against Sir Vernon's will.

Sir Vernon was in his best form; and the talk, led by him, was rapid and, at times, brilliant. But there was at least one of those present to whom it made no appeal; for Joan Cowper was painfully anxious as to the result of Lucas's interview with Sir Vernon. Several times she caught his eye; but, although he smiled at her down the table, his look brought her no reassurance. At last, when the servants had withdrawn after the last course, Joan rose, purposing to lead the ladies to the drawing-room. But Sir Vernon waved her back to her seat, saying that, before they left the table, there was something which he wanted them all to hear. Clearly there was nothing for it but to wait; but Joan made up her mind that, if Sir Vernon spoke of her publicly as engaged to Prinsep, not even the spoiling of his birthday party should stop her from speaking her mind.

Chapter II
Sir Vernon's Will

"All of us here," began Sir Vernon, with a well-satisfied look round the table, "are such good friends that we can be absolutely frank one with another. I am an old man; and I expect that almost all of you have at one time or another wondered—I put it bluntly—what you will get when I die. It is very natural that you should do so; and I have come to the conclusion that you had better know exactly how you stand. Carter here has, of course, as my legal adviser, known from the first what is in my will; and now I want all of you to know, in order that you may expect neither too much nor too little. I fear I am still a moderately healthy old man, or so my doctor tells me, and you may, therefore, still have some time to wait; but at my age it is well to be prepared, and I felt that you ought not to be left any longer in the dark."

At this point several of Sir Vernon's auditors attempted to speak, but he waved them into silence.

"No, let me have my say without telling me what I know already," he continued. "I know that you would tell me truly that nothing is further from your thoughts than to wish me out of the way. It is not because I am in any doubt on that head that I am speaking to you; but because this is a business matter, and it is well to know in advance what one's prospects are. Listen to me, then, and I will tell you, as far as I can, exactly how the thing stands.

"To several of you I have already made substantial gifts. You, John, and you, George, have each received £50,000 in shares of the Company. You, Joan, have £10,000 worth of shares standing in your name. These sums are apart from my will, and the bequests which I propose to make are in addition to these.

"As nearly as Carter here can tell me, I am now worth, on a conservative estimate, some eight or nine hundred thousand pounds. Carter works it out that, when all death duties have been paid, there will be at least £600,000 to be divided among you. In apportioning my property I have worked on the basis of this sum. I have divided it, first, into two portions—£100,000 for smaller legacies, and £500,000 to be shared by my residuary legatees.

"First, let me tell you my smaller bequests, which concern most of you. To you, Lucas, my oldest and closest friend, I have left nothing but a few personal mementoes. You have enough already; and it is at your express wish that I do as I have done. To my young friend and your ward, Ellery, I leave £5000. I understand that he will have enough when you die; but this sum may be welcome to him if, as I expect, I am the first to go. To you, Carter, I leave £20,000. You, too, have ample means; but our close connection and the work you have done so well for me and for the Company call for recognition. To Mrs. Carter—to you, Helen—I have left no money—you will share in what your husband receives—but I will show you later the jewels which will be yours when I die. To you, Mary, who, with Joan, have lived with me and cared for me, I leave £20,000, enough to make you independent. There are but two more of my smaller legacies I need mention. The rest are either to servants or to charitable institutions. But you all know that, for many years past, I have not been on good terms with my brother Walter. I have no mind, since I have other relatives who are far dearer to me, to leave him another fortune to squander like the last; but I am leaving in trust for him the sum of £10,000, of which he will receive the income during his life. On his death, the sum will pass to my dear niece, Joan, to whom I shall also leave absolutely the sum of £40,000. This, with the £10,000 which she had already, will make her independent, but not rich.

"You may be surprised, Joan, that I leave you no more; but, when I tell you of my principal bequests, you will understand the reason. The residue, then, of my property, amounting to at least £500,000, I leave equally between my two nephews, John Prinsep and George Brooklyn. You too, therefore, will both be rich men. As so large a sum is involved, I have thought it right to make provision for the decease of either of you. Should George die before me, which God forbid, you, Marian, as his wife, will receive half the sum which he would have received under my will. The other half will pass to John, as the surviving residuary legatee. Should John die, the half of his share will pass to Joan—a provision the reason for which you will all, I think, readily appreciate. I have not made provision for the death of both my nephews—for an event so unlikely hardly calls for precaution. But should God bring so heavy a misfortune upon us, the residue of my property would then pass, as the will now stands, to my nearest surviving relative."

While Sir Vernon was still speaking Joan had been trying to break in upon him. Prinsep was able to check her for a moment, but at this point she insisted on speaking. "Uncle," she said, "there is something I must say to you in view of what you have just told us. I am very sorry if my saying it spoils your birthday; but I must say it all the same. What you have left to me is more than enough, and certainly all that I expect, or have any right to expect. But I cannot bear that you should misunderstand me, or that I should seem, by saying nothing now, to accept the position. I want you to understand quite definitely that I have no intention of marrying John. I am not engaged to him; and I never shall be. It's not that I have anything against him—it's simply that I don't want—and don't mean—to marry him. I'm sorry if it hurts you to hear me say this; but you have publicly implied that we are to be married, and I couldn't keep silent after that."

Sir Vernon's face had flushed when Joan began to speak, and he had seemed on the point of breaking in upon her. But he had evidently thought better of it; for he let her have her say. But now he answered coldly, and with a suppressed but obvious irritation.

"My dear Joan, you know quite well that this marriage has been an understood thing among us all. I don't pretend to know what fancy has got into your head just lately. But, at all events, let us hear no more of it to-night. Already what you have said has quite spoilt the evening for me."

Then, as Joan tried to speak, he added, "No, please, no more about it now. If you wish you can speak to me about it in the morning."

Joan still tried to say something; but at this point Lucas cut quickly into the conversation. Actor-managers, he said, had all the luck. You would not find a poor devil of a playwright with the best part of a million to leave to his descendants. And then, with obvious relief, the rest helped to steer the talk back to less dangerous topics. Sir Vernon seemed to forget his annoyance and launched into a stream of old theatrical reminiscence, Lucas capping each of his stories with another. The cheerfulness of the latter part of the evening was, perhaps, a trifle forced, and there were two, Joan herself and young Ellery, who took in it only the smallest possible part. But Prinsep, Lucas, and Carter Woodman made up for these others; and an outsider would have pronounced Sir Vernon's party a complete success.

There was no withdrawal of the ladies that evening, for, after her discomfiture, Joan made no move towards the drawing-room. In the end it was Prinsep who broke up the party with a word to Sir Vernon. "Come, uncle," he said, "ten o'clock and time for our roystering to end. I have work I must do about the theatre and it's time some of us were getting home."

Then Joan seemed to wake up to a sense of her duties, and Sir Vernon was promptly bustled off upstairs, the guests gradually taking their leave.

Most of them had not far to go. Lucas had his car waiting to run him back to his house at Hampstead. Ellery had rooms in Chelsea, and announced his intention, as the night was fine, of walking back by the parks. The George Brooklyns and the Woodmans, who lived in the outer suburbs at Banstead and Esher, were staying the night in town, at the famous Cunningham, on the opposite side of Piccadilly, the best hotel in London in the estimation of foreign potentates and envoys as well as of Londoners themselves. George Brooklyn, saying that he had an appointment, asked Woodman to see his wife home, and left Marian and the Woodmans outside the front door of the Piccadilly theatre, while they crossed the road towards their hotel.

The guests having departed, Liskeard House began to settle down for the night. On the ground floor, indeed, there began a scurry of servants clearing up after the dinner. On the first floor Joan, having seen Sir Vernon to his room, sat in the long-deserted drawing-room, talking over the evening's events with her friend, Mary Woodman, and reiterating, to a sympathetic listener, her determination never to marry John Prinsep. Meanwhile, upstairs on the second floor, John Prinsep sat at his desk in his remote study with a heavy frown on his face, very unlike the seemingly light-hearted and amiable expression he had worn all the evening. Sir Vernon's birthday party was over, but there were strange things preparing for the night.

Chapter III
Murder

John Prinsep was a man who valued punctuality and cultivated regular habits, both in himself and in others. At 10.15 punctually each night a servant came to him to collect any late letters for the post. Thereafter, unless some visitor had to be shown up, he was left undisturbed, and no one entered his flat on the second floor of Liskeard House until the next morning. The servants, who slept on the floor above, had access to it by a staircase of their own, and did not need to pass through Prinsep's quarters.

No less regular were the arrangements for the morning. At eight o'clock precisely, Prinsep's valet called him, bringing the morning papers and letters and a cup of tea. At the same time, other servants began the work of dusting and cleaning the flat, a long suite of rooms running the whole length of the house. Prinsep's bedroom, opening out of his study, and accessible also from the end of the long corridor, was a pleasant room looking out over the old garden towards the back of the theatre.

On the morning after the birthday dinner, Prinsep's valet approached the bedroom door with some trepidation, for he had overslept himself and was at least five minutes late—an offence which his master would not readily forgive. Repeated knocks bringing no reply, Morgan slipped into the room, only to find that the bed had not been slept in, and that there was no sign that Prinsep had been there at all since he had dressed for dinner on the previous evening. Closing the door, Morgan walked back along the corridor to consult his fellow-servants. He found Winter, who was superintending the dusting of the drawing-room.

"Did you see the master last night?" he asked. Winter answered with a nod, and added, "Yes, I took some letters from him for the post as usual."

"Did he say anything about going out? His bed has not been slept in, and he's not in his room this morning."

Winter replied that Prinsep had said nothing, and the two men walked down the corridor together to take a look round.

At this moment there came a terrible scream from the study, and a scared maid-servant came running out straight into Morgan's arms. "Oh, Mr. Morgan—the master," she sobbed, "I'm sure he's dead."

The two men-servants made all haste into the study. There, stretched on the floor beside his writing-table lay John Prinsep. A glance told them that he was dead, and showed the apparent cause in a knife, the handle of which protruded from his chest, just about the region of the heart. Morgan went down on his knees beside the body, and felt the pulse. "Get out quick," he said, "and stop those girls from kicking up a row. He's dead, right enough."

Morgan's voice was agitated, indeed; but it hardly showed the grief that might have been expected in an exemplary valet mourning for the death of his master. Winter made no reply, but left the room to quiet the servants. Then he came back and telephoned first for the police and then for the dead man's doctor, who promised to be with them inside of half an hour. As he sat at the telephone he warned Morgan. "Don't disturb a thing. If we're not careful one of us may get run in for this job."

Morgan meanwhile had satisfied himself beyond a doubt that Prinsep was dead. Leaving the body he turned to Winter. "Some one will have to tell Miss Joan, I suppose. I'll go and find her maid. Meanwhile you stay on guard here."

Winter's guard was not for long. In less than ten minutes Morgan returned. "I've seen Miss Joan," he said, "and she's gone to tell Sir Vernon. Here are the police coming upstairs."

The telephone message had, by a lucky accident, found Inspector Blaikie already at Vine Street, and it was he, with two constables and a sergeant, who had come round to the house at once. The constables remained downstairs, while he and the sergeant made a preliminary examination. Winter told him that nothing had been disturbed, except that they had touched the body in order to make sure that Prinsep was dead, and used the telephone to communicate with the doctor and the police.

"No doubt about his being dead," said Inspector Blaikie, after a brief examination of the body. "Dead some hours, so far as I can see. And no doubt about the cause of death, either"—and he pointed to the knife still in the body. "Has either of you ever seen that knife before?"

Both Winter and Morgan took a good look at the shaft, but disclaimed ever having seen the knife. "It wasn't his—I can tell you that," said Morgan. "I know everything he had in the study, and I'm dead sure it wasn't here yesterday."

"Hallo," said the inspector suddenly, "this is curious. There's a mark on the back of the head that shows he must have been struck a heavy blow. It might have killed him by itself—must have stunned him, I should say. Well, we'll leave that for the doctors." So saying, the inspector got up from his knees and began to make a minute examination of the room. "Here, you two," he said to Morgan and Winter, "clear out of here for the present, and stay in the next room till I send for you."

Inspector Blaikie was a careful man. Everything in the room was rapidly submitted to a detailed examination, the results of which the sergeant wrote down as his superior dictated them. They were neither surprisingly rich nor surprisingly meagre. Of fingermarks there were plenty, but these might well prove to be those of Prinsep himself, or of other persons whose presence in the room was quite natural. Identifiable footmarks there were none.

Robbery, unless of some special object, did not appear to have been the motive of the murderer. Considerable sums of money were in the drawers of Prinsep's desk; but neither these nor the other contents of the drawers seemed to have been in any way disturbed. A safe stood unopened in a corner of the room. The dead man's watch and other valuables had been left intact upon him. Either the murderer had left in great haste without accomplishing his purpose, or that purpose did not include robbery of any ordinary kind.

Inspector Blaikie directed his special attention to the papers lying on the dead man's desk, which he seemed to have been working upon when he was disturbed. These, it did not take the inspector long to discover, related to the financial affairs of Walter Brooklyn who, as he soon ascertained later by a few questions, was the brother of Sir Vernon, a man about town of shady reputation, and known to be head over ears in debt. The papers seemed to contain some sort of abstract statement of his liabilities, with a series of letters from him to Sir Vernon asking for financial assistance.

"H'm," said the inspector to himself, "these may easily have a bearing on the case."

But there were other interesting discoveries to come. The inspector was now informed that the doctor had arrived. He ordered that he should be shown up immediately, and suspended his examination of the room to greet the new-comer. Dr. Manton had been for some years the dead man's medical adviser; but no other member of the Brooklyn family had been under his care. Something in common with him had perhaps caused Prinsep to forsake the staid family physician in his favour; but this hardly appeared on the surface. Prinsep was heavily built and sullen in expression: Dr. Manton was slim built and rather jaunty, with a habit of wearing clothes far less funereal than the normal etiquette of the medical profession seems to dictate. He entered now, flung a rapid and seemingly quite cheerful "Good-morning, inspector—bad business this, I hear," to Blaikie, and went at once down on his knees beside the body. "Bad business—bad business," he continued to repeat to himself, in a perfectly cheerful tone of voice, as he made his preliminary examination. He made a noise between his teeth as he touched the hilt of the knife still embedded in Prinsep's chest: then, as he saw the contusion on the back of the head, he said "H'm, h'm." Then he relapsed into silence, which he broke a moment later by whistling a tune softly to himself.

"Well," said the inspector, "what's the report?"

The doctor made no answer for a moment. Then he said, "Have him carried into the bedroom. I want to make a fuller examination. I'll talk to you when I've done."

"Very well," said the inspector; and he went to the door and called to the sergeant to bring up the two constables to move the body. Heavily they marched into the room, lifted up the dead man, and bore him away, the doctor following. But, as they raised the body from the floor, an interesting object came to light. Underneath John Prinsep's body had lain a crumpled pocket-handkerchief. The inspector pounced upon it. In the corner was plainly marked the name of George Brooklyn.

"Who's George Brooklyn?" Inspector Blaikie called out to the doctor in the adjoining room. The doctor came to the door, and saw the handkerchief in the inspector's hand. "Hallo, what's that you've got?" he said. "George Brooklyn is

Prinsep's cousin, old Sir Vernon's other nephew. An architect, I believe, by profession."

"Thanks. This appears to be his handkerchief," the inspector answered. "It was under the body."

"H'm. Well, that's none of my business," said the doctor, and turned back into the bedroom.

There, a minute or two later, Inspector Blaikie followed him, leaving the sergeant on guard in the room where the tragedy had occurred. But first he carefully packed up and transferred to his handbag the handkerchief, the papers from the desk, and certain other spoils of his search.

"Well, what do you make of it now?" he asked Dr. Manton.

The doctor had by this time drawn the knife from the wound, and this he now handed silently to the inspector, who examined it curiously, felt its edge, and finally wrapped it up and put it away in his bag with the rest of his findings. Then he turned again to the doctor.

"A shocking business, inspector," said the latter, still with his curiously cheerful air, "and, I may add, rather an odd one. The man was not killed with the knife, and the knife wound has not actually touched any vital part. He was killed, I have no doubt, by the blow on the back of the head—a far easier form of murder for any one who is not an expert. It was a savage blow. The wound in the chest, I have little hesitation in saying, was inflicted subsequently, probably when the man was already dead. As I say, it would not have killed him, and there are also indications that it was inflicted after death—the comparative absence of bleeding and the general condition of the wound, for example."

"H'm, you say the man was killed with a knock on the head, and the assassin then stabbed him in order to make doubly sure."

"Pardon me, inspector, I say nothing of the sort. I say that the blow on the back of the head was the cause of death, and that the knife wound was, in all probability, subsequent. Anything about assassins and their motives and methods is your business and not mine."

"I accept the correction," said the inspector, smiling. "But the inference seems practically certain. Why else should the murderer have stabbed a dead man?"

"I have no theory, inspector. I simply give you the medical evidence, and leave you to draw the inferences for yourself."

"But perhaps you can give me some valuable information. I believe you were Mr. Prinsep's doctor."

"Yes, and I think I may say a personal friend."

"What sort of man was he? Anything wrong, physically?"

"No; there ought to have been, from the way he used his body. But he had the constitution of an ox. He limped, owing to an accident some years ago. But otherwise—oh, as healthy as you like."

"And, apart from that, what was he like?"

"I got on well with him; but there were many who did not. A tough customer, hard in business and not ready in making friends."

"What terms was he on with his family—with Mr. George Brooklyn, for instance?"

"Come now, inspector, this is hardly fair. I barely know George Brooklyn. I don't think he and Prinsep liked each other; but there had been no quarrel so far as I know. I suppose you are thinking of the handkerchief."

"I have to think of these things."

While he was speaking the inspector opened his bag and took out the knife again.

"A curious knife this," he said. "Perhaps you can tell me whether it is a surgical instrument."

"Not so curious, when you know what it is. I do happen to know, though it has nothing to do with my profession. My son is a mechanical draughtsman, and he has several. Knives of this type are sold by most firms which supply architects' and draughtsmen's materials."

"H'm, what did you say was Mr. George Brooklyn's profession?"

"I believe he is an architect, and a very promising one."

"That, doctor, may make this knife a most valuable clue."

"I do not choose to consider it in that light. Clues are not my affair, I am glad to say."

"Well, they are my business, and I shall certainly have to make further inquiries about Mr. George Brooklyn."

"Oh, inquire away," said the doctor. "But I fancy you will find George Brooklyn quite above suspicion."

The inspector's eyes showed, just for an instant, a dangerous gleam. Then, "And is there anything else you can tell me?" he asked.

"Nothing else, I think," said the doctor. "I'm afraid you won't find it much of a clue." And with that and a few words more about the necessary inquest, the doctor took his leave.

The inspector went back into the study. "Ask those two men who are waiting to step in here, will you?" he said to the sergeant. Morgan and Winter were duly brought in. "Sergeant, while I talk to these two men, I want you to make a thorough examination of the rest of the house. Leave nothing to chance. House and garden, I mean. And make me a sketch plan of the whole place while you're about it."

"Now," said the inspector, when the sergeant had withdrawn, "there are a number of questions I want to ask you. First, who, as far as you know, was the last person to see the deceased alive? Which of you was in charge of the front door last night?"

"I was, sir," replied Winter.

"Well, then," said the inspector, "I will begin with you. Morgan can go back to the other room for the present, and I will send for him when I want him. Now, when did you yourself last see Mr. Prinsep?"

"At 10.30 last night, sir, when I went up to fetch his letters for the post."

"Did you notice anything unusual, or did he make any remark?"

"He just gave me the letters. He didn't say anything. He seemed in a bad temper, but that was nothing out of the ordinary."

"I see. There was nothing remarkable. Do you know if any one saw him after you?"

"Yes, sir. At about a quarter to eleven Mr. George Brooklyn called and asked for Mr. Prinsep. I told him I thought Mr. Prinsep was in, and he said he would find his own way up."

"And do you know when Mr. George Brooklyn came out?"

"Yes, I happened to catch sight of him crossing the hall to the front door about three-quarters of an hour later—somewhere about half-past eleven. We were in the dining-room clearing up, and several of us saw him go out."

"You say 'clearing up.' Had there been some entertainment in the house last night?"

"Yes, sir. It was Sir Vernon Brooklyn's family party. His seventieth birthday, sir. Besides those in the house there were Mr. and Mrs. George, Mr. Carter Woodman, sir—the solicitor, who is also Sir Vernon's cousin—and his wife, and Mr. Lucas—and, yes, Mr. Ellery."

"When did they leave?"

"They all left a minute or two after ten o'clock. Mr. and Mrs. George and the Woodmans are staying at the Cunningham, sir, and they walked. Mr. Lucas—the playwriter, sir—he went off in his car to Hampstead, and Mr. Ellery, he walked off in a great hurry."

"So far as you know, no one besides Mr. George Brooklyn saw Mr. Prinsep after 10.15."

"No. Of course, Miss Joan or Miss Woodman or Sir Vernon may have seen him without my knowing."

"One more question. Do you recognise this walking-stick?" The inspector had found this lying on the floor of the room. It might be Prinsep's; but it was best to make sure.

"No, sir. I've never seen it to my knowledge. But it may have been Mr. Prinsep's, for all that. He had quite a number."

"You've no idea, then, whose it was?"

"No, sir. Mr. Prinsep used to collect walking-sticks. He was always bringing new ones home."

"Now, I want to ask you another question. You see this knife—the one that was sticking out of the body. Have you ever seen it before?"

Winter's manner showed some hesitation. At length he said, "No, I can't say I have. I mean, it wasn't here to my knowledge yesterday."

"You seem to hesitate in answering. It's a curious sort of knife. Surely you would remember if you had seen it. Or have you seen one like it?"

"Must I answer that question, sir? You see, I'm not at all sure it was the same."

"Of course you must answer. It is your business to give the police all the help you can in discovering the murderer."

"Well, sir, all I meant was that I'd often seen Mr. George Brooklyn using that sort of knife when he was doing his work—he's an architect—down at Fittleworth. He used to bring his work down when he came to stay with Sir Vernon, and I know he had a knife like that."

"I see. But you can't say whether this is his."

"No. It might be; but all I know is it's the same pattern."

"And that's all you can tell me, is it?" Winter said nothing, and the inspector added, "Very well, that will do. Now I want to ask Morgan a few questions."

Morgan had little light to throw upon the tragedy. He had been out all the previous evening, after helping his master to dress for dinner, when he had noticed nothing extraordinary. He had come back soon after 11.30, and had gone straight to bed. Where had he been? He had spent the evening with friends at Hammersmith, had come back by the Tube with two friends, who had only left him at the door of the house. There he had met Winter and had gone upstairs with him to bed.

Asked if he knew the walking-stick, he was quite sure that it was not his master's, and that it had not been in the room on the previous day. About the knife he knew nothing, except that he had never seen it, or one like it, before.

The inspector had just finished his examination of Morgan when he was startled by a shout from the garden. Throwing up the window, he called to a constable who was running towards the house. The man's answer was to ask him to come as quickly as possible. Calling another constable to keep guard in the study, Inspector Blaikie hastened to the garden, directed by Morgan to a private stairway which led directly to it from the back of the house. This, Morgan informed him, was Mr. Prinsep's usual way of getting into the garden, and thence, by the private covered way, into the Piccadilly Theatre itself.

But before inspector Blaikie left the study, he did one thing. He 'phoned through to Scotland Yard, and made arrangements for the immediate arrest of George Brooklyn, who was probably to be found at the Cunningham Hotel.

Chapter IV
What Joan Found in the Garden

Joan Cowper usually knew her own mind. And, in her view, knowing your own mind meant knowing when to stop as well as when to go on. She had made her position clear at the dinner, and Sir Vernon could no longer pretend, she said to herself, that her marriage with Prinsep was a foregone conclusion. Sir Vernon, indeed, had said nothing more about the matter when she took him to his room in the evening, and they had separated for the night apparently on the best of terms. But Joan had known that she must prepare for a stormy interview on the morrow; and, as she dressed in the morning, her thoughts were running on what she should say to Sir Vernon, in answer to the reproaches he was sure to address to her.

Just as she was ready for breakfast, her scared maid came to her door, and said that Morgan wished to speak to her for a moment. Joan looked at the girl's face, and saw at once that something serious was amiss.

"Why, what's the matter?" she said.

"I don't know, miss; but there's something wrong upstairs, and they're sending for the police."

Joan hurried to the room where Morgan was waiting for her. With the impeccable manner of the good manservant, and almost without a shade of feeling in his voice, Morgan told her what had happened—how he and Winter had found Prinsep lying on the floor of his study, dead.

"You are sure that he is dead," she managed to ask. "Have you sent for a doctor?"

Morgan assured her that everything was being attended to, and said that he had come to her because some one would have to break the news to Sir Vernon. Would she do it?

Into Joan's mind came the thought of the interview she had expected, and of the interview she was after all to have. No question now of her marrying John Prinsep—there was no longer any such person as John Prinsep to marry.

"I suppose I must do it," she said.

Joan's composure lasted just long enough for the door to close behind Morgan. Then she flung herself down on a couch, and let her feelings have their way. She sobbed half hysterically—not because, even at this tragic moment, she felt grief for John Prinsep, but simply because the sudden catastrophe was too much for her. Tragedy had swooped down in a moment on the house of Brooklyn, sweeping out of existence the crisis which had seemed so vital to her only a few minutes ago. On her was the sense of calamity, bewilderment, and helplessness in the face of death.

She had felt no call to ask Morgan questions. John Prinsep's death—his murder—was a fact—a shattering event which must have time to sink into her consciousness before she could begin to inquire about the manner of its coming. She did not even ask herself how it had happened, or who had done this thing. As she lay sobbing, the one thought in her mind was that Prinsep was dead.

But soon that other thought, that call to action which had been presented to her at the very moment when Morgan told her the news, came back into her mind. She had given way; but she must pull herself together. Sir Vernon, old and weak as he was, must be told the news; and she must tell him. She must tell him at once, lest tidings should break on him suddenly from some other quarter. Already the police were probably in the house. With a powerful effort, Joan forced herself to be calm. Drying her eyes, she stood upright, and looked at herself in the glass. She would need all her power to break the news to the old man whom she loved—the old man who had loved John Prinsep far more than he loved her.

John Prinsep had been Sir Vernon's favourite nephew—the man who was to succeed him—had indeed already succeeded him—in the management of the great enterprise he had built up. He liked George and Joan; but Prinsep had always had the first place in both his affection and his esteem. This death—this murder—Joan told herself, might be more than he could bear. It might kill him. And it fell to her, who only the night before had flouted his will by refusing to marry John Prinsep, to break to the old man the news of his favourite's death.

Still, it had to be done, and it was best done quickly. Sir Vernon always lay in bed to breakfast, and it was to his bedroom that Joan went with her evil tidings. She did not try to break it to him gradually—she told him straight out what she knew, holding his hand as she spoke. He looked very old and feeble there in the great bed. But he took it more quietly than she had expected, unable apparently to take in at once the full implication of what she said. "Dead—murdered," he repeated to himself again and again. He lay back in the bed and closed his eyes. Joan sat beside him for a while, and then stole away. His eyes opened and he watched her to the door; but he did not speak.

Joan's first act on leaving Sir Vernon was to telephone to the family doctor—old Sir Jonas Dalrymple—and ask him to come round as soon as he could. Then she felt that she must have air: her head was swimming and she was near to fainting. So she went down the private staircase and out into the old garden which, now as ever, seemed so remote from the busy world outside. For some minutes she walked up and down the avenue of trees, along which were ranged the antique statues Lord Liskeard had brought home from Asia Minor. Then, in search of a place where she could sit and rest, she went towards the model temple which the same old scholar-diplomat had built to mark his enthusiasm for the world of antiquity.

But, as Joan came nearer the temple she saw, in the entrance, some indistinct dark object lying upon the steps. At first she could not be sure what it was; but, as she came close, she became sure that it was the body of a man, lying with the feet towards her in an unnatural attitude which must be that of either unconsciousness or death. Her impulse was to turn tail and run to the house for help; but, with a strong effort of will, she forced herself to go still nearer. It was a man, and the man, she felt sure, was dead. The face was turned away, lying downwards on the stone of the topmost step; and on the exposed back of the head was the mark of a savage blow which had crushed the skull almost like an egg-shell. Already Joan was nearly certain who it was, and an intense feeling of sickness came over her as she forced herself to touch the body and to turn it over enough to expose the face. Then she let the thing drop back, and started back herself with a sharp cry. It was her cousin, George Brooklyn, manifestly dead and no less manifestly murdered, who lay there on the steps of the Grecian temple.

Filled as she was with horror at the second tragedy of the morning, Joan did not lose her presence of mind. She staggered, indeed, and had to cling for a minute to the nearest of the old statues—the Hercules whose points John Prinsep had showed off to his guests only the night before. The tears which she had been keeping back burst from her now, and the weeping did her good. She regained her composure and realised that her first duty was to summon help. Slowly and unsteadily she walked towards the house. At the door leading to the garden she met one of the policemen who was helping the sergeant in his examination of the house. She tried to speak, but she could only utter one word, "Come," and lead the way back to the horror that lay there in the garden.

The policeman followed her. But as soon as they came in view of the temple and he saw what she had seen already, he ceased to advance. "One moment, miss," he said, "I must fetch the sergeant," and he started back to the house in search of his superior.

Joan stood stock still, only swaying a little, until the policeman came back with the sergeant. Then she watched the two men go up to the body, turn it over slightly to see the face, and then let it fall back.

"Begging pardon, miss," said the sergeant, turning to her, "but maybe you know who this gentleman is?"

With a violent effort Joan managed to answer, "George— my cousin—Mr. George Brooklyn," she said; and then, overcome by the strain, she fainted.

The sergeant was a chivalrous man, and he instantly left off his examination of the spot and came to Joan's help. Propping up her head he fanned her rather awkwardly. As he did so, he shouted to the policeman. "Don't stand there, you fool, looking like a stuck pig. Go and get some water for the lady."

The constable set off at a run, lumbering heavily over the grass. "And tell the inspector what's toward," shouted the sergeant after him. It was this shout that the inspector heard, and that made him throw up the study window and receive at once the constable's message.

By the time Inspector Blaikie reached the garden, the constable had returned with a glass of water, and Joan had recovered consciousness. She was sitting on the grass, her back propped against the pedestal of the statue, and the sergeant was trying to persuade her to go indoors. The inspector, after a hasty glance at the scene, added his entreaties; but Joan refused to go.

"No, I must see this through," she said, as to herself. "I'm all right now," she added, trying to smile at the police officer. "Let me alone, please." After a time they left her to herself and pursued their investigation of the crime.

Not only were the fact and manner of death plain enough: the actual weapon with which the blow had been dealt was also clearly indicated. Between the body and the statue lay a heavy stone club, evidently a part of the group of statuary against which Joan was resting. It was the club of Hercules, taken from the hand of the stone figure which stood only a few feet away from the body. On the club were unmistakable recent bloodstains, and clotted in the blood were hairs which seemed to correspond closely with those of the dead man.

The blow had been one of immense violence. The stone club itself was so heavy that only a very strong man could have wielded it with effect; and it had evidently been brought down with great force on the back of George Brooklyn's head by some one standing almost immediately behind him, but rather to the right hand. So much appeared even from a cursory inspection of the wound. It was also evident that the body did not lie where it had fallen. It had been dragged two or three yards along the ground into the temple entry, presumably in order that it might be well out of the way of casual notice. The dragging of it along the ground had left clear traces. A track had been swept clear of loose stones and rubble by the passage of the body, and two little ridges showed where the stones and dust had piled up on each side.

George Brooklyn was fully dressed in his evening clothes, just as he had appeared at dinner the night before. He had evidently come out into the garden without either hat or overcoat—or at least there was no sign of these on the scene of the crime. His body lay where it had been dragged— presumably by the murderer; and all the evidence seemed to show that death had been practically instantaneous. There was no sign of a struggle: the only visible mark of the event was the trail left where the dragging of the body had swept clear of dirt and pebbles the stone approach to the model temple.

All these observations, made by the sergeant within a minute or two of discovering the body, were confirmed by the inspector when he went over the ground. Footmarks, indeed, were there in plenty; but Joan explained that they had all been walking about the garden before dinner on the previous evening, and that nearly all of them had actually stood for some time just outside the porch of the temple. From the footprints it was most unlikely that any valuable evidence would be derived.

Had the situation been less grim Inspector Blaikie would have been inclined to laugh when he found that the man whose body lay in the garden was the very man for whose arrest he had just issued the order. His fear had been that George Brooklyn would slip away before there was time to effect an arrest. That fear was now most completely removed. If George Brooklyn had killed Prinsep upstairs, certainly fate had lost no time in exacting retribution.

The inspector's immediate business, however, was to see what clues to this second and more mysterious murder might have been left. And it soon appeared to him that valuable evidence was forthcoming. First, on the stone club, his skilled examination plainly revealed a fine set of finger-prints, blurred in places, but still quite decipherable. Moreover, these prints occupied exactly the spaces most natural if the weapon had been used for a murderous assault. The inspector carefully wrapped up the club for forwarding at once to the Finger-Print Department at Scotland Yard.

But good fortune did not end there. Close to the statue of Hercules from which the club had been taken he found, trodden into the ground, a broken cigar-holder. It was a fine amber holder, broken cleanly across the middle. Where the cigar was to be inserted was a stout gold band, and on this band was an inscription, "V.B. from H.L." Blaikie looked in vain for a cigar end. Probably the holder had dropped from a pocket and been trodden upon. Perhaps from the pocket of the murderer himself.

The inspector turned to Joan with his find.

"Have you ever seen this before?" he asked.

Joan gave a start of surprise. For a moment she stared at the cigar-holder without saying a word. Then she spoke slowly, and as if with an effort.

"Yes," she said. "Uncle Harry—I mean Mr. Lucas—gave it to Sir Vernon; but Mr. Prinsep always used it. I saw him using it last night."

"Miss Cowper," said the inspector, "this may be very important. Are you quite sure that you saw Mr. Prinsep using this holder last night, and, if you are, at what time?"

"Yes, quite sure. He was smoking a cigar in it when he went up to his room."

Joan had stayed in the garden while the inspector was examining the ground, because she seemed to have lost the power of doing anything else. If she went in she must go and tell Sir Vernon of this second tragedy, or else talk to him in such a way as deliberately to keep him in ignorance of it. The strain in either case would be, she felt, more than she could bear. It was better even to stay near this horrible corpse, and to watch the police making their investigations.

Meanwhile, Dr. Manton, and with him a police surgeon, had come into the garden and were making an examination of the body. When they had done, two stout constables placed it on a stretcher and carried it into the house. Joan followed almost mechanically, leaving the inspector still in the garden.

As she entered the house Winter told her that Mrs. George

Brooklyn and Mrs. Woodman were upstairs with Miss Woodman, and that Carter Woodman had telephoned to say that he was coming round at once. He had just heard, at his office, the news of Prinsep's murder; but of course he would know nothing yet of George's fate. And then it occurred to Joan that Mrs. George, who was upstairs, had probably heard nothing as yet of her husband's death. Was she to break the news again—this time to a wife whose love for her husband had been so great as to become a family proverb? "As much in love as Marian." How often they had laughed as they said it; and now it came home suddenly to Joan what it meant. Still, she must go upstairs and see them—tell them, if need be.

She found that they knew already. They had seen from a window the excitement in the garden, and Mary Woodman had run down to find out what the trouble was. So Mary had had to tell Mrs. George, and there they were sitting in silence, waiting for news that could be no worse, and could be no better.

Joan shortly told them what she knew. Marian listened in silence, sitting still and staring at nothing with a fixed gaze. She did not weep: she was as if she had been turned to stone. Joan thought that she looked more beautiful now than she had ever looked on the stage, when she set a whole theatre crying for the sorrows of some queen of long ago. She longed to offer comfort, but she dared do nothing. Complete silence fell on the room.

Meanwhile, below, Carter Woodman had arrived. He heard from Winter at the door the news of the second tragedy of the morning. At first he seemed half incredulous; but he was soon convinced that there was no room for doubt. With a sentence expressing his horror, he hurried through into the garden in search of the inspector, whom he found still seeking for further traces of the crime.

Carter Woodman took the position by storm. His tall, athletic presence dominated the group of men gathered round the statue. He insisted that he must hear the whole story, demanded to know what clues the police had found, and so bullied the inspector and everybody else as to get himself at once very heartily disliked. Before he had half done the police were quite in a mood to convict him of the murder, if they could find a shred of evidence.

But they had to respect his energy; for it was he who pointed out to them something which they had overlooked. It was a scrap of paper lying on the floor of the temple, seemingly blown into a corner, just beyond where the body had lain. A leaf clearly from a memorandum book, and, from the cleanness and the state of the torn edge, apparently not long torn out. On it was written, in a hand which Woodman at once identified as Prinsep's, "Come to me in the garden. I will wait in the temple—J.P." There was no address or direction. But it seemed to prove that Prinsep, who lay dead upstairs, had arranged with some one a meeting in the garden, where now George Brooklyn's body had been found.

It was Woodman, too, who made a valuable suggestion. "Look here, inspector," he said. "Most of this part of the garden, though it is hidden from the house by the trees, can be seen from the windows at the back of the theatre. Whoever was here with poor old George last night may quite possibly have been seen by some one from there. There are nearly always people about till late."

The inspector at once pointed out that the place where they were standing, and the temple itself, were completely hidden from the theatre by a thick belt of trees and shrubs. But Woodman insisted that the chance was worth trying. George or his assailant might have been in another part of the garden some of the time.

The inspector and Woodman accordingly went across to the theatre, to which the news had already spread. And there they quickly found what they wanted. A caretaker, who lived in a set of ground-floor rooms at the back of the house had distinctly seen John Prinsep walking up and down the garden shortly after eleven o'clock, or it might have been a quarter past, on the previous night. He had been quite alone, and the man had last seen him walking towards the shrubbery and the temple. Asked if he was quite certain that the person he saw was Prinsep he said there could be no mistaking Mr. Prinsep. He had on his claret-coloured overcoat and slouch hat, and no one could help recognising his walk. He had a pronounced limp, and walked with a curious sideways action. "It was Mr. Prinsep all right," the caretaker concluded. "I should know him out of a thousand."

This would have satisfied some men; and it appeared to satisfy Woodman. But the inspector held that it was desirable to look for corroborative evidence. No one else in the building seemed to have seen any one in the garden; but most of the staff had not yet arrived. The inspector made arrangements for each to be interrogated on arrival, and he and Woodman then went back into the garden through the private door opening on the covered way communicating between the theatre and the house. They continued their search; but no further clues were to be found.

Chapter V
Plain as a Pikestaff

Inspector Blaikie, when he had done all that he could on the scene of the double crime, went at once to report to his superiors and to hold a consultation at Scotland Yard. The officer to whom he was immediately responsible was the celebrated Superintendent Wilson—"the Professor," as his colleagues called him, in allusion to his scholarly habits and his pre-eminently intellectualist way of reasoning out the solution of his cases. "The Professor," in his earlier days as Inspector Wilson, had patiently found his way to the heart of a good many murder mysteries by thinking them out as logical problems. He had made his name by solving the great "Antedated Murder Mystery," when every one else had been hopelessly in fault; and a man's life and a great fortune had both depended on his skill in reasoning out the truth. He was a small man, with quick, nervous movements, and a curious way of closing his eyes and holding up his hands before him with the tips of his fingers pressed tightly together when he was discussing a case. He was reputed to have but a scant respect for most of his colleagues at Scotland Yard; but he made an exception in favour of Inspector Blaikie, whose pertinacity in following up clues worked in excellently with his own skill at putting two and two together. Blaikie, he would often say, could not reason; but he could find things out. He, Wilson, stuck there in his office, could not go hunting for clues; but he and Blaikie together were a first-class combination. He was sitting at his desk, busy with a mass of papers, when the inspector entered. He at once put his work aside and settled down to discuss the new case. Word of the second murder had already been sent to him over the telephone; and he had seen that the case was certain to make a stir. The connection of the victims with Sir Vernon Brooklyn and the Piccadilly Theatre was enough to ensure a first-class newspaper sensation. There was an unusual note of eagerness in his voice as he asked for the latest news.

"The trouble about this case, sir," said Inspector Blaikie, "is that it's as plain as a pikestaff; but what the clues plainly indicate cannot possibly be true. Perhaps I had better tell you the whole story from the beginning."

Superintendent Wilson nodded, put the tips of his fingers together, leant back in his chair, and finally closed his eyes. He had composed himself to listen.

"I went to Liskeard House shortly before half-past eight this morning, on receipt of a telephone message stating that a murder had been committed."

"Who sent the message?"

"One of the servants. They had found the body when they went in to clean the room in the morning. I went to the house, as I say. In a room on the second floor, a study, I found the body, which the servants identified as that of Mr. John Prinsep, by whom the second floor was occupied. Mr. Prinsep was managing director of the Brooklyn Corporation and nephew of Sir Vernon Brooklyn."

The superintendent nodded.

"The body was lying on the floor with the face upwards. A knife, which I have since found to be of a peculiar type used by architects and draughtsmen, was protruding from the chest in the region of the heart. On the side of the head was a very clearly marked contusion, obviously caused by a heavy blow from some blunt instrument, which cannot have been any object of furniture in the room. The dead man's doctor, Dr. Manton, and the police surgeon agree that this blow, and not the knife wound, was the cause of death. The knife did not touch any vital part, and the doctors believe that the wound in the chest was inflicted after death."

"You say 'believe.' Are they certain?"

"No; almost certain, but not so as to swear to it. I at once made an examination of the room. The dead man had evidently been sitting at his desk, and had fallen from his chair on being struck from behind on the left-hand side. On the desk was a mass of papers relating to the financial affairs of a Mr. Walter Brooklyn, a brother, I find, of Sir Vernon Brooklyn, and therefore uncle to the deceased. I have the papers here."

The inspector handed over a bundle which the superintendent placed beside him on the table. "Go on," he said.

"Lying on the floor, at some distance from the body, was this walking-stick, which may, or may not, have some connection with the crime. There were at least thirty or forty walking-sticks standing in a corner; but this was lying on the floor behind the study chair to the left—that is, at the point from which the murderer seems to have approached his victim. The servants say that they do not remember seeing the stick before; but they cannot be certain, as the deceased collected sticks. This is evidently a curio, made, I think, of rhinoceros horn."

The superintendent examined the stick for a moment, and then put it down beside him.

"Dr. Manton then arrived, and, after a preliminary examination, asked that the body should be removed to the adjoining bedroom. When it was lifted up there was revealed, lying beneath it, this handkerchief which, as you see, is marked in the corner with the name 'G. Brooklyn.' Mr. George Brooklyn, I have ascertained, is also a nephew of Sir Vernon Brooklyn. He is, moreover, an architect by profession, and might therefore easily have been in possession of the knife found embedded in the body. Winter, the butler at the house, has often seen him using a knife of this precise pattern."

"H'm," said the superintendent.

"I made inquiries among the servants. The last of them to see Mr. Prinsep alive was the butler, Winter, who collected from him his late letters for the post. That was at 10.30 or thereabouts. The deceased was sitting at his table, working at a lot of figures. He seemed in a bad temper, but that, Winter says, was nothing unusual. But from the same Winter I obtained a very valuable piece of evidence. At about a quarter to eleven Mr. George Brooklyn called to see the deceased. He said he would show himself upstairs, and did so. He was seen by Winter and the other servants leaving the house by the front door at about 11.30. It was on receiving this information that I telephoned to you asking for the immediate arrest of Mr. George Brooklyn, who was believed to be staying at the Cunningham Hotel."

"Yes," said the superintendent. "I sent two men round there. They were informed that Mr. Brooklyn had booked rooms, and that his wife had spent the night in the hotel. He had not been there since the previous day before dinner. I was about to take further steps when I received your second message."

"Quite so. Now I come, sir, to the really extraordinary part of the case. Immediately before telephoning to you I had received an urgent message to come down to the garden, where the sergeant was making investigations. In the garden I found a body, which was identified by a young lady who lives in the house—Sir Vernon Brooklyn's ward, I understand—as that of Mr. George Brooklyn himself. He was in evening dress, without hat or coat, and the body was lying on the steps of a curious sort of stone summer house—they call it the Grecian temple—where it had been dragged. The cause of death—the doctors confirm this—was a terrific blow on the back of the head, and the weapon was lying a few yards from the body. I have it here in the parcel." The inspector lifted the heavy club with an effort on to the table, and the superintendent gave an involuntary start of surprise as he saw the strange weapon that had been employed in this sinister tragedy.

"It is, as you see, sir, a heavy stone club. It is part of a group of statuary—a Hercules, they tell me—which stands in the garden about four yards from the summer-house or temple. It has obviously been detached for some time from the rest of the statue. On it are some bloodstains and hairs which correspond to those of the dead man. There are also finger-prints, which I suppose you will have examined. I took the precaution to secure finger-prints of both the dead men for possible use. They are here." The inspector handed over another parcel.

"I studied carefully the scene of the crime. The deed was evidently done almost at the foot of the statue, and the body was dragged from there to the temple, presumably to remove it from casual notice. At the foot of the statue I found this crushed cigar-holder, which Miss Joan Cowper—the young lady to whom I referred—identifies as habitually used by Mr. John Prinsep, and actually seen in his mouth at ten o'clock last night, when a party then held in the house broke up. I also found on the floor of the temple this crumpled piece of paper, presumably a leaf from a memorandum book," and the inspector handed over the brief scrawled note in John Prinsep's writing making an appointment in the garden.

What he said, however, was not quite accurate; for it was not he, but Carter Woodman, who had found the note.

"The writing of this note was identified by Miss Cowper as that of Mr. Prinsep. It is one of the puzzles of this affair."

"You mean that it would have fitted in better if John Prinsep's body had been found in the garden," suggested the superintendent.

"Exactly; as things are it is confusing. About this time Mr. Carter Woodman, Sir Vernon Brooklyn's lawyer, arrived. At his suggestion we went across to the theatre which overlooks the garden, although the place where the crime was committed and the body found is completely concealed by trees from both the house and the theatre. Our object was to find if any one from the theatre had seen anything of what happened. A caretaker stated that he had seen Mr. Prinsep walking in the garden some time between eleven o'clock last night and a quarter past. I made further inquiries, both in the house and at the theatre; but that, I think, exhausts the discoveries I have made so far." And the inspector stopped and wiped his face with a green handkerchief.

"You have stated the case very plainly," said Superintendent Wilson. "Now tell me what you make of it?" And he gave what can best be described as the ghost of a chuckle.

"Ah, that's just where the troubles come in, sir," replied the inspector. "I don't know what to make of it. As I said, it's as plain as a pikestaff, and yet it can't be. When I examined Mr. Prinsep's room I found abundant evidence pointing to the conclusion that he was murdered by Mr. George Brooklyn. But when I go into the garden, I find Mr. George Brooklyn lying dead there, under circumstances which strongly suggest that he was killed by Mr. Prinsep. Yet they can't possibly have killed each other. It's simply impossible."

"You say that there is strong ground for suspecting that Prinsep killed Brooklyn. What is the ground?"

"Well, first there's that cigar-holder. The second thing is the letter in his writing, though I admit that raises a difficulty. The third thing is that I'm practically certain the finger-prints on the club correspond to those I took from Prinsep's hands.

Then Prinsep was certainly seen walking in the garden."

"In short, Inspector Blaikie," said the superintendent, half smiling, "you appear to hold very strong prima facie evidence that each of these two men murdered the other."

The inspector groaned. "Don't laugh at me, sir," he said. "I'm doing my best to puzzle it out. Of course they didn't kill each other. At least, both of them didn't. They couldn't. You know what I mean."

"You mean, I take it, that they could only have killed each other and left their bodies where they were found, on the assumption that at least one corpse was alive enough to walk about and commit a murder and then quietly replace itself where it had been killed. It will, I fear, be difficult to persuade even a coroner's jury that such an account of the circumstances is correct."

"Of course it isn't correct, sir; but you'll admit that's what it looks like. It is quite possible for a man who has committed a murder to be murdered himself as he leaves the scene of his crime; but it's stark, staring nonsense for the man whom he has killed to get up, as if he were alive and well, and come after his murderer with a club. To say nothing of laying himself out again neatly afterwards. No, that won't wash, Yet the evidence both ways is thoroughly good evidence."

"We can agree, inspector, that these two men did not kill each other. But it remains possible, even probable, on the evidence you have so far secured, that one of them did kill the other, and was then himself killed by some third person unknown, possibly a witness of the first crime bent on exacting retribution. How does that strike you?" The superintendent thrust his hands deep into his pockets and leant back in his chair with a satisfied look, as if he had scored a point.

Inspector Blaikie's face, however, hardly became less doleful. "Yes, that's possible," he said; "but unfortunately there is absolutely nothing to show which set of circumstantial clues ought to be accepted and which discarded in that case. We do not know which of the two men was killed first. When Brooklyn went to see Prinsep, did he murder him then and there in the study, or did Prinsep decoy his visitor into the garden by means of the note we have found, and there kill him? Either theory fits some of the facts: neither fits them all. I don't know which to think, or which to work on as a basis. The evidence we have probably points in the right direction in one of the cases, and in the wrong direction in the other; but how are we to tell which is right and which is wrong? There is nothing to lay hold of."

"What about the medical evidence as to the time of death? Does that throw any light on the case?"

"None whatever, unfortunately. In both instances the doctors agree that death almost certainly took place at some time between 10.30 and 12 o'clock. But they say it is impossible to time the thing any more accurately than that."

"Come, that seems at least to narrow the field of inquiry. When were each of these men last seen alive?"

The inspector referred to his notes. "John Prinsep was seen at 10.30 by the servant, Winter, who went to fetch his letters for the post. He was seen in the garden at some time between 11 o'clock and 11.15 by the caretaker at the Piccadilly Theatre, Jabez Smith, and also, I have since ascertained, by a dresser named Laura Rose about the same time. No one seems to have seen him later than about 11.15. His body was found in his study this morning at ten minutes past eight by the maid, Sarah Plenty, and seen immediately afterwards by the household servants, William Winter and Peter Morgan."

"And George Brooklyn?"

"He was seen at about a quarter to eleven by Winter and other servants, when he called at Liskeard House and went up by himself to John Prinsep's room. He was seen again, by Winter and two other servants, leaving the house at about

11.30. He did not go home to his hotel, and neither his wife nor any one else I have been able to discover saw him again. His body was discovered at 9.30 this morning in the garden of Liskeard House by his cousin, Joan Cowper.”

“That certainly does not seem to help us very much. In the case of Prinsep, he may have died any time after 11.19. Brooklyn was still alive at 11.30.”

“Yes; but, if Brooklyn killed Prinsep, it seems he must have done so between 11.15, when Prinsep was still alive, and 11.30, when Brooklyn was seen leaving the house.”

“That does not follow at all. We know he came back after 11.30, since he was found dead in the grounds. The first question is, How and when did he come back?”

“I have made every possible inquiry about that. The front door was bolted at about 11.45, and Winter is positive that he did not come in again that way. There are two other ways into the garden. One is through the coach-yard. That was locked and bolted about 11, and was found untouched this morning. The other is through the theatre. Nobody saw him, and the caretaker says he could not have gone through that way without being seen. But it appears that the door from the theatre into the garden was not locked until nearly midnight, and it is just possible he may have slipped through that way. He seems to have been seen in the theatre earlier in the evening—before his call at Liskeard House at 10.45.”

“Was it a usual thing for Prinsep to walk about the garden at night?”

“Yes, they tell me that he often took a stroll there on fine nights before going to bed.”

The superintendent rubbed his chin thoughtfully. “I can only see one thing for it,” he said. “We have no evidence to show which of these men died first, and therefore, which, if either of them, killed the other. You must follow up both sets of clues until you get further evidence to show which is the right one. But remember that, even if one murder can be accounted for in that way, there is still another murderer somewhere at large—unless another unexpected corpse turns up with clear evidence of having been murdered by one of the other two."

The inspector laughed. "Well," he said, "it all seems a bit of a puzzle. It seems to me the next thing is to find out whether either of them had any special reason for murdering the other. If you agree, I shall work up the antecedents of the case, and do a little research into the family history."

"Yes, that's probably the best we can do for the present. But spread the net wide. Find out all you can about the whole family and the servants—every one who is known to have been in the house last night—every one who could have any reason for desiring the death of either or both of the murdered men."

"I suppose one of them must have murdered the other," said the inspector reflectively.

"I see no sufficient reason for thinking that," replied his superior. "It looks to me more like a very carefully planned affair, worked out by some third party. But we mustn't take anything for granted. Your immediate job is certainly to follow up the clues you have found. Even if they do not lead where we expect them to lead, they will probably lead somewhere. A deliberately laid false clue is often just as useful as an ordinary straightforward clue in the long run."

"Oh, I'll keep my eyes open," said the inspector, "and as there is a third party involved in any case, it's worth remembering that he could not easily have got into the house after midnight at the latest, and I'm blest if I see how he could have got out of it and left all the doors properly fastened unless he had an accomplice inside."

"That is certainly a point. Every one who slept in the house is certainly worth watching. What about the men-servants?"

"Only two—Morgan and Winter—sleep in the house.

Morgan says he came back about 11.30, after spending the evening with friends in Hammersmith. He and Winter went up to their rooms together soon after. Morgan's room can only be reached through Winter's. Winter says he lay awake for some hours—he is a bad sleeper—and heard Morgan snoring in the next room all the time. He did not go to sleep until after he had heard two o'clock strike. He says he is a light sleeper, and Morgan could not have passed through his room without waking him."

"That seems to clear Morgan, if Winter is speaking the truth. What about Winter himself? A good deal seems to turn on his testimony."

"Winter is a very old servant. He has been in the family since he was a boy. He doesn't strike me as at all the kind of man to be mixed up in an affair of this sort. Morgan is rather a sly fellow—much more the sort of man one would be inclined to suspect."

"You are probably right; but we must not let Winter off too easily. Suppose it is true that one of these two men did kill the other. Isn't an old devoted family servant, if he saw the crime, Just the man to take his revenge? There have been many crimes with far less strong a motive."

"I will certainly have Winter watched, and Morgan too. But I'm not at all hopeful. It's too well planned to be a sudden crime, and I'm sure Winter's not the man for a high-class job of this sort."

"Do the best you can, and keep me fully informed about the case. If I have a brain-wave, I'll let you know. At present I can't see light any more than you."

With that unsatisfactory conclusion the two detectives parted. Superintendent Wilson, left alone, walked quickly up and down the room, chuckling to himself, and every now and then marking off a point on his fingers, or pausing in his walk to examine one of the clues which the inspector had left in his keeping. He appeared to find it a fascinating case.

Chapter VI
A Pause for Reflection

When Inspector Blaikie got to his own room, he sat down with a sheet of paper in front of him, and on it made out, from his notes, a list of all the persons whom he knew to have been in the house the previous night. It was a long list, and he made it out more to set his subconscious mind free to work than with any idea that it would throw a direct light on the problem. Having made his list, he began to write down, after each name, exactly what was known about its owner's doings and movements on the night before. He left out nothing, however unimportant it might seem; for he had fully mastered the first principle of scientific detection—that detail generally gives the clue to a crime, and that therefore every detail matters.

He began with those who seemed least likely to have had any hand in the business. First there were the four maid-servants. They had gone to bed before eleven. They slept two in a room, and there seemed no reason to doubt that, as they said, they had all slept soundly. He did not dismiss them from his mind, but he had nothing against them so far.

Then there was the lady's maid, Agnes Dutch. She had slept alone on the first floor, in a little room next to that of Joan Cowper. She had felt tired, she said, and had gone to bed at 10.30, after making sure that Miss Joan would not want her again. She seemed a nice, quiet girl, and, although she seemed very upset in the morning when the inspector saw her, that was no more than was to be expected. There was nothing against her either. Besides, Mary Woodman had not gone to bed until after twelve, and she said that she was certain the girl was in her room until then. She had been sitting in the big landing-lounge reading, and both Joan's and the maid's doors opened on to the lounge.

What of Mary Woodman herself? She had been with Joan until about eleven, and had then sat for an hour reading. No one had seen her during that hour, or heard her go to bed afterwards. But Mary notoriously got on with everybody and had not an enemy in the world. Every one had told the inspector, without need of his asking the question, that she was the very last person to have anything to do with a murder. Besides, the whole thing was clearly a man's job. The inspector filed Mary Woodman in his mind for future reference; but he felt quite sure that she knew nothing about the crimes.

Then, to finish the women, there was Joan Cowper. She had discovered George Brooklyn's body in the garden, and her manner after the discovery seemed to be sign enough that it had come to her as a horrifying surprise. Certainly, she had known nothing about George Brooklyn's death; but she might, for all that, be in a position to throw some further light upon the crimes. He had asked her in the garden how she had spent the previous evening; and she had answered without hesitation. After seeing Sir Vernon to his room shortly after ten, she had sat with Mary Woodman in the lounge until eleven o'clock, and had then gone to bed. Her maid had come to her rather before half-past ten and she had told her she would be needed no more that night. Mary Woodman, who had sat on in the lounge, confirmed this, and stated that Joan had not left her room before midnight. Certainly there seemed to be nothing to connect Joan with the crimes. She was a fine young lady, the inspector reflected. She had borne up wonderfully.

Next there were the men, and it was among them that the criminal, if, as Blaikie suspected, he was one of the intimate circle of Liskeard House, would probably be found. Sir Vernon Brooklyn was clearly out of it. He was a feeble old man whose hand could not possibly have struck those savage blows. He was reported to be very fond of both his nephews; and he had undoubtedly gone to bed at a quarter past ten. So much for him. He might know things or suspect, but he could have had no hand in the murders. At present, the inspector had been told, he was prostrated by the news of Prinsep's death, and his doctor had forbidden any mention of the matter in his presence. He did not even know yet that George Brooklyn was dead.

The only other men who had slept in the house were the two servants—Winter and Morgan. Morgan seemed to be cleared of suspicion, at least if Winter had told the truth. But might not Winter himself have had a hand in the affair? The superintendent had dropped a plausible hint, and there might be something in it. Inspector Blaikie wrote it down as possible, but unlikely. Two other menservants, who had waited at dinner, did not sleep in the house, and had left soon after half-past eleven. They had been busy clearing up until the very moment of their departure, and it seemed plain that they had enjoyed neither time nor opportunity for any criminal proceeding. Besides, they were strangers, imported for the evening from the restaurant attached to the theatre. As robbery had evidently not been a motive in either murder, there was the less reason to think seriously about them. They could have had no motive.

Next, the inspector turned to a consideration of the guests who had been at the dinner. These were, first, George Brooklyn and his wife. About George he had already noted down all that he knew. What of Mrs. George? Inquiries which the sergeant had made established that she had gone straight back to her hotel—the Cunningham—soon after ten o'clock. George had left her in the care of the Woodmans, parting from them at the door of the theatre on plea of an appointment. Mrs. George—or, as she was better known both to the inspector and to all London, Isabelle Raven, the great tragedy actress—had then sat talking with Mrs. Woodman in the sitting-room which they shared at the hotel until "after eleven," when she had gone to bed, expecting that her husband might come in at any moment. She had gone to sleep and had only discovered his absence when she woke in the morning. She had been worried, and after a hasty breakfast she had hurried across to Liskeard House with Helen Woodman to make inquiries. There she had been met with the fatal news. She was now lying ill in her room at the Cunningham Hotel, with Mrs. Woodman in faithful attendance upon her.

This recital clearly brought up the question of the Woodmans, man and wife. When they returned to the hotel with Mrs. George, Carter Woodman had gone to one of the hotel waiting-rooms to write letters, leaving the two women together. He said that he had remained at work till 11.45 or so, when he had gone down to the hall and asked the night porter to see some important letters off by the first post in the morning. This was corroborated by the night porter, who had so informed the sergeant. Carter Woodman had then gone straight to bed—a statement fully confirmed by his wife. This seemed fairly well to dispose of any connection of either the Woodmans or Mrs. George with the tragedy.

Harry Lucas? Sir Vernon's old friend had left in his car for Hampstead at ten minutes past ten after a few farewell words with Sir Vernon. He had reached home soon after 10.30, and had gone straight to bed. This had been already confirmed by police inquiries at Hampstead during the morning.

Robert Ellery? He had left the house soon after ten, saying that he intended to walk back to his room at Chelsea. The inspector had not yet followed his trail; but he now made up his mind to do so, though he had not much faith in the result. Still, here was at least a loose end that needed tying.

When he had made his list and tabulated his information, Inspector Blaikie did not feel that he had greatly advanced in his quest. Not one of the people on the list seemed in the least likely either to have committed the murders, or to have been even an accessory to them. He began to feel that he had not yet got at all on the track of the real criminal, or at least of the second one, if one of the two men had really killed the other. Was it some one quite outside the circle he had been studying, and, if so, how had that outsider got access to the house? He might have slipped in without being noticed, but it did not seem very likely, and it was far more difficult to see how he had slipped out. But, after all, George Brooklyn had got back somehow after 11.30, and, where he had come, so might another. Perhaps some one had slipped in and out by way of the theatre.

So the inspector made up his mind to go over the whole scene again, and, above all, to find out more about the persons with whom he had to deal—their histories and still more their present ways of life: their loves and, above all, their animosities, if they had any. There, he felt, the clue to the mystery was most likely to be found.

Accordingly, on the following morning—the second after the tragedy—Inspector Blaikie presented himself early at the office of Carter Woodman and sent up his card. Sir Vernon was still far too ill to be consulted, and the next thing seemed to be a visit to his lawyer, who, being both confidential adviser and a close relative, would be certain to know most of what there was to be known about the circumstances surrounding the dead men. Woodman had offered all possible assistance, and had himself suggested a call at his office.

The inspector presented his card to an elderly clerk who was presiding in the outer office, and was at once shown in to the principal. Again he was struck, as he had been on the morning before, with the lawyer's overflowing vitality. At rather over forty-six, Woodman still looked very much the athlete he had been in his younger days, when he had accumulated three Blues at Oxford, and represented England at Rugby football on more than one occasion. He had given up "childish things," he used to say; but the abundant vigour of the man remained, and stood out strongly against the rather dingy background which successful solicitors seem to regard as an indispensable mark of respectability. Carter Woodman, the inspector knew, had a big practice, and one of good standing. He did all the legal work of the Brooklyn Corporation, and he was perhaps the best known expert on theatrical law in the country.

Woodman greeted the inspector cordially, and shook his hand with a force that made it tingle for some minutes afterwards.

"Well, inspector," he said, "what progress? Have you got your eye on the scoundrels yet?"

The inspector shook his head. "We are still only at the beginning of the case, I am afraid. I have come here to take advantage of your offer to give me all the help you can."

"Of course I will. It is indispensable that the terrible business should be thoroughly cleared up. For one thing, I am very much afraid for Sir Vernon; and there certainly would be more chance of his getting over it if we knew exactly what the truth is. Uncertainty is a killing business. He has not been told yet about Mr. George Brooklyn's death."

"You will understand that, as it is impossible for me to see Sir Vernon, I shall have to ask you to tell me all you can about any of the family affairs that may have a bearing on the tragedy. As matters stand it is most important that I should know as much as possible about the circumstances of the two dead men. To establish the possible motives for both crimes may be of the greatest value. There is so little to go upon in the facts themselves that I have to look for evidence from outside the immediate events."

"Am I to understand that you have no further light on the crime beyond what you gained when the bodies were found?"

"Hardly that, Mr. Woodman. I have at least had time to think things over, and to conduct a few additional investigations. But I shall know better what to make of these when I have asked you a few questions."

"Ask away; but I shall probably be able to answer more to your satisfaction if you tell me how matters stand. I think I may say that I know thoroughly both Sir Vernon's and the late Mr. Prinsep's affairs."

"Well, you know, Mr. Woodman, the prima facie evidence in both cases seemed to point to a quite impossible conclusion. In each case, what evidence there was went to show that the two men had murdered each other. This could not be true of both; but we have so far no evidence to show whether it ought to be disbelieved in both cases, or only in one. That is where further particulars may prove so important."

"I will tell you all I can."

"Let us begin with Mr. Prinsep. Was he in any trouble that you know of?"

The lawyer hesitated. "Well," he said at length, "it is a private matter, and I am sure it can have no bearing on the case. But you had better have all the facts. There had been some trouble—about a woman, a girl who is acting in a small part at the Piccadilly Theatre."

"Her name?"

"Charis Lang. Prinsep had been, well, I believe somewhat intimate with her, and she had formed the opinion that he had promised to marry her. He came to see me about it. He denied that he had made any such promise, and said he was anxious to get the matter honourably settled. I wrote to the woman and asked her to meet me; but she refused—said it was not a lawyer's business, but entirely a private question between her and Mr. Prinsep. I showed him her letter, and he was very much worried. He informed me that Mrs. George Brooklyn—she used to be leading lady at the Piccadilly—had known the girl in her professional days, and I approached her and told her a part of the story. She took, I must say, the girl's side, and said she was sure a promise of marriage had been made. She wanted to take the matter up; but George Brooklyn objected to his wife being mixed up in it, and undertook to see Miss Lang himself. He was to have done so two nights ago—the night of the murders—and then to have gone back to tell Prinsep what had happened. I have no means of knowing whether he actually did so."

"This is very important. Can you give me Miss Lang's address?"

"I have it here. Somewhere in Hammersmith. Yes, 3 Algernon Terrace. But she is at the theatre every evening, and you could probably find her there."

"I must certainly arrange to see her. Can you tell me anything further about the young woman? For instance, is she—well—respectable?"

"I have told you all I know. Mrs. George might know more."

"Thank you. Now, is there anything else you know about Mr. Prinsep that might have a bearing on his death?"

"Nothing."

"Had he any financial troubles?"

"None, I am sure. He had a large salary from the Brooklyn Trust, besides a considerable personal income, and he always lived well within his means."

"Had he any enemies?"

Again the lawyer paused before answering. Finally, "No,"

he replied, "no enemies."

The inspector took the cue.

"But there were some people you know of with whom he was not on the best of terms?" he asked.

"I think I may say 'yes' to that. He had a temper, and there had been violent disputes on several occasions with Mr. Walter Brooklyn—Sir Vernon's brother."

"One moment. Was he on good terms with Mr. George Brooklyn?"

Again a pause. "No, I can't say he was—but they were not enemies. George thought he had behaved badly to Charis Lang, and said so. Also, George was strongly against Prinsep's marrying Miss Joan Cowper, which Sir Vernon had set his heart on."

And then, in question and answer, the whole episode at the dinner, the announcement of Sir Vernon's will, and Joan's dramatic refusal to marry Prinsep, gradually came out. The inspector felt that now at last he was learning things.

"Did Miss Cowper know about Miss Lang?"

"Not that I am aware of. But I can't be sure. Mrs. George may have told her."

"And what would you say were the relations between Miss Cowper and Mr. Prinsep?"

"He was half in love with her—in a sort of a way. At any rate he certainly wanted to marry her. She was most certainly not in love with him. I don't think she had any strong feeling against him; but it is impossible to be sure. She would have done almost anything rather than marry him, I am certain."

"Had Miss Cowper, so far as you know, any other attachment?"

"That is a difficult question. She is very thick with Robert Ellery, the young playwright, you know; but whether she is in love with him is more than I can tell you. He is obviously in love with her. It was the common talk, and everybody, knew about it except Sir Vernon."

"This Mr. Ellery—can you tell me anything about him? He was at the dinner, was he not?"

"Yes, he's a ward of old Mr. Lucas, one of Sir Vernon's oldest friends. A good deal about with Joan, and a frequent visitor at Sir Vernon's country place. A nice enough fellow, so far as I have seen."

"Was he on good terms with Mr. Prinsep?"

"Prinsep did not like his going about with Joan, I think. Otherwise, they seemed to get on all right."

"Now, Mr. Woodman, I want to ask you a somewhat difficult question. I should, of course, ask Sir Vernon himself, if he were well enough. You know, presumably, the terms of Sir Vernon's will. Do you feel at liberty to tell me about its contents? They might throw some light on the question of motive."

The lawyer thought a moment. "I don't see why I shouldn't tell you the whole thing—in confidence," he said. "Sir Vernon told them all that night what was in his will, and you certainly ought to know about it. The greater part of his property was to be divided at his death between his two nephews, who have now unhappily predeceased him."

"Yes, and in the event of the death of either or both of the nephews, what was to happen?"

"If Mr. George Brooklyn died, half of his share was to go to Mrs. George and half to Prinsep. If Prinsep died, half of his share was to go to Miss Joan Cowper. Sir Vernon explained that his arrangements were based on her marrying Prinsep."

"Then, under the will, Miss Cowper now gets half Mr. Prinsep's share. Does she get half Mr. George's share also?"

"No, a part of it goes to Mrs. George, and the remainder in both cases to the next of kin."

"I see. And who is the next of kin."

"Joan's step-father, Mr. Walter Brooklyn."

"Ah! I think you mentioned that Mr. Walter Brooklyn was on bad terms with Mr. Prinsep."

"Walter Brooklyn was on bad terms with most people who knew him. His step-daughter left him after her mother's death, and came to live with Sir Vernon. I am afraid Walter Brooklyn is not a very likeable person."

"On what terms was he with Sir Vernon?"

"He was always trying to get money from him. He had ran through one big fortune, his wife's—including all the money left in trust for Miss Cowper. He leads a fairly expensive life in town, supported, I understand, partly by his bridge earnings and partly on what he can raise from his friends."

"Did Sir Vernon give him money?"

"Yes, far more than I thought desirable. But Sir Vernon had a very strong sense of family solidarity. Latterly, however, Walter Brooklyn's demands had become so exorbitant that Sir Vernon had been refusing to see him, and had handed the matter over to Prinsep, whom Walter was finding a much more difficult man to deal with."

"Do you know whether Prinsep had been seeing Mr. Walter Brooklyn lately?"

"Yes; I know he saw him the day before the murder. Walter was always after money. He'll probably begin sponging on Miss Cowper in a day or two."

"You certainly do not give Mr. Walter Brooklyn a good character."

"No; but I think every one you ask will confirm my estimate."

"I will look into that. Now, are there any other particulars in the will I ought to know about? I should like to know approximately what Sir Vernon is worth."

"Not far short of a million."

"You don't say so. Then any one interested in his will had a great deal at stake. Are any others interested besides those you have mentioned?"

"There are a number of smaller legacies. Miss Cowper was left £40,000. My sister, Miss Mary Woodman, and I are left £20,000 each. The rest are quite small legacies."

"I think that is almost all I need ask you. But is there any other particular you think might help me in my inquiry?"

"As to that, I cannot say; but there are two points I have been intending to mention. The first is that I know Mr. Walter Brooklyn called at Liskeard House a few minutes after ten on the night of the murder. My wife and I saw him go up to the porch and ring the bell just after we had come out of the house."

"This is very important. Do you know anything more?"

"No, it was merely a chance that I noticed him and pointed him out to my wife. Mr. and Mrs. George may also have seen him. They were with us. He went into the hall. That is all I can tell you."

"Where did you go when you left the house?"

"Straight back to the hotel where I was staying. I did not go out again that night. I heard nothing about the tragedy till they rang me up about it at my office the next morning."

"Who rang you up?"

"One of the servants at Liskeard House. I do not know which it was."

"And what was the other point you wished to mention?"

"Only that I know Mr. Walter Brooklyn was in exceptional financial difficulties, and had been trying in vain to raise a loan. This has happened very opportunely for him."

"But, of course, Sir Vernon may alter his will."

"If he recovers enough to do so, he may. But I doubt if he will. He always told me that he could not bear the thought of leaving money out of the family. And much as he disapproves of Walter Brooklyn, he is still attached to him."

"H'm. Well, thank you very much, Mr. Woodman. What you have told me has been very helpful. Perhaps I will call again and tell you what success I meet with in following it up. I may, of course, have more to ask you later."

The inspector rose and Woodman gave him his hand. He went out of the office with his hand tingling.

"Certainly a man who impresses himself upon one," said he, laughing softly to himself. "And what he had to say was most enlightening."

Chapter VII.
The Case Against Walter Brooklyn

Inspector Blaikie left Carter Woodman's office with the feeling that a new and unexpected light had been thrown on the tragedy, and that he had at least found a quite sufficient motive for both crimes. If Walter Brooklyn had committed the murders, he stood to gain directly a considerable slice of Sir Vernon's huge fortune. Moreover, a considerable slice of the remainder would go to his step-daughter, Joan Cowper, and he might hope to despoil her again, as he had despoiled her of her mother's money. Evidence against Mr. Walter Brooklyn might be lacking; but certainly there was no lack of motive. Moreover, the man seemed, from Woodman's description, quite a likely murderer. The inspector decided that his next job was undoubtedly to discover whether there was any direct evidence against Walter Brooklyn.

To begin with, he said to himself, what had he to go upon? Of direct evidence, not a shred; but where the direct evidence pointed obviously in the wrong direction, it was necessary to consider very seriously the question of motive. Walter Brooklyn, he reflected, would not stand to inherit Sir Vernon's money unless both nephews were cleared out of the way. He had, therefore, a motive for both murders together, but not for either of them except in conjunction with the other. This seemed to point to the conclusion that, if Walter Brooklyn had committed either of the murders he had committed both. On the other hand, it still remained possible that one of the two men had killed the other, and that Walter Brooklyn, knowing this and realising his opportunity, had then disposed of the survivor. Or, after all, the indications might again be as deceptive as those which followed hard upon the discovery of the murders.

What Woodman had told the inspector provided, however, at least one clear line of investigation which could be followed up immediately. If Woodman and other people had seen Walter Brooklyn approaching Liskeard House and ringing the front-door bell soon after ten o'clock on the night of the murders, it ought not to be difficult to get further information about his movements. Had he been admitted to the house; and if so, when had he left, and why had no mention of his visit previously been made to the inspector? The best thing was to call at Liskeard House at once and make inquiries. Inspector Blaikie set off immediately.

The bell was answered by a maid-servant, and the inspector asked for a few words with Mr. Winter. He was shown into a small side-room, and within a minute Winter joined him. The inspector plunged at once into business.

"Since I have left you there have been certain developments which make it desirable that I should ask you one or two questions. I want to know whether, on Tuesday night, any one called at the house during the evening?"

"Well, sir, of course, there were the guests at dinner that night. You have their names."

"Did any one else call—later in the evening, for example?"

"Yes, there was Mr. George. As I told you, he came at about a quarter or ten minutes to eleven, and left at about 11.30."

"Did anybody else visit the house that night?"

"No—there was no one else."

"Now, I want you to be very careful. Are you positive that no one else called?"

"Yes—I mean, no. I had quite forgotten. At a few minutes after ten Mr. Walter Brooklyn—Sir Vernon's brother—came. He sent up his name to Sir Vernon, and asked him to see him at once. He said it was about something important."

"Did Sir Vernon see him?"

"No. He sent down word by one of the temporary men-servants he couldn't see him. He told him to see Mr. Prinsep or to write."

"Then, did Mr. Walter Brooklyn go up to see Mr. Prinsep?"

"No. He seemed mighty annoyed, he did. Said to me things were coming to a pretty pass when a man wouldn't see his own brother. Then he took himself out of the house in a rage, and I shut the door after him."

"Did you see anything more of him?"

"No, that's the last I saw. He didn't come back; for I was on duty here till the place was bolted up for the night."

"Did Mr. Walter Brooklyn often come to the house?"

"Well, he'd been a number of times lately to see Mr. Prinsep."

"Had he been to see Sir Vernon?"

"No. You see, Sir Vernon's been away in the country for some time."

"But when he was in London, did Mr. Walter Brooklyn come to see him?"

"He used to. Then I believe there was a bit of a quarrel. Last time he was in London Sir Vernon told me he would not see Mr. Walter, and I was to tell him to see Mr. Prinsep if he came. I sent up on Tuesday because I didn't know if the instructions still held."

"Then there had been a quarrel?"

"Hardly what you would call a quarrel. What we understood was that Mr. Walter wanted money, and Sir Vernon wouldn't give it him."

"Did any one else see Mr. Walter Brooklyn on Tuesday?"

"Yes, the maid—Janet—must have seen him."

The inspector sent for Janet, who confirmed what Winter had said. It seemed plain enough that Walter Brooklyn had called at about ten minutes past ten, had been refused an interview with Sir Vernon, and had left a few minutes later. Thereafter, no one about the house had seen any more of him.

Before he left the inspector obtained from Winter Mr. Walter Brooklyn's address. He lived at his club, the Byron—named after the playwright, not the poet—only a few steps down Piccadilly. The inspector made that his next place of call.

The club porter, with the aid of the night porter, gave him the information he needed. Walter Brooklyn had dined in the club on Tuesday, had gone out at about ten o'clock and had returned just about midnight. The night porter had noticed nothing unusual about him when he came back. It was about his usual hour. He had gone straight upstairs, the man believed—probably to his room, but the porter could not say.

So far there was nothing very much to go upon. Walter Brooklyn might have committed the murders—he had certainly been out until midnight. But this was nothing unusual, and there was no evidence that he had been in the house. What evidence there was seemed to show that he had not.

But Inspector Blaikie still lingered in talk with the two porters, asking further questions which produced quite unilluminating answers. Soon they found a common interest in the cricket news, and plunged into a discussion of the respective chances of Surrey and Middlesex for the County

Championship. The night porter, who was a north-countryman and a partisan of Yorkshire, cut in every now and then with a sarcastic comment. He was especially scornful of the day porter's pride in the number of amateurs included in the Middlesex eleven. "Call them gentlemen," he said. "They get paid, same as the players, only they put it down as expenses."

But at this point the argument broke off; for the day porter suddenly changed the subject.

"Let me have a look at that stick, will you?" he said to the inspector.

Inspector Blaikie, who had been twirling the stick about rather obtrusively, at once handed it over. It was the stick found in Prinsep's room, and he was carrying it about with him solely with the hope that some one might recognise it, and enable him to discover to whom it had belonged. It was a peculiar stick, and likely to be noticed by those who saw it. The shaft was of rhinoceros horn, linked together with bands of gold; and it had a solid gold handle.

"What do you make of it?" the inspector asked.

"I was going to ask you how you got hold of it," answered the porter.

"Why do you ask?"

"Only because it is surely Mr. Walter Brooklyn's stick. I have often seen him carrying it."

"Take a good look. Are you quite certain it is his?"

"Either it is, or it's one just the same. It's a most unusual pattern, too."

"Yes, rhinoceros horn, I should say. Could you swear to it?"

"Hardly that. There might be two of them. But I've not seen Mr. Brooklyn with his for a day or two."

"Try to remember—was he carrying this stick when he went out on Tuesday?"

The porter paused a minute. "Yes, I think he was," he said. "But, no, you mean in the evening. You'll have to ask the night porter here that. He was on duty from nine o'clock."

The inspector turned to the night porter. "Do you recognise this as Mr. Brooklyn's stick?"

"Yes, I'm pretty sure it's his."

"And do you remember whether he was carrying it on Tuesday night when he went out?"

The man hesitated some time before replying. Finally, "No," he said, "I can't say. Maybe he was—I rather think he was. But I'm not sure."

"And when he came in?"

"He had a stick, I remember. He rapped at the door with it. I expect it was this one. No, I don't think it was. It was a plain stick, I'm almost sure."

"Remember that this may be of the utmost importance. You can't remember whether or not Mr. Brooklyn had a stick when he went out?"

"Not for sure. I think he had."

"But you can't say whether it was this stick?"

"No, not for certain."

"And when he came in?"

"He had a stick; but I'm almost sure it wasn't this one."

"Would any one else be likely to know?"

"I don't think so. There was no one else about."

At this point the day porter struck in. "I wonder why you're so curious about that stick," he said.

"That, I am afraid, is my business," said the inspector. "Now, can you tell me where Mr. Brooklyn usually goes of a night?"

"Sometimes to a theatre or variety show. But most often he goes to play bridge at his other club."

"Where is that?"

"It's a small place—the Sanctum, in Pall Mall. Only a few minutes from here."

After a few words more the inspector took his leave en route for Duke Street. The stick he held in his hand had become a clue of the first importance. Its presence in Prinsep's study seemed to show that its owner had been there on the fatal night. More and more Walter Brooklyn was becoming involved. But how had he got in? That was the mystery still.

At the Sanctum, Inspector Blaikie at first drew a blank—a blank which he had expected. Walter Brooklyn had not been to the club on Tuesday. Nothing had been seen of him since the previous Saturday night.

"So you've heard nothing of him this week?" said the inspector, preparing to take his leave.

"Beg pardon, sir," replied the porter. "It had almost slipped my memory. Mr. Walter Brooklyn rang up one night this week on the telephone. I have a note of the call somewhere."

"What was it about?"

"He asked if a registered parcel had come for him, because if it had he wanted it sent round to him at once by hand."

"Sent to his other club?"

"No. He wanted it sent to Sir Vernon Brooklyn's, Liskeard House, Piccadilly. He gave us the name and address over the 'phone."

"Did you send the parcel?"

"No. Because we told him no parcel had come."

"Has it arrived since?"

"No."

"When was this call you mention?"

The porter referred to his book. "It was about 11.30, or a bit before. The call before was at 11.20."

"On what day?"

"On Tuesday of this week."

"The night of the murder," thought the inspector. "And did Mr. Brooklyn say where he was speaking from?"

"Yes, he was at Liskeard House, where he wanted the parcel sent."

So Walter Brooklyn, who had apparently failed to secure admittance to the house just before 10.15, had somehow got into it afterwards, and was there at 11.30. He, like George Brooklyn, had slipped into the house unseen. That fact, with the fact of the stick, seemed to the inspector to determine his guilt, or at least his complicity in the crimes, or one of them. The stick and the telephone message, taken together, proved that he had been in Prinsep's room.

The inspector next produced the stick. The porter recognised it at once as the one Walter Brooklyn always carried. He had never seen him with another. He was more sure than the porters at the Byron. He was prepared to swear to the stick. "But," he added, "you've gone and lost the ferrule."

The inspector had noticed that there was no ferrule; but it had not seemed important. It might have dropped off anywhere. He therefore followed up a different line.

"When did you see this stick last?"

"On Saturday, when Mr. Brooklyn was here, he was showing off a billiard stroke with it out there in the hall. It had a ferrule then, all right. I happened to notice it."

No further information was forthcoming, and the inspector passed on to his next business. He went straight back to Liskeard House, and up to Prinsep's study. Exhaustive search there failed to reveal any trace of the missing ferrule.

"I may as well try the garden," said the inspector to himself. "But it's almost too good to be true."

Nevertheless, there in the garden the inspector lighted on

the ferrule, lying in a heap of gravel near the base of the statue. He cursed himself for missing it before, and then blessed his luck that had enabled him to retrieve the blunder. There could be no doubt that it was the right ferrule. The stick was an outsize and it fitted exactly. The nail-marks and the impression left by the rim on the stick coincided exactly. The ferrule was a little out of shape, as if it had been wrenched, and there was a scratch on it where it was bent. But, when the inspector had bent it back into shape, there could be no doubt about the fit. Walter Brooklyn had been in the garden as well as in Prinsep's study, and had been on the very spot where the murder of George Brooklyn had taken place. Inspector Blaikie was more than satisfied with his day's work. Out of seemingly insignificant beginnings, he had built up, he felt, more than enough evidence to hang Walter Brooklyn. He went in the best of spirits to report to his superior officer.

Chapter VIII.
A Review of the Case

The inspector found Superintendent Wilson in his room. As he told his case, the superintendent kept his eyes closed, but every now and then he gave an approving nod. His subordinate had done well, and it was only right that this should be recognised. The inspector's spirits rose higher still as he saw the impression he was making.

Having told the full story, he came to the point on which he wanted his superior's assent.

"And now, sir, I think, as we have abundant evidence, I must ask you to get a warrant made out at once for Walter Brooklyn's arrest."

It was then the inspector received his first check.

"Not quite so fast, my friend," said the superintendent. "Do you mean that, in your opinion, it is proved that Walter Brooklyn committed these murders?"

"Surely," said Inspector Blaikie, "after what I've just told you, there can't be the shadow of a doubt about it."

Superintendent Wilson gave a short laugh, and sat upright in his chair. He was beginning to enjoy himself.

"Ah, but I think there can. Come now. Let us take first only the murder of John Prinsep, leaving out of account for the moment the murder of George Brooklyn. Now, what evidence have you as to the murder of John Prinsep?"

"First, that Walter Brooklyn's walking-stick has been found in his room, and secondly that Walter Brooklyn rang up from Liskeard House at about 11.30 that night. He must have rung up from Prinsep's room. There are only two telephones in the building, one in the porter's room downstairs, connecting with the offices on the ground floor, and the other, on a separate line, in Prinsep's room. He couldn't have used the downstairs 'phone, because it was out of order that night. Winter told me that."

"Assume that you are right. Still, there is at least as strong evidence that George Brooklyn was in the room that night, too. Remember his handkerchief you picked up, and the draughtsman's knife. And in any case he was seen leaving the house at 11.30, and we know from the discovery of his body in the grounds that he came back afterwards."

"Yes, I know that," said the inspector.

"And do you mean to tell me that, in face of that evidence, you can prove to a jury that it was Walter, and not George Brooklyn, who killed Prinsep?"

"Perhaps not, if the case were taken alone. But it has to be considered together with the other—the murder of George Brooklyn. The double incrimination seems to me decisive."

"Wait a bit. Next let us take George Brooklyn's case, leaving aside for the moment that of Prinsep. Now, there, what evidence have you?"

"The finding of the ferrule in the garden, and the strong motive Walter Brooklyn had to put both nephews of Sir Vernon out of the way."

"Motive by itself, however strong, is not enough; and the ferrule evidence is rather slender. It may have been dropped previously."

"Walter Brooklyn had not been to Liskeard House for more

than a week before the murder, and the ferrule was on his stick only three days before."

"I allow you that point. But, even if his stick was in the garden, it does not follow that he was there. He may have lost it earlier. Prinsep may have had it for all we know. Moreover, what of the evidence which seems to show that Prinsep murdered George Brooklyn? He was seen in the garden just before eleven o'clock. The cigar-holder which he habitually used, and had been using that very evening, was found broken on the spot where the murder was done. Moreover, I have in my possession now a far more decisive piece of evidence. You told me that you were sure the finger-prints on the stone club found in the garden were those of Prinsep. You were perfectly correct. The Finger-Print Department has compared them with the impressions of John Prinsep's hands, and these coincide beyond a doubt with the marks left on the stone. You have not yet seen the reproductions, inspector. Here they are."

The superintendent took some papers and photographs from a drawer, and handed them across the table to the inspector, who pored over them for some time without speaking. Finally, he said, with something of a sigh,—

"There can be no doubt they are the same. And, as you say, this throws a quite new light on one of the murders. It seems to prove that George Brooklyn was killed by Prinsep."

"I do not regard it as proof positive: but it is certainly very strong evidence, especially as the marks on the club are just where a man would take hold in order to deal a smashing blow. The murderer used both hands, you notice. The prints are quite distinct for both the thumbs."

"Yes, that is clear enough, although none of the impressions is quite complete. Somehow a part of the marks had got rubbed off before the club was properly examined."

"These accidents will happen. It is only fortunate that the marks were not destroyed beyond hope of identification.

Perhaps you yourself, inspector, or one of your subordinates, handled the club carelessly. Or perhaps some one else handled it before you came on the scene."

"No. I was most careful, and no one touched it after I appeared except myself. The sergeant did not allow it to be touched at all until I arrived. Miss Cowper, who first discovered the body, told me she had not even noticed the weapon, much less handled it. She was too upset to notice anything except the body."

"Well, I suppose it does not greatly matter, as the identification of the prints is still quite clear. There remains, of course, the bare possibility that, while Prinsep did handle the club, he did not actually kill George Brooklyn. But it is certain that the club was the weapon used. The fragments of hair clotted with blood which are still on it came quite definitely from the head of the deceased. The only doubt in my mind is whether Prinsep was a powerful enough man to strike such a blow. But I suppose we must take it that he was. It was a terrific blow, I understand from the medical evidence."

"Yes, but a man not unusually strong can, by using his opportunities, get in a very big blow. I do not think there is much in that."

"Quite so. Then I take it you agree that, in face of the evidence, it would be quite impossible to arrest Walter Brooklyn on the charge of having murdered George Brooklyn?"

The inspector sighed. "Yes," he said, "you are right. I thought the case was getting straightened out, but it now seems darker than ever." Then a thought came into the inspector's mind; and his expression brightened. "But," he went on, "if Prinsep murdered George Brooklyn, that makes it certain that George Brooklyn cannot have murdered him. It means that the evidence against Walter Brooklyn holds so far as the murder of Prinsep is concerned."

"I think you are forgetting a difficulty. Prinsep was last seen in the garden shortly after eleven. But George Brooklyn was seen leaving the house at 11.30. After that, he must somehow have come back, got into the garden, and been murdered. That would take some time."

The inspector nodded.

"But Walter Brooklyn, who rang up his club from Prinsep's rooms at 11.30, was back at his club before midnight. That leaves very little time. If the theory you advance is true, how do you fit in the times? George Brooklyn could hardly have got back into the garden and got himself killed, before a quarter to twelve. It would take Walter Brooklyn five minutes to get out of the house and back to his club. That leaves less than ten minutes for Prinsep to go up to his room and for Walter Brooklyn to murder him."

"That sequence of time is difficult; but it is not impossible. Crime is usually a pretty rapid business. Probably Walter and George came back into the garden together, and the two murders followed in rapid succession. Prinsep killed George, and he and Walter went upstairs together. Then Walter killed him while they were discussing his affairs. You remember the papers I found lying on the table?"

"Perhaps, but that seems to me exceptionally quick work—so quick that my instinct is to doubt whether it is the right explanation. After all, there is no direct evidence that Walter Brooklyn did murder Prinsep."

"Surely the walking-stick and the telephone message together are very strong evidence?"

"Not strong enough, I am certain, to obtain a conviction. The telephone message was sent some time before George Brooklyn was killed. And don't forget that, a moment ago, you thought your evidence that Walter Brooklyn had murdered George Brooklyn equally strong. Yet already you are practically convinced that he did not."

"I am still convinced that he was there when the murder

took place in the garden."

"Ah, that is another matter. He may have been present at both murders, and yet committed neither."

"I see now what you are driving at. You mean that there may be a fourth man involved?"

"That may be so; but I was not quite sure on that point. What the evidence seems to me to establish beyond reasonable doubt is that some meeting of the three men—Prinsep and George and Walter Brooklyn—took place at Liskeard House that night. That meeting was followed by—probably resulted in—the death of two of the three. There may have been others present. That is for you to find out. But I am clear that the next step is to discover what this meeting was about, and who was there. If we knew that, it would probably throw a new light on the whole situation."

"In the circumstances, there is still, it seems to me, every reason for arresting Walter Brooklyn. He was certainly present, whether he committed murder or not."

"I think it will be best to leave him at large for the time being. We have, I think, ample evidence of his presence in the house, but not of his having had a guilty hand in the murders. I think, instead of arresting him, it will be far better for you to see him, and find out all you can about what happened that night."

"Very well. I will try to see him at once. Ought I to warn him that what he says may be used against him?"

"I must leave that to your judgment. And now, inspector, I fancy you are a bit discouraged by the result of our talk. You came here with your mind made up, and you have found that the case is not so straightforward as it was beginning to appear. But that is no reason at all for being discouraged. The evidence you have gathered is of the greatest value. It has enabled us to put our hand on some one who, we are practically sure, knows all about the murders, whether or not he actually committed one of them. Once again, let me congratulate you on a very fine day's work."

The inspector was only in part reassured by Superintendent Wilson's conclusion. He had been watching his superior intently, and had noticed the keen critical joy with which he had demolished the apparently overwhelming case against Walter Brooklyn. The inspector had been compelled to admit, even to himself, the force of his superior's arguments; but, when he left the room, he remained, somehow in spite of this, convinced that Walter Brooklyn was not merely an accessory, but the actual murderer of one, if not of both men, and with a strong suspicion that the apparently conclusive evidence that Prinsep had killed George Brooklyn had a flaw in it somewhere, if only he could find it.

But he could not attend to his instincts for the moment. His next business was to see Walter Brooklyn, and find out from him all he could. At the least, Walter must know a great deal. Most probably he knew the whole story. But how much would he tell?

Chapter IX.
Walter Brooklyn's Explanation

Inspector Blaikie made a hasty meal, and then set off for Walter Brooklyn's club. He found Mr. Brooklyn there, and was soon alone with him in a private room. Before the inspector could even introduce himself and state his business, he found the offensive turned against himself. He had thought over the interview carefully beforehand, and had made up his mind that, whatever his private opinion might be, it was his duty to hear, without prejudice, whatever Walter Brooklyn had to say, and to put aside for the moment all suspicions, resting only on the undoubted fact that the man had been present in the house that night. He might be able to explain his presence, or he might not. The interview would show. Till the chance had been given, the inspector was determined to keep an open mind.

But the conversation did not begin at all as he had anticipated. As he got out the first few words about the purpose for which he had asked for an interview, Walter Brooklyn struck in abruptly.

"See here, inspector, I fail to see that it is any of your business to come nosing about in my affairs. I find you have been asking the porter downstairs a whole lot of questions. From your manner, the fellow has jumped to the conclusion that you suspect me of having had a hand in these murders.

You've set all the servants simmering, and by now it's all round the club that I murdered my nephew or something like it. I tell you I'm damned if I'll stand it. Blast your impudence. Since you have come here, I think you owe me an explanation."

Walter Brooklyn's manner seemed to the inspector quite extraordinarily violent. But he noticed something else while Brooklyn was speaking—the man's amazing physical strength. He could not be less than sixty; but as he stood there, in a half-threatening attitude—with difficulty, it seemed, holding himself in—Inspector Blaikie could not help thinking that here was the very figure of a man to have struck the blows on both the dead men's skulls. Here, moreover, was a man, obviously passionate and lacking in self-control—just the sort of person to resort to violence if his will were crossed. The inspector's open mind was rapidly closing up before Brooklyn had finished his first speech. Nevertheless, he answered quietly enough,—

"I am sorry, Mr. Brooklyn, if any of my inquiries have caused you inconvenience. But you must understand that it is my duty to investigate these murders, and to ask any questions that may be necessary for that purpose. You apparently know——"

But here again Walter Brooklyn struck in.

"Necessary inquiries, of course," he said. "But what I want to know is what you mean by coming round here and practically telling my club servants that I have committed murder. Necessary inquiries, indeed!"

"If you know, Mr. Brooklyn, what was the matter of my conversation with the club servants, you can hardly fail to realise why the inquiries were necessary."

"Most certainly I fail to see it. These murders have nothing to do with me."

"That may be; but even so it is necessary to establish that fact. You know, I suppose, that your walking-stick was found in Mr. Prinsep's room the morning after the murder. I want you to tell me how it got there."

"I dare say you say you found it there. I know that, if it was there, it was not I who put it there. I don't believe it was there at all. I lost it last Tuesday afternoon."

"And where did you lose it, may I ask?"

"If I knew that, my man, I should have been after it soon enough. I must have left it somewhere. Not that it's any business of yours what I did with it."

"Pardon me, Mr. Brooklyn. You will admit that the fact that it was found in Mr. Prinsep's room calls for some explanation. If you do not know where you left it, I shall have to do my best to find out. May I ask where you went last Tuesday afternoon?"

"I don't see why I should tell you."

"I think, Mr. Brooklyn, that, unless you wish to find yourself in the dock on a criminal charge, you had far better do so."

For a moment it seemed as if Walter Brooklyn would make a personal attack on the detective, or at least turn him then and there out of the room. But he seemed to think better of it. "Ask your questions," he said.

"First, then, where did you call when you were out on Tuesday afternoon?"

"I went first to see Mr. Carter Woodman—I presume you know who he is—at his office in Lincoln's Inn. Then I took a taxi to the Piccadilly Theatre, where I saw that young hound, Prinsep, and one or two others."

"Who were the others?"

"An actress-girl there—a Miss Lang. She was the only one."

"Did you see them separately or together?"

"Separately."

"And then where did you go?"

"Back to Mr. Woodman's office. I told him I had lost the stick, and thought I must have left it there. He had a look, but it wasn't there. He said I must have left it in the taxi, and I supposed I had."

"When did you notice the loss?"

"On leaving the theatre."

"So you might have left the stick there, or in the taxi, or at Mr. Woodman's?"

"Yes. If you found it in Prinsep's room, I suppose he must have found it in the theatre, and taken it up to his room."

"Why didn't he give it back to you when he saw you later in the evening?"

"Saw me later in the evening! He didn't see me later in the evening."

"But you were at Liskeard House on Tuesday evening."

"Look here, young man. I don't know what you're driving at. I tell you I did not see Prinsep except in the afternoon."

"But you were at Liskeard House in the evening."

"I tell you I was not. Yes, by Jove, though, I was—in a sense. I went to the door and asked for Sir Vernon, but he was not at home."

"When was that?"

"About ten o'clock, I suppose."

"And you did not go into the house then?"

"No, only into the outer hall."

"That, Mr. Brooklyn, is not the occasion to which I was referring. You came back to Liskeard House still later on Tuesday evening."

Walter Brooklyn glared at the inspector. "Young man,"

he said, "I will thank you not to tell me where I was. I know that for myself."

"You admit, then, that you came back to the house."

"I admit nothing of the sort. I was not in the house at all. I've told you already that I did not go there."

The inspector discharged his bombshell. "Then how did it occur that you rang up the Sanctum Club from Liskeard House at 11.30 on Tuesday evening?"

This was too much for Walter Brooklyn. "Infernal impudence," he said. "I don't know where you picked up these cock-and-bull stories. I did not ring up the Sanctum from Liskeard House, because I was not there. And now I've had enough of your questions, and you can go." And he strode to the door and held it open. "Get out," he said.

The inspector picked up his hat. "I had some further questions to ask you," he said. "Perhaps another time I shall find you in a better mood. Good evening." And he left the room as hastily as he could without compromising his dignity, not quite certain whether Walter Brooklyn would complete the performance by throwing him downstairs. Brooklyn, however, merely relieved his feelings by slamming the door.

In the hall the inspector found the porter. "Had a pleasant interview?" asked the latter, familiar with Walter Brooklyn's ways.

"Not exactly pleasant, but decidedly illuminating," said the inspector, as he went upon his way.

Chapter X
Charis Lang

Inspector Blaikie, when he left the Byron Club, was quite convinced that Walter Brooklyn was the murderer. Not merely one of the murderers, but the murderer of both men. The evidence against Prinsep he was more than ever inclined to discount in face of the impression which Walter Brooklyn had made upon him. Not only the man's manner, but even more his physique, had convinced the inspector of his guilt. Here at least was a man who combined great physical strength with an obviously ungovernable temper—just the combination of qualities which seemed most clearly to fit the case. After all, he had never believed much in finger-prints. They showed, no doubt, that Prinsep had actually held in his hand the weapon with which the murder was committed; but did that prove that he had done the deed? He might conceivably have taken hold of the club for some quite different purpose. The prints were not conclusive evidence—on that point he permitted himself to differ from his superior, who had seemed to think that they were. They needed explaining, certainly; but there were other possible explanations. Moreover, if Prinsep had been careless enough to leave his finger-prints all over the club, was it not curious that not a trace of them had been left on the dead man's clothing, though he had obviously been dragged by the collar from the statue into the little antique temple so as to be out of the way. A starched collar was about the likeliest possible place for clear impressions of fingers. But there was not the trace of a finger-mark on it. The man who dragged the body to the temple steps had certainly worn gloves.

Then a very curious point struck the inspector. All the finger-prints had been partly obliterated, as if some one had handled the club subsequently. But, in the morning he had been careful that no one should do so, and he was fairly certain that no one had. Then another significant point occurred to him. No other finger-prints had been found on the club. Then, if some one else had handled it subsequently, that some one else had worn gloves. But, in the garden that morning, not one of those present had been wearing gloves. The obliterating marks had been made before the discovery, and therefore also presumably before the crime. The inspector almost felt that he could reconstruct the scene. John Prinsep had held the club; but later, Walter Brooklyn, wearing gloves, had handled it. As usual, the evidence of the finger-prints, true as far as it went, was misleading. Only the partial obliteration of the marks had given the key to the truth. The new explanation, moreover, fitted in exactly with his observation of the absence of finger-prints on George Brooklyn's crumpled collar.

It was true, of course, the inspector reflected, that all this was only hypothesis. He could not prove absolutely that the obliterations had been made by a pair of gloved hands holding the club with murderous purpose, and still less could he prove that the gloved hands were Walter Brooklyn's. His conjecture was not evidence in a court of law; but it served to confirm him in his own opinion. He could now, with good hope, go in search of further evidence.

What, then, ought his next step to be? His talk with Walter Brooklyn had opened up certain fresh lines of inquiry. He must see Woodman again, and find out what had been the business on which Brooklyn had twice visited him on the Tuesday. And he had better see this Miss Lang of the Piccadilly Theatre, in case she could throw any light on the case. And he must try to trace Walter Brooklyn's stick. He felt sure that Brooklyn had told him a lie about this, and that he had really left it in Prinsep's room in the evening. But it was his business to make every inquiry, and to test Brooklyn's story by every possible means.

By this time—for it was now nine o'clock—Woodman would certainly have left his office. The inspector felt that he had done a good day's work, and could with a good conscience leave further activity for the morrow. He went home, and straight to bed, in his tiny bachelor flat in Judd Street.

When Inspector Blaikie woke the following morning he at once began to turn the case over in his mind. It was now Thursday, and the inquests had been fixed for Friday. It would be necessary that day to decide on the procedure to be followed. Ought the police to produce the evidence which they had gathered, or would it be better to make the proceedings as purely formal as possible, and to reserve all disclosures for the trial which would surely follow? The Inspector's instinct was against any premature showing of his hand; but he would have to discuss the matter with Superintendent Wilson, with whom the final decision would rest. That could stand over until he had seen Woodman and the unknown Miss Lang. He would arrange to see the superintendent in the afternoon.

The inspector went out and breakfasted in one of those huge "Tyger" restaurants which cater for the servantless flat-dwellers of London. Then he went to Scotland Yard, arranged to see the superintendent after lunch, and 'phoned through to Woodman arranging an eleven o'clock appointment at his office. Next he got on the phone to the Piccadilly Theatre, and discovered that Miss Lang was expected there at about midday. He left a message stating that he would call to see her. She lived, as he knew, at Hammersmith, and was not on the telephone. He also rang through to the sergeant on duty at Liskeard House, who reported that there were no fresh developments.

At eleven o'clock punctually, the inspector entered Carter Woodman's outer office. The old clerk, seated there at his desk, looked up at him suspiciously from a heap of papers. Rather brusquely, the inspector announced that he had come to see Woodman by appointment. The man went to tell his master, and Carter Woodman promptly appeared at the door of the inner room to bid his visitor welcome. Coming towards the inspector, he gripped him firmly by the hand. "Well, my lad, how goes it?" he said. "Have you found the scoundrels? You must come in and tell me all about it."

The inspector felt himself almost carried bodily into the inner room, and seated breathless in a chair, while Carter Woodman took up a commanding position on the hearthrug. "Quite right to come to me," he said. "You must treat me as if I were Sir Vernon—as his man of business I regard myself as in charge of his affairs. Now let me know exactly what you have done so far, and I'll see if I can help you. But, first, have you any fresh clue as to the identity of the murderers?"

Inspector Blaikie reflected, as Woodman was speaking, that powerful physique seemed to run in the Brooklyn family. Woodman was only a distant relative; yet he had many of the physical characteristics which the inspector had noticed in Walter Brooklyn. But there the resemblance seemed to end. Woodman's bluff and hearty manner, which seemed to have big reserves of strength and self-control behind it, was in marked contrast to Walter Brooklyn's passionate and excitable temperament. Woodman belonged to a very definite type—the successful city man who combined keen business acumen and a sharp eye for a bargain with a hail-fellow-well-met manner and an ability to make himself instantly at home in almost any society.

The inspector, engrossed with his own thoughts, said nothing in immediate reply to Woodman's question; and the latter, after a pause, repeated it, remarking cheerfully, "What, daydreaming, are we? Won't do in a detective, you know. Not at all what we expect of you, eh?" And, after putting his hand for a moment on the inspector's shoulder, he abandoned his place of vantage before the fireplace and sat down in his desk-chair facing his visitor.

"I saw Mr. Walter Brooklyn yesterday—not, I am afraid, a very pleasant interview. He seemed to resent very much my asking him any questions—in fact he all but threw me downstairs," the detective added with a laugh.

"What took you to see him?" asked Woodman. "I suppose it was about our seeing him outside the house."

"It had come to my knowledge that Mr. Walter Brooklyn was actually in Mr. Prinsep's room at Liskeard House at 11.30 on Tuesday night."

"Good Lord, man, you don't say so. Are you sure? Why, who in the world told you that?"

"Nobody actually saw him there; but he telephoned at that time to his club, said that he was speaking from Liskeard House, and asked if a registered parcel had arrived for him, as he wanted it sent round there at once."

"Dear me, inspector, this throws a new—and a most distressing—light on the case. Did you discover from Mr. Brooklyn what he was doing at Liskeard House?"

"No, and it was exactly on that point that I came to see what you could tell me."

"My dear chap, I'm as surprised as you are to know that he was there at all."

"I understand from Mr. Brooklyn that he had seen you earlier in the day. It might help if I knew what was the business then."

"You probably know enough about Walter Brooklyn to guess that it was about money."

"I had guessed so; but I am glad to have it definite. Can you give me rather more particulars?"

"I think I may, though, strictly speaking, the matter ought to be confidential. Mr. Walter Brooklyn had been trying for some time to get Sir Vernon to pay his debts, as he had done on several previous occasions. This time Sir Vernon handed the matter over to John Prinsep, partly because he was away from town, and partly because he thought he could trust Prinsep to handle the matter more successfully than if he did it himself. Prinsep thereupon saw Walter Brooklyn, and also consulted me. On my advice, he refused to make any payment without a very clear understanding that this was to be the last application. Walter Brooklyn tried all means to get the money without conditions, and in particular refused to disclose in detail what his liabilities were. Prinsep would not give a penny unless his conditions were met. On Tuesday afternoon Walter Brooklyn came down by appointment to see me, and I tried to get him to accept the conditions. He refused, and declared his intention of seeing Prinsep again. I told him he must do what he liked about that. I believe he saw Prinsep. Anyhow, later in the afternoon he came back, and made another attempt to get me to urge that the conditions should be modified. I refused of course, and he left. I have not seen him since."

"So far as you know, he had made no appointment with Prinsep for the evening?"

"I know nothing about that. He may have done. He did not tell me."

"When he came back to you the second time, did he tell you that he had lost his walking-stick, and ask if you had found it in the office after he left?"

"Yes, I believe he did. It was not here. I said he had probably left it in the taxi."

"And that is all you know about the matter?"

"Yes, of course I know something about the extent of Walter Brooklyn's liabilities. They are considerable."

"We can go into that if it becomes necessary. But can you tell me—would it be likely that, if Walter Brooklyn arranged a meeting with Prinsep about money, George Brooklyn would also have been present? It seems they were both there that evening?"

"I should not have expected so; but it is certainly not impossible. Prinsep might have called in George, as he was co-heir to Sir Vernon's money, to help him make it quite plain that the money would only be paid if the conditions were met. Or, of course, it may have been an accident. George Brooklyn might have been with Prinsep when Walter called. Have you any reason to believe that it was so?"

"Well, we know that Walter Brooklyn, although he denies it, was in Prinsep's room at about 11.30. We know that George Brooklyn left the house at about that time, and he must have come back at some time later to the garden, if not to the house. It seems at least likely that they met either before or after 11.30."

"Yes, that seems probable. But I am afraid I know no more than I have told you."

"Perhaps you can help me a little more. I am getting interested in this Miss Lang, who seems to turn up at every point in the story. It now appears that Walter Brooklyn went to see her at the theatre on Tuesday afternoon. He saw her and Prinsep there separately."

"I know nothing about that. I told you he went off to see Prinsep; but I have no idea what he can have been doing with Miss Lang."

"Did Walter Brooklyn know Miss Lang?"

"Quite probably. He had a large theatrical acquaintance.

But I did not know he was friendly with her."

"But you said that Mr. George Brooklyn was to have seen Miss Lang on Tuesday evening."

The lawyer nodded.

"And now," the inspector continued, "we find Walter as well as George Brooklyn mixed up with her. May not she have had something to do with the evening meeting at Liskeard House?"

"Really, inspector, that is a matter for you. I have never seen the young woman, and I know no more about her than I have already told you. You had better see her yourself."

"That is what I propose to do; but I thought you might be able to throw some light on Walter Brooklyn's dealings with her."

"None at all, unfortunately. I wish I could; for there is nothing I want more than to get this horrible business cleared up."

The inspector saw that there was nothing more to be learned from Carter Woodman at that stage. He accordingly took his leave, and went in search of Charis Lang, who, he was beginning to feel, might well hold the clue to the whole mystery. His original idea had been to see her at her home; but he had decided that it would be better to talk to her at the theatre, where the event in which she was concerned had actually taken place. Accordingly, he took a taxi to the Piccadilly Theatre, and sent up his card to Miss Lang, who had just arrived, and been given his note and message.

When he was shown into Charis Lang's room, Inspector Blaikie had his first surprise. He had been expecting, without any good reason, to be confronted with a beauty of the picture post card type, some little bit of fluff from the musical comedy stage. But he saw at once that Charis Lang was not at all that kind of woman. She was a girl whom no one but an idiot—and

Inspector Blaikie was far from being an idiot—would think of calling pretty. Beautiful, some people would call her, but less from any regularity of feature than from an effect of carriage and expression—a dignity without aloofness, a self-possession that was neither hard nor unwomanly. The inspector did not think her beautiful—she was not of the type he admired—but he said to himself that here was obviously a woman of character. And he at once changed his mind about the right way of tackling Miss Lang. She was, he recognised, a person with whom it would pay to be quite frank.

"I understand," she began, "that you wish to ask me some questions about"—she hesitated a moment—"this terrible affair." The inspector could see that she was deeply moved.

"Yes, Miss Lang," he replied, "I have come to ask you for certain information. We have, of course, every desire to trouble you as little as possible."

"Oh," she interrupted, "I only wish I had more to tell you. By all means, ask me what you will."

"I am afraid some of my questions may seem to you rather impertinent."

"No, inspector. I understand it is your business to get at the truth. I shall answer, whatever you may ask."

"Then, first of all, will you tell me about Mr. Walter Brooklyn. I understand that he came to see you last Tuesday here. Is that so?"

"I confess I am surprised at the question. I thought it was about Mr. George Brooklyn and Mr. Prinsep that you wished to question me. But I can answer at once. Mr. Walter Brooklyn did come to see me."

"Do you know Mr. Walter Brooklyn well?"

"No, hardly at all. Indeed, until that day I had scarcely spoken to him. I had met him a few times in large gatherings at Liskeard House and elsewhere."

"Then he is not a friend of yours?"

"By no means." The answer was so decided as to startle the inspector.

"Have you any objection," he asked, "to telling me on what business Mr. Walter Brooklyn visited you on Tuesday?"

"It is not a thing I like to speak about; but I am fully prepared to tell you. Mr. Brooklyn came to make to me a dishonourable suggestion that I should help him to extract money from Mr. Prinsep."

"In what way?"

"Mr. Prinsep had refused to give Mr. Walter Brooklyn a certain sum of money which he wanted. He came to ask me to bring pressure to bear on Mr. Prinsep to give it to him. He suggested that I had a hold over Mr. Prinsep—I suppose I must tell you what made him think that too—and that if I was to ask he would get the money."

"And on what ground did he ask you to do this?"

"He threatened that if I did not he would tell Sir Vernon about me and Mr. Prinsep. He made the most horrible insinuations."

"You were friendly with Mr. Prinsep?"

"Two years ago John Prinsep asked me to marry him, and I accepted him. Our engagement was kept secret at his request."

"Miss Lang, I am sorry if I give you pain; but I must ask you whether you were engaged to Mr. Prinsep at the time of his death."

The answer came clearly, but in a voice totally devoid of expression. "I do not know," said Charis Lang. "The engagement had at least not been formally broken off."

"And of course you rejected Walter Brooklyn's proposal?"

"I did."

"Did you tell Mr. Prinsep about it?"

"No. It was not a matter I could bring myself to mention to him."

"You understood that Walter Brooklyn intended to carry the story to Sir Vernon?"

"Yes, and of course Sir Vernon would have been very angry. He has always wanted John to marry his ward, Miss Cowper."

"What had Walter Brooklyn to gain by telling Sir Vernon?"

"I suppose he thought that Sir Vernon would soon make John give me up, and that between them they could fix up for John and Miss Cowper to marry. Or perhaps he relied on my telling John, and thought John would let him have the money to prevent him from going to Sir Vernon."

"Yes, that seems the most probable explanation. And did you see Mr. Prinsep after your meeting with Walter Brooklyn?"

"Yes, for a few moments. He had seen Mr. Brooklyn, too, and was very angry. Mr. Brooklyn had used the same threat to him as he used to me."

"And how had Mr. Prinsep taken it?"

"He had refused to give Mr. Brooklyn a penny, and said he would see Sir Vernon himself."

"In order to tell him of your engagement?"

Again came the answer, painfully given, "I do not know."

"I am sorry, Miss Lang, but I have not quite done. Did you see Mr. George Brooklyn on Tuesday?"

"Yes, he came here to see me after he had left Liskeard House in the evening."

"At what time was that?"

"It was after ten o'clock—probably about a quarter past. I am off the stage for a long time then."

"Was Mr. George Brooklyn a friend of yours?"

"Yes, in a way. At least, Mrs. George Brooklyn is a very

dear friend. I used to understudy her when she was Isabelle Raven. She was the Isabelle Raven, you know."

"Yes. Then there was nothing unusual in Mr. George Brooklyn's coming to see you here?"

"I don't think he had ever been to my room before. I had often met him at his own house or at Liskeard House."

"Did he come for some special purpose?"

"Yes, he came to see me about my engagement to Mr. Prinsep."

"Do you mind telling me more exactly what you mean?"

"Until recently, Mr. Prinsep always behaved to me as if we were engaged. Lately, his manner to me had changed. When I spoke to him about it, he laughed it off, and I tried to go on treating him as I had done. But about a fortnight ago I had a letter from Mr. Carter Woodman—you know him, I expect— saying he would like to discuss with me certain matters placed in his hands by Mr. Prinsep. I wrote back saying that I could not conceive that there was anything in my relations with John that called for a lawyer's interference. Then I took the letter to John, and we had a real quarrel about it. I asked him if I was to consider our engagement at an end; but he put me off, and before I could get him to answer we were interrupted. I did not see him again until Tuesday, and then only for a minute. I meant to try to clear matters up, and to tell him I could not go on like that; but he was called away, and I had no chance. Then in the evening George Brooklyn came to see me."

"Will you tell me what happened then?"

"He asked me point-blank whether I had been engaged to John. I said that I certainly had been, but that I didn't know whether I still was. I told him that I still loved John; but I asked him to let John know—he had promised to see him when he left me—that I considered our engagement definitely at an end, unless he desired to renew it."

"Miss Lang, my questions must have been very painful, and it has been very good of you to answer them so freely. I think there is only one thing more I need ask. At what time did Mr. George Brooklyn leave you?"

"A few minutes after half-past ten. I went on the stage again almost immediately afterwards."

"And you did not see Mr. George Brooklyn again?"

"No."

"You saw no more of either Mr. Prinsep or Mr. Walter Brooklyn, I suppose?"

"Yes, as it happens, I caught sight, out of my window, of Mr. Prinsep walking in the garden behind the theatre. That must have been about a quarter past eleven."

"And that is all you saw. He was alone?"

"Yes. I saw no one else."

"Then I have only to thank you again for the way in which you have told me what you know." And with that the inspector took his leave, feeling that, as a result of his talk, he had scored another good point against Walter Brooklyn. Quite apart from the murders, the man really deserved hanging for his behaviour to Charis Lang—at least that was how Inspector Blaikie felt about it. He must get enough evidence to convince his reluctant superior, and thereafter twelve good men and true, that Walter Brooklyn was the murderer. John Prinsep, perhaps, was not such a bad riddance: certainly he had been behaving like a cad. But then, Charis Lang was in love with him, and that was enough to cover a multitude of sins. For her sake at least the murderer must be brought to justice. Moreover, George Brooklyn seemed to have been a good sort. The inspector was inclined to dismiss the idea that he had had anything to do with the killing of Prinsep, even though his talk with Prinsep after leaving Charis Lang might have afforded full provocation, if, as seemed likely, Prinsep had refused to marry her. The inspector's last thought was that it was still a tangled enough skein that he had to unravel. But some at least of the knots had been successfully untied.

Chapter XI
Joan Takes Up the Case

Charis Lang had kept her composure during that trying interview with the inspector, and had forced herself to tell him everything she had to tell that could even indirectly bear upon the murders. She had felt that this was her duty; and in her the sense of duty was unusually strong. But the telling had cost her a terrible effort, and when the inspector went away, and there was no longer need to hold herself up bravely, her fortitude gave way. She had told things which, until then, she had not admitted even to herself; and what hurt her most was that, in telling the truth and nothing but the truth, she had been compelled to let John Prinsep's character appear in the worst light. Not, she told herself, that it mattered to him any longer; but she loved him, and it was horrible to her that she should have to drag his memory in the mud. Moreover, was he not suspected of having killed George Brooklyn, and would not her account of him have made such an act seem more probable? She did not believe that he had done so, and, as she thought over her conversation with the inspector, she felt that she had been false to his memory; and yet she knew that there was nothing else she could have done.

But why had Walter Brooklyn been so dragged into the case by the detective? Until Inspector Blaikie had come to see her, she had been quite without a theory of the events of Tuesday.

She had been stunned by the fact of Prinsep's death, and she had hardly troubled to think who could have killed him. Now it was clear that the police believed that Walter Brooklyn had something to do with it. An odious man, by all accounts, and one who had proved himself odious beyond measure in his dealings with her. Yet not a man she would readily have suspected of murder with violence. Underhand crimes—dirty, little crimes—she said to herself, would be more in keeping with what she knew of him. And then, despite his treatment of her, she accused herself of being uncharitable. After all, there was some dignity about murder; and her feeling, biased no doubt by her personal experience, was that Walter Brooklyn was not even fit to be a murderer.

Charis felt that she could not go on to the stage that afternoon as if nothing had happened. She had forced herself to play her part—and had played it as well as ever—since the tragedy; but for that afternoon at least she must be free, and her understudy must take her place. Having been forced to tell her story to the inspector, she felt all the more need to tell it again to some one more sympathetic—to some real friend capable of understanding what she had suffered and of sharing in her sorrow. Speedily her mind was made up. She must see Isabelle, Mrs. George Brooklyn. Isabelle, too, was in trouble at least as hard as her own. Isabelle had lost her George, as she had lost John Prinsep.

Then she remembered. Some people said that John had killed George Brooklyn, and some said that George Brooklyn had killed John Prinsep. She had heard that there was evidence, though she did not know what it was. Could either of these things be true, and, if there was even a chance that either might be true, how could she go and talk about it to Isabelle?

She did not find an answer to her questions; but all the same she made up her mind to go. She was capable of conceiving the thought that the two men might have quarrelled, and that the one might have killed the other; but she was not capable of believing the thought which she could conceive. She knew that they might quarrel—that they had done so often enough; but they would not kill. And even if they had—she barely formulated the thought—what did it matter now? She and Isabelle were both desolate and in need of comfort. She would go.

So Charis, having made—to her understudy's secret delight—her arrangements at the theatre, set off to find Isabelle—for that was the name by which she still called Marian Brooklyn. Isabelle, she knew, was still at the hotel— the Cunningham—and she had not far to go. In a few minutes the two women were in each other's arms. It was not a question of who had killed their lovers; they both needed comfort, and they sought together such comfort as could be found.

By-and-by, Charis found herself telling the story of the inspector's visit. She had never before spoken openly to Mrs. George about John Prinsep; but now she told the whole story, only to find that most of it was known to Marian already. Marian told her how Carter Woodman had come to see her, and asked her to use her influence to break the entanglement between Charis and John Prinsep, and how she had indignantly refused and had threatened to go and tell John straight out that he ought to marry her. Charis did not try to defend Prinsep: she realised that there could be no defence for what he had done; but she told Marian that she had loved him, and that she believed he had loved her—in a way—and would certainly have married her but for his fear of Sir Vernon's opposition. She told Marian that it was quite clear from the inspector's manner that he suspected Walter Brooklyn of one, if not of both, murders, and at last she told her of Walter Brooklyn's visit to herself, and of the infamous threat he had made.

To Charis's surprise, Marian Brooklyn altogether refused to consider the possibility of Walter's guilt. She had seen him outside Liskeard House as they left on the Tuesday evening, and she agreed that he might possibly have gone there to carry out his threat of telling Sir Vernon. But she was quite convinced that he had had nothing to do with the murders, and she was very doubtful whether he would really have carried out his threat against Charis. "Walter Brooklyn," she said, "is a thoroughly bad lot. In money matters you couldn't trust him an inch. But I do not believe he would really have done a thing like that—I mean, either murdered anybody, or really told Sir Vernon about you. He might threaten, but I don't believe he'd do such a thing, when it came to the point."

Then Marian Brooklyn realised what seemed to her the most horrible thing about the situation. "Poor Joan," she said, "it will be simply terrible for her if Walter Brooklyn is really suspected. She has trouble enough with what has happened, already, and with Sir Vernon on her hands in such a state that nearly everything has to be kept from him. If her stepfather is going to be dragged into court, I don't know what she will do."

All Charis could suggest was that it would be best that she should know nothing about it until it could no longer be kept from her; but to this Marian Brooklyn did not agree. "I think, dear, she had better know at once. Joan is not easily frightened; and I am sure she would wish to be told."

And so it was finally settled. Marian Brooklyn said that she would go to Liskeard House at once and try to see Joan. At first she suggested that Charis should come with her; but finally they agreed that she had better go alone. Charis, a good deal more at ease after her talk with her friend, went back to the theatre with every intention of appearing at the evening performance.

Marian Brooklyn found Joan at home. Indeed, since Tuesday she had not left the house, save for an occasional breath of air in the garden. With the police continually making inquiries, Newspaper reporters laying constant siege to the house, and

Sir Vernon so ill that the fact of George Brooklyn's death had still to be kept from him, and George's absence explained by all manner of subterfuges, Joan and Mary Woodman had been going through a terrible time, made the worse, in Joan's case at least, by the sense of helplessness in face of a great calamity. Her duties in looking after Sir Vernon did not prevent her from thinking: rather they were such as to make thought turn to brooding. Her thoughts seemed to go round and round in an endless and aimless circle; and, as the days passed, the strain was telling on her far more than on Mary Woodman, who was not blessed—or cursed—with the faculty of imagination. Mary did her duty quietly and sympathetically, and with little sign of inward disturbance. Joan did her duty, too, but she was eating out her soul in the doing of it. Her face, as she came into the room to greet Marian, was haggard with lack of sleep. She had not quite lost that look of composure and self-possession that was normally hers; but it was easy to see that the strain on her had been severe.

Marian did not quite know how to begin what she had to say; but Joan saved her from her embarrassment by beginning at once to speak about Sir Vernon. He had been very bad indeed; he was still very bad, but she thought he was beginning to rally. It had been terribly difficult—having to keep from him the news and prevent him from taking any part in the investigation. He had asked more than once to see the police; but the doctor said that absolute rest was indispensable, and that any further shock or excitement would almost certainly still be fatal to him. Joan told Marian that she and Mary had their hands so full that they knew little or nothing of what was going on, and had no idea what progress the police were making towards the solution of the mystery.

This gave Marian the opening for which she had been waiting. "It was about that, darling," she said, "I came to see you. I did not want the police to come asking you more questions until you were prepared."

Joan expressed her surprise. "Prepared, Marian—prepared for what do you mean?"

"Well, dear, I thought I had better tell you. The police think they have a clue."

"A clue? Do you mean they know who did it?"

"No, dear. I don't mean that they know; but there is somebody whom they suspect. Of course, it is their business to suspect people; but I thought I ought to tell you."

"Of course, it is their business to find out who did it. I am only glad it isn't mine—and yet I can't help wondering. I keep thinking about it, even though I try hard to put it out of my mind."

"That is only natural, dear. It is the same with me. I find myself wondering——"

Joan interrupted, "And the worst of it is that one's thoughts take one no further. Mine just go round and round, I haven't the ghost of an idea who it was."

"What I came to tell you, Joan, was this. Of course, it can't be true; but the police suspect—your stepfather."

Joan had been standing, leaning with one arm on the mantelpiece; but at Marian's words she went very white, and her body swayed. She gripped the mantelpiece to steady herself, and felt her way to a chair. For a moment she said nothing. Then, so low as to be just audible, her answer came. "Marian, tell me at once what makes you think that."

"I don't think it, my dear. But, unfortunately, the police do. That man, Inspector Blaikie, has quite convinced himself of it. I had better tell you exactly what I know."

Then Marian told Joan all about the inspector's visit to Charis Lang. Joan listened in silence, barely moving. Her colour came back slowly, and, as she realised that the police had built up a real case against her stepfather, a look of determination came into her face.

"I wonder if he knows," she said. "I must go to him at once."

Marian said to herself that Joan was bearing it wonderfully well. There was no fear that she would collapse under the shock. Indeed, she could see that the news had really done her good. During the days since the crime she had been suffering above all because she felt helpless and useless. The danger to her stepfather gave her a sense of work to do. It roused her and brought into play the reserves of strength in her character. Marian had so far held back the reason for Walter Brooklyn's visit to Charis Lang; but she felt that it was only fair to Joan to tell her the whole truth, however bad it might be. If she was to help Walter Brooklyn, she must certainly know the worst that could be said against him.

There was no doubt at all in Joan's mind. Badly as Walter Brooklyn had used her, and though she had refused to live any longer under his roof, she was quite certain that he was incapable of murder, above all of the murders of the two victims of Tuesday's tragedy. Even when Marian told her the purpose with which Walter Brooklyn had been to visit Charis Lang, that in no way altered her view. "He would never have told Sir Vernon," she said. "It was only too like him to threaten; but he would never have done it. I know him, and I'm sure of that."

Joan was keenly anxious to find out what evidence the police could possibly have against her stepfather; but of this Marian could tell her hardly anything. She could only suggest that probably Carter Woodman would know about it. Mrs. Woodman was still with her at the hotel; but Carter had been away the previous night, and she had not seen him. Joan said that she would try to see Carter at once, and then, when she had found out all she could, she would go to see Walter Brooklyn.

So far from being prostrated by the news, Joan was moved

by it to take action at once. She telephoned through to Carter Woodman at his office, and asked him particularly to come and see her at Liskeard House that afternoon. Woodman tried to put her off; but when she said that, if he could not come to her, she would go at once to him, he at last agreed to come. Within an hour he was with her, and Joan plunged at once into business by asking him to tell all he knew about the police and the progress they had made.

Woodman seemed reluctant to talk; but, on being pressed, he told her most of what had passed at his first talk with the inspector, leaving out, however, anything which would tend to connect Walter Brooklyn with the crime, and thereby creating the impression that the police were totally at a loss. But Joan was not to be put off so easily. "It's no use, Carter," she said, "your trying to spare my feelings. I know that the police suspect my stepfather, and I want to know on what evidence they are trying to build up a case against him. Surely you must know something about that."

Faced with the direct question, Carter Woodman told her most of what he knew. He said that the police had found out that Walter Brooklyn had been in the house that night, and that he had actually telephoned to his club from Prinsep's room at about half-past eleven. He told her that Walter Brooklyn's walking-stick had been found in Prinsep's room, and that Walter had almost thrown the inspector downstairs when he went to question him about his movements. What surprised him, he said, was that Walter Brooklyn had not been arrested already.

At this Joan broke out indignantly, "You don't mean that you believe he did it?"

"My dear Joan, I only wish you had not asked me such a question. But what am I to think? It is clear that he was in the house, and somebody must have done it, after all. I'm sorry for you; but I think you are under no illusions about your stepfather's character."

"I tell you that he could never have done a thing like that. I know he's a bad man, in many ways. But he's not that sort. Surely you must understand that."

But Carter Woodman did not seem to understand it. Apologetically, but firmly, he made it quite clear to Joan that he was disposed to believe in Walter Brooklyn's guilt, or at least that he saw nothing unlikely in the supposition that he might have committed murder. Joan, who had intended to ask Woodman to go to work for the purpose of clearing her stepfather, soon saw that there was nothing to be gained by making such a request. In his present mood, at least, Carter Woodman would be far more likely to search for further evidence of Walter Brooklyn's guilt. Joan had found out from him most of what she wanted; and, seeing that there was nothing further to be gained by enlisting his help, she got rid of him as soon as she decently could.

When Woodman had gone, Joan sat down to think the matter over quietly. She was absolutely certain that her stepfather was in no way guilty of the murders; but, after what Woodman had said, it seemed only too clear that he must have been on the spot when one of them at least was committed. That meant that he knew the truth; but, for some reason or other, he had evidently not told the police what he knew. That, Joan felt, was not altogether surprising. Probably the police had somehow got him into one of his rages; and she knew that, if that were so, it was just like him to have refused to say a word. It was more than ever necessary for her to see him and get at the real truth of what he knew. Only if she had that to go upon could she help him; and, as Carter Woodman would do nothing, she felt that she must devote all her energies to clearing him of the suspicion. He would have to have a good lawyer of his own, of course; but Joan must see him, and compel him to bestir himself about his defence.

For one thing, he was certain to be in low water; and she must at once promise to pay all the expenses of the case.

She admitted to herself that, in the light of what Charis Lang and Woodman had told her, the police seemed to have a strong case against Walter Brooklyn. Her mind went back to Woodman's words, "After all, somebody must have done it"; and she realised that, for the police "somebody" might mean Walter Brooklyn quite as readily as any one else. She, knowing him as no one besides knew him, might be sure of his innocence; but that was no reason why others should share her conviction. No, if Walter Brooklyn was to escape from the coils in which he was enmeshed, it would be because decisive evidence was forthcoming that he had not committed the murders. And that decisive evidence would have to be deliberately searched for by some one other than the police, who, intent on proving the case against Walter Brooklyn, would not be likely to seek for clues which would invalidate their own case. And, if she did not undertake this task, who would? She felt that the duty was hers.

But if, as she was sure, Walter Brooklyn had not committed murder, then who had, and what had her stepfather been doing in Liskeard House that night? It was true that, by Carter's account, he had denied his presence there; but it did not surprise Joan at all that her stepfather should have lied to the police. If he was determined not to tell what he knew, his only possible course was to deny that he had been present. She would have to point out to him that, as his presence in the house had been definitely established, the only possible course remaining was to tell the police everything that he knew.

But what could it be that he was holding back? If he had been present when murder was done, he must be concealing the name of the murderer. That puzzled Joan; for she did not see whom Walter Brooklyn could possibly be intent on shielding. Quixotism was as unlike him as deliberate murder.

Moreover, who could the murderer have been? She searched her mind in vain for any hint of a clue. There was literally no one whom she could suspect. The whole thing appeared to her merely inexplicable.

She realised, however, that the best way—perhaps the only way—of clearing her stepfather was to bring the real murderer to light. But there might be two different murderers. Joan was inclined to regard it as quite possible that Prinsep might have killed George Brooklyn; but it was utterly inconceivable that George should have killed anybody. Far more clearly than her stepfather, he was not that kind of man. So that the best line of inquiry seemed to be to search for the murderer of John Prinsep. But, she remembered, it was in this case that the police had their strongest evidence against Walter Brooklyn. There was little or nothing, so far as she knew, to connect him with the death of George; but he had been in Prinsep's room, and there his stick had been found. Surely he must know who had killed John Prinsep. She could do nothing until she had seen him; but seeing him might well clear up the whole tragedy once and for all.

Joan was still lying back in her chair, with closed eyes, trying to think the thing out, when Winter announced that Mr. Ellery was in the lounge, and would like to see her if she felt equal to it. She had not seen Ellery since that fatal Tuesday evening, when he had left with the other guests, announcing his intention of walking back to Chelsea. Doubtless, he had felt that to come sooner would be an intrusion; but she knew enough of his feelings to be sure that it had cost him a struggle to keep away. She was glad—very glad—he had come; for just what she wanted was some one to whom she could talk freely, some one on whose help she could rely in trying to clear her stepfather. Robert Ellery, she knew, would be ready to believe as she believed, and to do everything in his power to help her in her trouble. These thoughts flashed through her mind as she went to the lounge where he was waiting.

Chapter XII
Robert Ellery

It had been a struggle for Ellery to keep away. He had heard nothing of the tragedy until Wednesday evening, when he had been to dine with his guardian, Harry Lucas, at Hampstead. There had been, of course, nothing in the morning papers, and he had not seen an evening paper. He had, indeed, spent the day in a long country walk, returning to Hampstead across the Heath in time to dress for dinner at his guardian's house, where he always kept a change of clothes, and often stayed the night. His walk had been taken with a purpose—no less a purpose than going thoroughly with himself into the question of his feeling for Joan Cowper. He had been a silent witness of the scene at Sir Vernon's party, when Joan had declared outright that nothing would ever make her marry John Prinsep. That outburst of hers had meant a great deal to him. He had hardly concealed from himself before the fact that he was head over ears in love with Joan; but he had always taught himself to regard his love as hopeless, and tried to make himself believe that he ought to get the better of it, and accept as a foregone conclusion Joan's marriage with Prinsep. He had been told by Sir Vernon himself that they were engaged, and, of course, no word on the matter had passed between him and Joan.

Her definite repudiation of the engagement had therefore come to him as a surprise, and, for the first time, had allowed him to think that his own suit might not be altogether hopeless. Joan liked him: that he knew well enough; but loving was, of course, another story, and he hardly allowed himself, even now, to hope that she loved him. But he made up his mind, after what had passed, first to spend the day in the country, thinking things over, or rather charging at full speed down the Middlesex lanes while the processes of thought went on of their own momentum. Then, he promised himself to tell his guardian in the evening exactly how matters stood, and to ask for his advice. Harry Lucas had known well how to make himself the friend and counsellor, as well as the guardian, of the young man.

Ellery went straight upstairs and dressed without seeing his guardian. But, as soon as they met in the smoking-room before dinner, he saw that something very serious was the matter. Lucas had expected that Ellery would already have heard the news; but, when he found that he knew nothing, he told him the story in a few words, explaining how the bodies had been discovered, but saying nothing about clues or about any opinion he may have entertained as to the identity of the murderer—or the murderers. Lucas himself had been down to Liskeard House to offer his help: he had seen Sir Vernon for a few minutes, and had talked with Joan and Mary Woodman. He had also seen Superintendent Wilson at Scotland Yard, and offered any help it might be in his power to give. But, beyond the bare facts discovered in the morning—startling enough in themselves—he knew little, and, of course, at this stage the inquiries of Inspector Blaikie were only at their beginning.

Ellery asked no questions at first. The news seemed for the moment to strike him dumb, and the first clear thought that arose in his mind was that, now at least, there could be no more question of Joan marrying Prinsep. Ellery had most cordially disliked and distrusted Prinsep, and he could not pretend to feel any great sorrow at his death. But he had greatly liked George Brooklyn, and, after his first thought, it was mainly the terrible sorrow that had come upon all those who were left that filled his mind. For a time he and Lucas spoke of nothing but the depth of the tragedy that had come upon the Brooklyns.

But, by-and-by, Ellery's curiosity began to assert itself. After all there was mystery as well as tragedy in the events of Tuesday night; and mystery had always exercised over him a strong fascination. "I feel a beast," he said to his guardian, "for thinking of anything but the sorrow of it all; but I'm damned if I can help wanting to find out all about it."

"My dear Bob, that's perfectly natural. It would be so in any one; but it's more than natural in your case. You write detective novels; and here you are faced with a crime mystery in real life. You would be more than human if you didn't want to unravel it. Besides, seriously enough, it wants unravelling, and I don't think the police are going to have an easy time in finding out the truth."

Then Lucas told him of the strange clues that had been discovered—how all the evidence seemed to point to the conclusion that Prinsep had murdered George Brooklyn, and equally to the conclusion that George had murdered Prinsep.

"Of course," Lucas added, "that is physically quite impossible; and personally, I'm not in the least disposed to believe that either of them killed the other. I'm sure in my own mind that some one else killed both of them; but I haven't a ghost of an idea who it can have been."

"And so there's nothing been found out to throw suspicion on anybody else?"

"So far as I know, nothing at all. You'd better do a bit of detective work on your own account."

Ellery said nothing in reply to that. While they had been talking, he had been turning over in his mind the question whether, after what had happened, he could possibly speak to his guardian about his love for Joan. He had told himself firmly that he could not; but, just when he had thought his mind made up, he found himself beginning to speak about it all the same. He was so full of it that he could not keep from declaring it.

"Was Joan really engaged to Prinsep?" he asked.

Harry Lucas had a good idea of Ellery's reason for asking the question. But he gave no hint of this in his answer, preferring to let the young man speak or not of his own affairs, as might seem to him best.

"No—that she never was," he replied. "Long ago, Sir Vernon had set his heart on their marrying, and he always persisted in treating it as settled. Joan, I know, had told him again and again that she would not marry Prinsep; but he always put her off, and said that it would all come right in the end. Between ourselves, I don't think Prinsep was really very keen on marrying Joan; but he was prepared to do it because Sir Vernon wanted it, and he was afraid he would not get the money if he refused. I don't know that I ought to speak like that about him now that he's dead: but you know very well that I disliked him, and it's no use pretending that I didn't."

Ellery felt his spirits rising as he heard what Lucas said—and again he accused himself of being a beast for feeling cheerful on such an occasion. No more was said then, and during dinner, while the servants were in the room, they talked of other things—of the play which Ellery was writing, of where he had been during the day, of many indifferent matters. They were both glad when dinner was over, and they could return to the smoking-room and be again alone.

Then it was that Ellery told Lucas of his love for Joan. And then he had his surprise; for he found that his guardian had discovered that for himself long ago, and that he was being strongly encouraged to persist in his suit. "My dear boy," said Lucas, "of course you're in love with Joan, and I shouldn't be a bit surprised if you find out before long that she's in love with you. She's a very fine young woman, and I couldn't wish you better fortune than to win her. I hope you will, when the time comes. But, of course, you can't make love to her just now. You will have to wait until this terrible affair is over."

"But, if I see her how can I possibly help telling her now— now that other fellow is out of the way? I know I shall simply blurt it out, and probably spoil my chance for good and all."

Lucas gave him some sage advice. He should go and see Joan, and offer to help in any way he could. But on no account must he make love to her yet awhile. From which it may be seen that Harry Lucas, up to date as he thought himself, had still some old-fashioned ideas about propriety.

Ellery stayed the night at Hampstead, and went to bed in a mood of cheerfulness which, he told himself, was quite unforgivably brutal. He would go and see Joan the next day. He would try to follow his guardian's advice: but, if he failed, well, he would fail, and he was not sure that to fail would be quite such a disaster as Lucas made out. After all, she had not been engaged to Prinsep; and why should he not say he loved her?

The next morning Ellery left, after an early breakfast, without seeing his guardian, and went off for another long walk across the Heath and over to Mill Hill. His mood had changed, and he now told himself that to go and see Joan would be an intrusion, and that he must at least let some days pass before he went. He felt he could not see her without telling her of his love, and he was sure that to tell her now would be wrong. He tried to put the thing out of his mind, and, as long as he kept walking, he succeeded fairly well. But when, after a long day, he found himself back in his lodgings at Chelsea, he was soon aware that he would be fit for nothing else until he had seen her.

He tried to go on with his work; but after a few attempts he put it aside as useless. Then he sat down to try to bring his mind to bear on the crime. He felt that he, as an amateur expert in "detecting," ought to be able to see some light upon the conditions of the crime; but he could see none. At length he was obliged to tell himself that he had not nearly enough information to go upon, and that he could not hope to make any progress without going himself over the scene of the crime and hearing more of what the police had done. But how could he do that without going to Liskeard House? And how could he go there without seeing Joan? As he went to bed, he told himself that he could do nothing. But he was a healthy fellow, and his perplexity did not long interfere with his slumbers. Tired out by his long walk, he slept like a top.

He was still in bed and asleep on the following morning when the landlady knocked at the door and told him that a gentleman, who would not state his business, was waiting to see him downstairs. Dressing hastily, he went down, and found a stranger standing before the fireplace. His visitor handed him a card, on which he read, "Inspector Gibbs, New Scotland Yard." So they had come to ask him something about the murders.

Inspector Blaikie, who had enough to do in following up the trail of Walter Brooklyn, had no time to act on his resolution to see Ellery and get from him an explanation of his movements on Tuesday after leaving Liskeard House. His colleague, Inspector Gibbs, had therefore been entrusted with this task. The police were not seriously disposed to think that Ellery had anything to do with the murders; but every one who had been at the house that night was worth interrogating, and Ellery was therefore to be questioned like the rest.

Inspector Gibbs was a very polite young man, excellently groomed, and with an air of treating you as one man of the world treats another. Very politely he explained the purpose of his visit, and told Ellery that he must not suppose that, merely because the police asked him certain questions, there was any suspicion at all attaching to him. "But we must, you know, get all our facts quite complete." Ellery said that he fully understood, and was prepared to answer any questions to the best of his power. "But the plain fact is," he said, "that I know nothing at all about it."

He was first asked at what time he had left Liskeard House on Tuesday evening, and replied that it was a few minutes past ten—he could not say more exactly. No, he had not returned there later in the evening—he had gone straight back to Chelsea. At what time had he reached his rooms in Chelsea? About midnight. Not till he made that answer did it occur to him that there was anything in his movements it might be difficult to explain.

"About midnight?" said the inspector, with a note of surprise in his voice. "But you said you went straight back after leaving Liskeard House."

"What I meant was that I went nowhere else in particular in between. As a matter of fact I walked back, and spent some time strolling up and down the Embankment before I returned to my rooms. I went down to Chelsea Bridge and walked right along the Embankment to Lots Road, and then back here to Tite Street. It was just about midnight when I let myself in."

"I see. And did you meet any one after you came in?"

"No; but my landlady may have seen me come in. There was still a light in her room, which looks out over the front door."

Before the inspector left he saw the landlady, and confirmed this with her. She had seen Ellery come in at about midnight. There was nothing unusual in his taking a long evening stroll by the river on a fine night.

But before he saw the landlady the inspector had further questions to ask of Ellery himself. "You say, then, that you were walking about for close on two hours between Liskeard House and Chelsea Embankment. Is there any one who can corroborate this?"

Ellery thought for a moment. "Yes, there ought to be," he said. "I met a friend who lives somewhere down here in Chelsea, at Hyde Park Corner, at about a quarter past ten, and he left me at the Lots Road end of the Embankment at about half-past eleven. We were together all that time."

"Will you give me his name and address?"

Ellery paused for a moment, and then gave a nervous laugh. "Upon my word," he said, "this is devilish awkward. I don't know the chap's address—I never have known it. All I do know is that he lives somewhere down the west end of Chelsea—not far from World's End, I think he said."

"I dare say we can trace him," said the inspector. "You had better tell me his profession as well as his name. Perhaps you know where he works."

"Good Lord, this is worse than ever," said Ellery. "I can't for the life of me remember what the fellow's name is. It has slipped clean out of my memory." Then, seeing a heightened look of surprise on the inspector's face: "You see," he added, "I hardly know him really. He's only a casual acquaintance I've met a few times at the Club." He paused and glanced at his visitor, in whose manner he was already conscious of a change.

"Come, come, Mr. Ellery, surely you must be able to remember the man's name. It's not————"

"I only wish I could. I almost had it then. It's something like Forrest or Forrester or Foster, I'm nearly sure. But it isn't any of those. I'm nearly certain it begins with an 'F.'"

"Isn't it rather curious that you should have been walking about London for so long with a man you hardly know, and whose name even you can't remember?"

"It may be curious, inspector, and you may think I'm making it all up. I can see you're inclined to think that. But what I've told is exactly what happened. I expect the name will come back to me soon—I have a way of just forgetting things like that every now and then."

"A most unfortunate way, if I may say so. I can only hope that your memory will soon come back. You realise, I suppose, that the consequences of your—lapse may be serious?"

"Oh, nonsense, inspector. I don't see anything so curious about it. I often get talking with chaps I don't know from Adam; and I'm quite capable of forgetting the name of my dearest friend. What happened was that we were both walking home towards Chelsea, it was a beautifully fine night, and we got into an interesting conversation—about plays. I'm a playwright, you know, and I think he must be an actor. I mean, from the way he talked."

"Well, Mr. Ellery, I should advise you to make a strong effort to find that gentleman again, or to remember his name. No doubt it's quite all right; but it will be best for you to have your alibi confirmed."

Ellery saw that Inspector Gibbs was not quite sure whether to believe or disbelieve his story. After all, it did sound a bit fishy. It would be awkward, and quite fatal to his plans of acting as an amateur detective, if the police began seriously to suspect him of having had a hand in the murders. That would put a visit to Liskeard House—and to Joan—more than ever out of the question.

Ellery promised to devote the day to an attempt to trace his missing acquaintance, and the inspector departed, with a last word of advice given as by one man of the world to another. But Ellery had an unpleasant feeling that until that fellow—what the devil was his name?—was run to earth, his movements would be carefully watched by the police. Which was not at all the development he had been expecting.

The Chelsea Arts Club, where he had certainly sometimes met the fellow, seemed the best place to begin the search, and

Ellery accordingly went round there to make his inquiries. But he drew blank. No one could place a fellow who lived in Chelsea—probably an actor—whose name was neither Foster nor Forrest nor Forrester, but something more or less like that. Every one he asked said it was too vague a description, or offered him suggestions which he at once rejected. Ellery began to feel that his job was not going to be easy. As he left the Club he was more than a little depressed, especially as he felt sure that a heavy-footed individual, who kept some distance behind, was under instructions to follow him. The police boots were unmistakable; he noticed them across the road as he came down the Club steps, and turning round a moment later, he saw their wearer following none too discreetly in his wake. "If that is the police idea of shadowing a man," he said to himself, "I don't think much of it. But perhaps they don't mind my knowing." Then he considered whether it was worth while to try giving his watcher the slip. But that, he reflected, would only make things worse, and get him suspected all the more. He must let himself be followed, and he might as well take it cheerfully. "With cat-like tread, upon the foe we steal," he whistled, and laughed as he heard the feet of the law clumping along behind him.

Chapter XIII
An Arrest

Inspector Blaikie had made arrangements to see Superintendent Wilson after lunch; and at half-past two they were closeted together in the superintendent's office. The decision about the inquest could be no longer delayed: it was imperative that the police should make up their minds how far they would place the facts which they had discovered before the coroner's jury. The police nearly always hate a coroner's jury—at least in cases in which murder is suspected or known. They dislike the premature disclosure of their hardly gathered clues before their case is complete: they dread the misdirected inquisitiveness of some juryman who may unknowingly give the criminal just the hint he wants. Above all, they object to looking like fools; and whether they present an incomplete case, or withhold the information they possess, that is very likely to be their fate in the presence of the good men and true and in the columns of the newspapers the next morning.

The Brooklyn case had created an immense popular excitement. Neither Prinsep nor George Brooklyn was much known to the general public; but Sir Vernon was still a great popular figure, and pictures of Isabelle Raven—Mrs. George Brooklyn—remembered as the finest actress of a few years ago, had been published in almost every paper. The reporters had, indeed, little enough to go upon; for after the first sensational story of the discovery of the bodies, they had been put off with very scanty information. Nothing connecting Walter Brooklyn with the crime had yet been published; but Inspector Blaikie knew that, as the club servants had fastened on that side of the story, it was certain to reach some of the papers before many days passed. Still, it was a moot point whether or not it would be best to keep all reference to Walter Brooklyn out of the inquest proceedings, if it were possible to do so.

Inspector Blaikie would usually have been inclined to favour any plan which aimed at keeping the coroner's jury in the dark. That was, in his view, a part of the duty of a good police officer. But, on this occasion, he had become so firmly convinced of Walter Brooklyn's guilt that he was set on a different method of proceeding. What he wanted was to be allowed to arrest Walter Brooklyn at once, in advance of the inquest, and then to tell the coroner's jury the full story of the evidence against him, in the hope that its publication in the Press would result in the offering of corroborative evidence from outside. He felt more and more certain that Brooklyn had committed both the murders; but he was not so sanguine as to suppose that he had yet enough evidence to assure a favourable verdict—that is, a verdict against Walter—from a jury. There was at least a specious case to be made out in favour of the view that Prinsep had killed George, and a skilful barrister would make much of this, using also every shred of evidence for the view that George had killed Prinsep, in the hope of so muddling the mind of the jury that they would not dare to bring in any verdict other than "Not Guilty." But only a very little further evidence would give him enough to hang Walter Brooklyn on one if not both of the charges. It was worth while even to submit to the foolish heckling of a coroner's jury, if by doing so he could hope to get the further evidence he wanted. His case so far, he recognised, depended on an inference; and it would be just like a jury to turn him down.

Juries, in his view, always did the wrong thing if you gave them half a chance. Still, in this case it was worth while, in the hope of getting further evidence, even to endure their folly.

This reasoning of Inspector Blaikie's failed to commend itself to Superintendent Wilson. He, too, saw that the case against Walter Brooklyn was not conclusive, and, unlike the inspector, he was not himself by any means convinced that Walter Brooklyn was guilty. But he thought he knew a way of bringing the matter to a supreme test, and of making the suspected man either proclaim his own guilt, or remove the most serious ground of suspicion against him. His idea was that, at least during the first stages of the inquest, the police should say nothing of those discoveries which implicated Walter Brooklyn, but that they should arrange for Walter himself to be called up to give evidence as if there were no suspicion against him. He could be used to identify the deceased; and a hint to the coroner would ensure that he should be asked to give an account of his movements on Tuesday evening. He would then have either to admit or to deny having been in Prinsep's room—either to tell at last what he must know about the murders, or to perjure himself in such a manner as would leave no doubt of his complicity, and little of his guilt.

Superintendent Wilson, then, would by no means agree to the execution of a warrant for Walter Brooklyn's arrest before the inquest; for he still thought that he might be innocent and might be persuaded to tell openly what he knew—a chance which his arrest would altogether destroy. But he agreed that, if Walter Brooklyn plainly perjured himself at the inquest, his arrest would be indispensable, and there would be no purpose in leaving him longer at large. He agreed, therefore, to take at once the necessary steps to procure the warrant, and he arranged that it should be handed to the inspector, for execution if and when the need arose. But on no account must it be executed until after the inquest, or save in accordance with the conditions which he had laid down. Only if Walter's guilt or complicity, and his refusal to tell freely what he knew, were plainly shown, would the superintendent agree to the arrest. Meanwhile, of course, the man should be watched.

So it happened that, although the inquest was for the most part a purely formal affair, Walter Brooklyn was among those who were called upon to give evidence. With most of its proceedings we need not concern ourselves: we know well enough already almost all that the coroner's jury was allowed to know. Indeed, we know a good deal more; for Inspector Blaikie, in his evidence, said not a word either of Walter Brooklyn's walking-stick, or of the telephone message which he had sent from Liskeard House. No Club servant was called, and there was no reference to the meeting with Charis Lang, who was not in any way brought into the case. Carter Woodman, indeed, gave evidence; but he had been warned in advance by the inspector, and he said nothing which could appear to implicate Walter Brooklyn.

To the reporters and to the members of the police who were present, crowding to suffocation the confined space of the coroner's court, it became more and more evident that the inquest was not likely to throw any light upon the mystery. They heard, from the police witnesses, from the household servants, and from Joan Cowper, how the bodies had been found. Walter Brooklyn and others gave purely formal evidence of identification: the doctors for once told a plain story. George Brooklyn had been killed by a savage blow on the back of the head, dealt without doubt by a powerful man with the stone club of Hercules, which was produced in court with the bloodstains still upon it. Prinsep, too, had probably been killed by the blow on the back of his head, dealt with an unknown instrument. The knife thrust at the heart, which had missed its object, had been made subsequently, and would not by itself have caused sudden death. Inspector Blaikie's evidence, indeed, promised to be more exciting; for he told of the finding of George Brooklyn's handkerchief under Prinsep's body, produced a knife, similar to that found in the body, which he had found in George Brooklyn's office, showed the broken fragments of Prinsep's cigar-holder found in the garden, and photographs of fingerprints found on the stone club and others taken from Prinsep's hands. This was exciting enough; but it did more to mystify than to enlighten the public and the reporters. Still, it was excellent copy; and the reporters, and later the editors and sub-editors, made the most of it. Then, when the inquest seemed practically over, the coroner, a sharp little man who had attended strictly to business and said as little as possible throughout the proceedings, acted on the hint given him by the police, and ordered Walter Brooklyn to be recalled. Walter's manner, when he gave his earlier evidence and was asked no more than a couple of formal questions, had shown plainly to the inspector, and also to Joan and Ellery, who were sitting together, that he was surprised at being let off so lightly. As the inquest went on, and nothing was said to draw him into the mystery, his expression, troubled and puzzled in the earlier stages, gradually cleared, and, up to the moment when he suddenly found himself recalled, he had been growing more and more sure that the suspicions of the police against him had been somehow dispelled. But now, in an instant, he realised that they had been deliberately keeping back everything that could seem to connect him with the case, not because they did not suspect him still, but because they had carefully set a trap into which they hoped that he would fall. For a moment, a scared look came into his face; but, when he stepped again into the witness stand, he wore his usual rather ill-humoured and supercilious expression. Immaculately dressed and groomed, he was a man who looked precisely what he was—an elderly, but still dissipated, man about town.

This time the questions which the coroner asked were far from formal. He began with what was plainly a leading question,—

"It has been suggested to me, Mr. Brooklyn, that you may be able to throw some further light on this tragedy. This morning you were given no opportunity to make a general statement; but I desire to give you that opportunity now. Is there anything further that you are in a position to tell us?"

"I know no more of the affair than I have heard in this court to-day—or previously from the police." Walter Brooklyn added the last words after a noticeable pause. "Nevertheless, there is a statement that I want to make. It has been suggested, not in this court, but earlier to me by Inspector Blaikie—that I was in Liskeard House on Tuesday evening. I desire to say that I called at Liskeard House shortly after ten o'clock and waited for a few minutes in the outer hall. Then I went away; and since that time—perhaps twenty past ten on Tuesday night—I have not been in either the house or the garden. Of the circumstances of the tragedy I know nothing at all except what I have heard at this inquest or from the police."

Walter Brooklyn's statement created a sensation; for here was the first hint of a suspicion entertained by somebody as to the real murderer. Clearly the police had been keeping something back—something which would incriminate the man who was now giving evidence. Of course, after interrogating Walter Brooklyn the police might have discovered their suspicions to be groundless, and therefore have said nothing of them. But, if this were so, why had they recalled him in this curious fashion, and why should Brooklyn go out of his way to draw public attention to himself, and to make certain that his doings would be fully canvassed in the newspapers? No, the way in which he had been recalled showed that the police were acting with a definite purpose. They were trying to get Walter Brooklyn to make a statement which would clearly incriminate him, and, if they really had evidence of his presence in the house, they had certainly succeeded.

This explanation, natural and largely correct as it was, was not quite a fair account of Superintendent Wilson's motives. His object had been not merely to get Walter Brooklyn to incriminate himself, but also to give him a chance of clearing himself if he could give a satisfactory explanation of his presence in the house. The fact that the man had repeated on oath an obvious lie seemed to him a good enough reason for ordering an arrest. He nodded across the court to the inspector.

But the coroner's court had not yet quite done with Walter Brooklyn. A juryman, quick to be influenced by the general suspicion which was abroad, signified his desire to ask a question. "Where did you go after leaving Liskeard House?" he rapped out.

The coroner interposed. "Since that question has been asked," he said, "perhaps it would be well if you would give us an account of your movements on Tuesday night."

Walter Brooklyn seemed to think for a minute before replying. "Well," he said, "I strolled about for a bit round Piccadilly Circus and Shaftesbury Avenue, and then I went home to the club."

"At what time did you reach your club?"

"I should guess it was shortly before midnight."

"That is a considerable time after you left Liskeard House."

"I am merely telling you what happened."

"The club porter could probably confirm the time of your return?"

"Yes, I imagine so."

"And is there any one who would be able to substantiate your account of what you did between 10.15 and midnight? Were you strolling about all that time?"

"Yes, I suppose I was."

"Were you alone?"

"Yes."

"Then there is no one who could confirm your story?"

"Probably not. But I did meet one or two people I knew."

"None of them is here now?"

"No."

"Do you desire that the inquest should be adjourned in order that they may be called?"

"No. What on earth for? I don't know whether I could find them, anyway."

"Then I think there is nothing further I need ask you."

And with that, a good deal bewildered, Walter Brooklyn was told to leave the witness box. He went back to his seat, but a minute later got up and left the court.

Many pairs of eyes followed him as he walked slowly towards the door, and the more experienced spectators nudged one another as Inspector Blaikie rose quickly in his place and went out after him. Joan, in her place in the court, saw her stepfather leave; but she did not notice that the inspector had followed. Ellery, who did notice, said nothing; for though he realised what was about to happen he saw that there was no means of preventing the arrest.

Meanwhile, the coroner was rapidly summing up the evidence. Murder, he told the jury, was clearly established in both cases; and they need have no hesitation as to their verdict on that point. But who had committed the murders? If they were satisfied that in either case the evidence established the guilt of some definite person, it was their duty to bring in a verdict against that person. In his opinion, however, the evidence was wholly inadequate to form the basis of any positive conclusion. It might be that John Prinsep had been killed by George Brooklyn—the finding of the handkerchief and his known visit to the house were certainly suspicious circumstances. It might be, on the other hand, that George

Brooklyn had been killed by John Prinsep—the note in Prinsep's writing found in the temple, the cigar-holder, and his known presence in the garden were all grounds for suspicion. But both these sets of clues could not point to the truth, and the jury had no means of determining on which the greater reliance should be placed. Indeed, both sets of clues might be misleading, and certainly neither was by itself enough to form the basis of a verdict. The murders might both be the work of some third person—and one of them must be the work of a third person—but no evidence had been placed before them which would justify a verdict against any particular person. Suspicion, he would remind them, was a very different thing from proof, and even with their suspicions they must not be too free in face of the very slender evidence before them.

After the coroner's summing up, it was clear that only one verdict was possible. After only a moment's consultation, the foreman announced that their verdict in both cases was "Wilful Murder by some person or persons unknown." The coroner made a short speech thanking every one, and the court adjourned. Joan was glad to breathe fresh air again after her first experience of the suffocating atmosphere of a court.

By this time Walter Brooklyn was safe under lock and key. As he reached the door of the court half an hour earlier, he felt a touch on his sleeve, and, turning, saw Inspector Blaikie immediately behind him.

"Well, what do you want now?" he said sullenly.

The inspector beckoned him into a corner, and there showed him the warrant duly made out for his arrest. Walter Brooklyn glanced at it. For a moment he drew himself up to his full height and grasped his stick tightly as if he were considering the prospects of a mad struggle for liberty. Then he gave a short laugh. "I will come with you," he said; and then he added suddenly, with a fury the more impressive because its utterance was checked—"you damned little fool of a policeman."

"Come, come, Mr. Brooklyn," said the inspector. "I'm only doing my duty." Walter Brooklyn made no reply, and the inspector added: "Are you ready now?"

"Call a taxi," said Walter. "I suppose you will not walk me handcuffed through the streets," he added bitterly.

"Certainly not," said the inspector, and he hailed a passing taxi, and signed to his prisoner to get in.

A small crowd had collected by this time, and stood gaping on the pavement as the taxi drove away.

Chapter XIV
Mainly a Love Scene

Joan had fully intended to see her stepfather before the inquest and to warn him of his danger and get him to tell the truth to her at least. When Ellery came to visit her on the Thursday afternoon—the inquest was on Friday—she had been on the point of setting out for his club, with the set purpose of making him tell her the whole story. Just before dinner time, she knew, was the most likely hour for finding him at home. There would probably be difficulty in persuading him to talk freely, even to her; but she thought that she would know how to manage him. It was still too early to start, however, and she had ample time to see Ellery first. A talk with him was just what she wanted. He would sympathise with her, and, she was sure, he was just the man to help her where Carter Woodman had failed. He would throw himself into the case, and aid her to find out what she ought to do in order to clear her stepfather of the suspicion which lay upon him. Since her talk with Woodman, she had come to realise fully how grave that suspicion was; but she was sure that Bob—she and Ellery had called each other by their Christian names ever since they were children—would not only take her word for it that Walter Brooklyn could not possibly be guilty of the crimes, but be ready to use his wits and his time in proving the suspected man's innocence. She did not quite tell herself that he would do all this because he was in love with her; but neither did she quite admit to herself that she would not have asked him unless she had been in love with him.

There was some embarrassment—of which Joan was fully conscious—in Robert Ellery's manner as he rose to greet her. "I hope I'm not in the way," he said awkwardly, blushing as he said it.

"My dear Bob, I'm so glad you've come. I've been pining for some one to whom I could really talk."

"I wasn't at all sure whether I ought to come. I thought you might prefer to be alone, and you must have your hands very full with Sir Vernon. Of course, I'd have come sooner if I had thought you wanted me." Again Ellery coloured.

"I want you now, anyway. And it isn't simply that I want to talk. I want to do something, and I want your help."

To help Joan! What thing better could Ellery have asked for? He would do anything in the world to help her. But what sort of help did she need? He longed to tell her that he was hers to command in any way she chose—because he loved her; but all he found himself saying was, "I say, that's awfully jolly of you—to let me help you, I mean"—conscious of the banality of the words even as he spoke them.

Joan went straight to the point. "Bob, the police suspect my stepfather of being mixed up with this horrible affair. In fact, I'm sure they think he is actually guilty of murder. They've got hold of something that seems to incriminate him."

Ellery made an inarticulate noise of sympathy.

"Of course, Bob, you and I know he didn't do it. You do think he couldn't have done it, don't you?"

"It would certainly never have occurred to me to suspect him."

"Of course, he's quite innocent, and it's all some horrible mistake. He couldn't have done such a thing. But I want you to help me prove he didn't."

"My dear Joan, are you quite sure the police really suspect him? Of course, they have to make inquiries about everybody. Why, I was quite under the impression that they suspected me."

"Suspect you? How dreadful! What do you mean?"

"Well, I had a most inquisitorial visit from the police this morning; and a man in obvious police boots has been following me about all day."

He spoke lightly; but Joan took what he said very seriously indeed. "My dear Bob," she said. "This is positively awful. But why ever should any one think you—had anything to do with it?"

"Oh, just because I failed to give a 'satisfactory explanation'—I think that is what they call it—of my movements on Tuesday night. You know I walked home after dinner. Well, I wandered round a bit and didn't get home till midnight. So they argue that I had plenty of time to kill half a dozen people, and insist that I must either prove an alibi—or take the consequences. What do you say? Do you think I did it?"

"My dear Bob, don't joke about it. It's far too serious, if the police are going to drag you into this terrible business."

"No, really, it isn't serious at all—now at any rate. I am in a position, fortunately, to produce a conclusive alibi. You see, I wasn't alone, and I've found the chap who was with me most of the time, and sent him round to Scotland Yard to tell them it's all right. I expect the gentleman with the boots will be out of a job before long."

"You're sure it's really all right?"

"Of course it is, or I shouldn't have said a word about it. And I dare say what you have heard about the police suspecting old Walter isn't a bit more serious."

"Oh, but it is. From their point of view, I'm afraid they have a very strong case." And Joan told him all that she knew—both what she had heard about Charis Lang from Marian Brooklyn, and what Carter Woodman had told her. Finally, she told Ellery that she had made up her mind to go at once to her stepfather, and try to make him tell her the truth.

As Joan told her story, Ellery could not help saying to himself that it looked bad for old Walter. He did not know Walter Brooklyn very well; but all he did know was unfavourable, and he had never heard any one—even Joan herself—say a good word for him. Left to his own reflections, Ellery would not have hesitated to suspect Walter Brooklyn of murder; for he realised at once that the wicked uncle had everything to gain by putting his two nephews out of the way. But Joan knew the man, and he did not; and, if Joan was positive, that was good enough for him. He was so completely under her influence that the idea that Walter Brooklyn was guilty was dismissed almost as soon as it was entertained. Ellery would make it his business to get Walter Brooklyn cleared—he would work for the old beast with the feeling that he was working for Joan himself. Entering at once into Joan's plan, he applauded her determination to go and see her stepfather, and placed himself unreservedly at her service.

"You're a dear," she said.

While they had been discussing Walter Brooklyn's story, Ellery's embarrassment had quite left him; but these words of Joan's, and her look as she spoke them, brought it back in double force. He felt the blood rushing to his head, and became uncomfortably aware that he was going red in the face. Also, he could not take his eyes off Joan, and somehow it seemed that she could not take her eyes off him. They gazed at each other, with something of fear and something of embarrassment in their looks, and each was conscious of a heart beating more and more insistently within. For at least a minute neither of them spoke. Then Ellery said one word and put out his hand towards her. "Joan," he said, and his voice sounded to him strange and unreal. He felt her hand grasp his, almost fiercely, and an acute sensation—it has no name—ran right through him at the touch. In an instant, her head was on his shoulder and his arms were round her. She was sobbing, and his cheek was caressing hers. "Poor darling," he said at last.

Joan had meant that talk with Robert Ellery to be so practical, so entirely the opening of a business partnership. She and Bob were to clear her stepfather together; and, when they had done that, who knew what might come after? But there was to be no intrusion of sentiment until the work in hand was completed. In the event, things had not gone off at all as she intended. From the moment of his coming, she had felt a sense of danger—something poignant, yet intensely welcome—in their meeting. This feeling had been dispelled for the time while she told him her tale, and she had half said to herself that now she was safe. Then, in a moment, security had vanished, the sense of tension had come back far more strongly than before, she had felt herself merely a passive thing—as he was another passive thing—in the control of great elemental forces beyond herself. Without a word said, it seemed, a marriage had been arranged.

There was, indeed, no need for words between them on this matter of matters that had joined them indissolubly together. They were sitting now on the couch, holding each other's hands. They could talk business—speak of what must be done to clear Walter Brooklyn—while with the contact of their bodies love interpenetrated them. And Joan could say to herself already that this most unbusinesslike proceeding was the best stroke of business she had ever done. For the immediate purpose she had in view, it had immensely strengthened their partnership. For these twain had become one flesh, and what was near her heart needs must be near his also.

As they sat there together, they formed their plan of campaign. It was obviously impossible to make a beginning until Joan had done her best to make Walter Brooklyn tell what he knew. If he were to refuse, their task would be so much the harder; but even the hardest task now seemed easy to them with the power of their love behind them. Whatever his attitude might be, they would still be ready to do their best for him. But surely he would tell Joan. There was no time to be lost. He must be seen at once, and Ellery set to work to advise Joan about the questions she ought to ask.

"It seems clear enough that he was in the house. I suppose he will be able to explain that. But we mustn't be content with getting just his explanation of what he was doing here. Try to find out exactly what he did and where he went that day. We may need to be able to account for every minute of his time."

Joan said that she quite saw how every detail mattered. If he would tell her anything, he would probably be willing to tell the whole story. At all events, she would do her best. It would be wisest, they agreed, for her to go alone; for Walter Brooklyn would very likely refuse to talk if Ellery were with her. But he would walk round to the club with her, and wait while she tried to get her stepfather to see her.

So Joan and Ellery walked round to the Byron Club together. There was a strange pleasure—quite unlike anything they had known before—in merely walking side by side. They belonged to each other now. But the answer to Ellery's inquiry of the Club porter was that Mr. Brooklyn was out, and that he had left word he might not return to the Club that night. Joan did not at all like the expression on the porter's face as he gave this information. She saw that he at any rate had strong suspicions, presumably put into his mind by the police.

Asked whether he could say where Mr. Brooklyn was, the porter did not know. He might, perhaps, be at his other Club, the Sanctum, in Pall Mall. Or again, he might not. He had not said where he was going.

Inquiries at the other Club were equally barren. Mr. Walter Brooklyn had not been there that day. He might come in, or he might not. And again Joan saw from the porter's manner that here too her stepfather was under suspicion of murder.

Joan left at each Club a message asking Walter Brooklyn to ring her up at Liskeard House immediately he came in. This was all that could be done for the moment; and to Liskeard House they returned, having suffered a check at the outset of their quest. Ellery promised to spend the evening scouring London for traces of Walter Brooklyn; and in the mind of each was the half-formed thought that he might have fled rather than reveal what he knew. Each knew that the other feared this; but neither put the thought into words. They arranged to meet again on the following morning, and Ellery was to ring up later in the evening to report whether he had traced Walter, and to hear whether any message had come to Joan from either of the Clubs. Then, after the manner of lovers, they bade each other farewell a dozen times over, each farewell more lingering than the last. At length Ellery went; for he was due at Scotland Yard, where he hoped to find that his alibi had been accepted, and the last trace of suspicion removed from him. It would be awkward to be followed about by the man in police boots wherever he went with Joan, and it would be awkward to have the police know exactly what they were doing in Walter Brooklyn's interest. The police boots had followed Joan and him on their visits to the two Clubs, and now, as he left Liskeard House, Ellery saw their owner leaning against a lamp-post opposite, and gazing straight at the front door. Never, he thought, had a man looked more obviously a detective—or rather a policeman in plain clothes. Even apart from the boots, he was labelled policeman all over—from his measured stride to the tips of his waxed moustache. As Ellery turned down into Piccadilly, he heard the man coming along behind him.

Chapter XV
To and Fro

It was by a fortunate accident that Ellery had been able so soon to establish his alibi. After drawing blank at the Chelsea Arts Club, he had had very little of an idea where he should try next. He was almost certain that it was there he had been introduced to the man, and the only course seemed to be that of waiting until he turned up again, or his name somehow came back to mind. Still, it was just possible that Ellery had met the man at his other Club in the Adelphi, and he got on a bus and went there to pursue his inquiries. His success was no better, although he remained there to lunch and made persistent inquiries of his fellow-members for an actor whose name began with an F. The afternoon found him walking rather disconsolately down the Strand not at all certain where to go next. Just outside the Golden Cross Hotel, fortune did him a good turn; for he ran straight into the very man he was looking for. Ellery turned back with him, and explained the difficulty he was in, and his acquaintance promised to go at once to Scotland Yard, and try to set matters right with Inspector Gibbs. He was so friendly that Ellery had some difficulty in admitting that he had forgotten his name; but he got round it by asking for his address, in case of need. The other's answer was to hand him a card, on which was written:—

William Gloucester,

11 Denzil Street, S. W. 3.

"Of course," said Ellery to himself. "But it didn't begin with an F after all."

This meeting put Ellery at his ease; and he felt that he could now go and see Joan with a clear conscience. Leaving Gloucester to go to Scotland Yard, and asking him to tell the inspector that he would come round later, he set off for Liskeard House, and found himself charged with the task of clearing, not himself, but Walter Brooklyn. He also found himself engaged to be married.

These events made it all the more essential to make quite sure that the police were no longer inclined to look on him with suspicion; and, on leaving Joan, he went straight to Scotland Yard, and was soon received, not by Inspector Gibbs, but by Superintendent Wilson, who, having received the inspector's report on Gloucester's visit, had made up his mind to have a look at Ellery himself. The superintendent at once put him at his ease by telling him that his explanation, and his friend's corroboration of it, appeared to be quite satisfactory. Ellery's reply was to say that, in that case, perhaps he might be relieved of the presence of the heavy-footed individual who had been following him about all day. The superintendent laughed. "Yes, I think we can find something more useful for him to do," he said. "I hope you have not resented our—shall I say?—attentions. We were bound to keep an eye on you until we were certain." And the superintendent at once gave instructions on the house-phone that the man who had been watching Ellery need do so no longer, but should report to him in a few minutes in his room.

Ellery assured him that it was quite all right; but that he was glad to be relieved of the man, because he wanted to do a little private detecting on his own. "I know you people have got your knife into Walter Brooklyn; but I'm sure he had nothing to do with it, and I mean to do my best to find out who had." Ellery said this deliberately, in the hope of getting the superintendent to show something of his hand; but that wary official merely wished him luck—for "we policemen," he said, "are always glad to have a man's character cleared, though you may not think it"—and politely bowed him out. So far as he could see, no one followed him as he left the building, and he went back to Liskeard House. He had said that he would 'phone; but he found it quite beyond his power to keep away.

Joan was busy with Sir Vernon when he arrived; but she came to him before long. No message had come from Walter Brooklyn, and she was getting anxious. Was it possible that he had been arrested already? Ellery promised to make inquiries, and to use every possible effort to find her stepfather; but, though he tried that evening every place he could think of in which Walter Brooklyn might be, no trace of him could be found, and there was no sign that he had been arrested. Resumed inquiries early the next morning were equally fruitless. Brooklyn had not been back to either of his Clubs, and no message had been received from him. It was under these circumstances that Joan failed to see her stepfather before the inquest opened. She was greatly relieved to see that he was present, and promising herself that she would talk to him as soon as it was over, she did nothing while the inquest was actually in progress. She passed a note to him asking him to come round and see her at Liskeard House immediately the court rose, and he nodded to her in reply across the room. She therefore felt no anxiety when he rose and left his seat before the proceedings came to an end. Thus it came about that he was arrested without her having a chance to ask him to tell his story of the events of Tuesday night.

The explanation of Walter Brooklyn's absence was simple enough. By Thursday, life at his Clubs had been made unendurable for him by the manner, and evident suspicions, of the Club servants. He became conscious that his fellow-members were also talking about him, and he decided to go away. He had been summoned to appear at the inquest on the following morning; but he could at least have a quiet night before returning to his troubles. While Joan and Ellery were hunting London for him, Walter Brooklyn was doing himself well at a hotel in Maidenhead. He had intended to return there after seeing Joan; but the inspector's hand on his shoulder warned him that he would sleep the coming night in jail.

At Vine Street, Brooklyn asked to be allowed to see a solicitor. The request was at once granted; and, in response to an urgent message, Mr. Fred Thomas, of New Court, arrived within half an hour. Thomas was not Brooklyn's regular solicitor; for Carter Woodman had managed most of his business affairs. But Thomas was a Club acquaintance and a man about town himself—professionally a lawyer with few illusions and a large, if rather disreputable, practice, mainly among racing men. Walter Brooklyn's first idea was that Thomas should make an effort to get him admitted to bail when he was brought up before the magistrate next morning, and he mentioned the names of several persons who might be prepared to stand surety for him. But Thomas at once destroyed his hopes. There was no chance, he said, of securing bail on a charge of murder: he was afraid his client would have to make up his mind to stay where he was for the present. At any rate, Thomas would see to it that he was made as comfortable as could be. There were ways of doing these things, and Thomas was an expert hand at dealing with the police. What he could do would be done; but the main thing was for his client to give him every fact that could possibly be helpful in preparing the defence. They began to discuss the case.

Meanwhile, Ellery, who had guessed at once the reason why the inspector had followed Walter Brooklyn out of the coroner's court, had not been idle. He had left his place a minute or two later, merely whispering to Joan that there was something he must do at once. He had come out of the court just in time to see the inspector and Walter Brooklyn get into a taxi and drive off. Hailing another taxi, he had told the driver to follow, and his car had drawn up at Vine Street Police Station a moment after the other. He had seen Brooklyn and the inspector pass into the building, and had then paid his driver, and stood disconsolately outside wondering what he should do. Finally, he went into the station and asked for Inspector Blaikie, sending in his card. He was kept waiting for some minutes, and then the inspector came to him, and asked what he wanted.

"You have arrested Mr. Walter Brooklyn, have you not?" Ellery asked.

The inspector replied that he had.

"Is it possible for some one to come and see him? I suppose he will be here overnight."

The inspector shook his head. "He will be here for the night," he said, "but you can't see him. He has already sent for his lawyer."

"I don't want to see him myself. But his stepdaughter, Miss Cowper, is very anxious to have a talk with him."

"Oh, that's another matter. It might be arranged. I don't say it could, but it might. The right course would be for her to see his lawyer, and for him to apply on her behalf. I couldn't do anything on my own responsibility."

"Then, if I brought her here, you couldn't allow her to see him."

"No, I'm afraid I couldn't. The regulations are very strict."

Ellery tried to move the inspector. He failed, but he was not inclined to give up hope. He went straight to Scotland Yard and asked for Superintendent Wilson. Reminding that official that, earlier in the day, he had wished him luck in his effort to clear Walter Brooklyn, Ellery obtained without difficulty permission for Joan to see him in his cell. Armed with a signed permit, he drove straight to Liskeard House.

He found Joan with his guardian, Harry Lucas, who had brought her back in his car from the court. Lucas, too, had seen the inspector leave the court, and had guessed his purpose. He had also guessed Ellery's object in leaving a moment later. In the car, he had already told Joan what he feared; and they had agreed that the best thing was to go back to Liskeard House and wait for news. Walter Brooklyn would come there if he was still a free man; and if not, Ellery would either come, or telephone to tell Joan what had happened.

Joan therefore received Ellery's bad news without surprise; and she gave him a grateful kiss—she had told Lucas of their engagement while they were waiting—when he showed her the permit to visit her stepfather Lucas's car was at the door, and he offered to take Joan round at once. He took the driver's seat himself, telling his chauffeur to await his return, and Joan and Ellery got in behind.

Chapter XVI
A Link in the Chain

Fred Thomas came away a good deal dissatisfied from his discussion with his client. Walter Brooklyn, he felt, had given him little enough to go upon. He persisted in affirming that he had not been in Liskeard House that night, and in denying absolutely that he had either rung up his Club and given a message or left his walking-stick in Prinsep's room. Yet surely, Thomas argued, the police, if they had proceeded to the drastic step of an arrest, must have some definite proof that he had been in the house, or at any rate some clear indication of his complicity. He did not believe that his client was being frank with him; and, while he had not said this outright, a hint of what he thought had produced a violent outburst of bad temper from Brooklyn, and almost caused him to tell his legal adviser to clear out and come back no more. This had served to confirm Thomas's idea that Brooklyn was lying, and his thought, as he went away, was that, if he tried again, probably Brooklyn would tell him the truth when he cooled down and came to realise more fully what his position was. In his experience imprisonment had a wonderfully sobering effect. Meanwhile, Thomas made up his mind to see Carter Woodman, and try to find out from him more definitely how matters stood. Woodman, presumably, would want Walter Brooklyn to get off, even if he believed him to be guilty. He would probably not want a member of the Brooklyn family to be convicted of murder, whatever the truth might be. Thomas had not long left Walter Brooklyn when Joan arrived to see him. She had come into the police-station alone, leaving Lucas and Ellery outside in the car to wait for her return. While they waited, Ellery told his guardian more about his engagement to Joan, and received from him very hearty congratulations. "You didn't take my advice, my boy," Lucas said; "but now that things have come out right, I'm most heartily glad that you didn't. I have hoped for this for a long time. I'm very fond of you both, and I can see there's no doubt about your being fond of each other." Which was very pleasant hearing for Ellery; for he had a great liking for his guardian, and he knew that his friendly countenance would be likely to stand him in good stead with Sir Vernon Brooklyn, of whom he was more than a little afraid. "You must back me up with Sir Vernon," he said; and Lucas readily promised his help.

It was three-quarters of an hour before Joan came out of the police-station. She seemed well satisfied, smiling back at the policeman who accompanied her to the door. "He has told you?" asked Ellery, as he held open the door of the car.

"What he had to tell," Joan replied. "It was not very much; but it makes everything different. Let us go back and talk it over."

Lucas drove straight back to Liskeard House, and there, in Joan's room, the three held a consultation. "He was not here at all," she told them. "I mean he did not come back to the house on Tuesday night. The telephone message must be all a mistake."

"Do you mean that he knows nothing at all about it?" asked Ellery.

"I am quite sure that he knows nothing. He has told me exactly what he did after leaving here and up to the time when he went back to his Club."

"You may think I ought not to ask this, Joan," said Lucas; "but are you quite sure of what you say?"

"Absolutely sure. He was telling me the truth, I know."

"Then I suppose," Ellery put in, "we can produce witnesses to prove that he was somewhere else when he was supposed to be here. But who the devil did send that telephone message if he did not?"

Lucas put in a word. "Never mind that for the moment. The main thing now is to prove that he did not send it. Who was with him and where was he?"

"Ah, that's just the difficulty. He has told me exactly where he went; but I don't see how we can find any one to prove it."

"Do you mean that he was alone all the time, and no one saw him?" asked Ellery.

"Well, not quite that; but something very like it, I'm afraid."

Then Joan was allowed to tell her story. Walter Brooklyn, after being refused an interview with Sir Vernon, had left Liskeard House at about a quarter past ten. He had stopped for a minute or two outside the Piccadilly Theatre, wondering what to do next. Then he had walked slowly along Piccadilly and into the Circus. There again he had hung about for a few minutes, and had then gone slowly along Coventry Street as far as Leicester Square. He had walked round the Square, and outside the Alhambra had stopped for a few minutes to talk to a woman of his acquaintance—"not at all a nice woman, I am afraid,—and he knows no more about her than that her name is Kitty, and that she is often to be found about there. He doesn't even know her surname. It was about a quarter to eleven when he met her."

Then he had gone on past the Hippodrome and up Charing Cross Road as far as Cambridge Circus. He had stopped for a few minutes outside the Palace, but had not spoken to any one, and then he had walked down Shaftesbury Avenue and back into Piccadilly Circus. In Cambridge Circus he had lighted a cigar with his last match; but it had gone out. Just outside the Monico he had stopped a man he did not know—"fellow came out of the place, he looked like a waiter, don't you know"—and had borrowed a match and re-lighted his cigar. Then he had crossed the Circus again, and walked back down Piccadilly as far as the turning leading to Liskeard House. He had half a mind, he said, to go in and ask to see Prinsep; but after hanging about for a few minutes he had given up the idea, crossed the road, and walked down St. James's Street with the idea of looking in at his other Club. But he had decided not to go in, and had walked past the door down Pall Mall and into Trafalgar Square. At the top of Whitehall he had looked at his watch, and the time had been 11.45. Just before that, he had hung over the parapet on the National Gallery side of the Square for a minute or two; but he had no conversation with any one. On leaving the Square, he turned up Regent Street and made his way, walking a good deal faster, along Jermyn Street and up St. James's Street, and so back to his Club in Piccadilly. He had thus again passed Liskeard Street, but on the opposite side of the road. When he got in, he had gone straight to bed.

This account of Walter Brooklyn's movements was quite convincing to Joan and her two listeners; but they had to admit that there was not much in it to persuade others of its truth. According to his own account, he must have been in the neighbourhood of Liskeard House at 11.30 when the 'phone message was supposed to have been sent; and not one of his movements between 10.15 and midnight seemed to be at all easy to confirm by any independent testimony. When Joan had finished her narrative, they all felt that, if Walter Brooklyn's vindication was to depend on an alibi, his chances were not particularly good. Still, if he had not been in the house, the police could after all have very little against him beyond a suspicion.

At this point Mary Woodman came into the room to say that Sir Vernon would be very pleased if Mr. Lucas would come and sit with him for a while, and Lucas, promising to obey her order to be very quiet and not to allow the patient to excite himself, was led off to the sick room.

"I tell you what, Joan," said Ellery, who had been sitting still, with a prodigious frown on his face, trying to think the thing over, "we've jolly well got to establish that alibi. We don't know what else the police may have; but we're safe enough if we can prove that he wasn't here that evening. Unless we can establish positively that he wasn't there, the circumstantial evidence will go down with a jury."

"But how can we establish it? I only wish we could."

"We're going to. We're going to find those people he spoke to, and we're going to hunt London for people who saw him strolling about. After all, he's very well known, and lots of people must have seen him. I know we shall be able to prove he's telling the truth."

"You're a dear to say so, and I don't see what we can do but try. How do you propose to set about it?"

"First of all, I propose that we make a map of the wanderings of Ulysses—shall we call it?—showing exactly where he went, whom he spoke to and when, and so on. That will help us to see exactly what's the best way of getting to work."

So Ellery took a sheet of paper, and they sat down side by side at the table. Under Joan's directions, Ellery made a map of Walter Brooklyn's journeyings on Tuesday evening. It took an hour to do, and this is what it looked like when it was done, with notes to help them in prosecuting their inquiries.

"It isn't very hopeful, I'm afraid," said Joan, as they looked together at the finished plan; "but I'm afraid it is all we have to go upon."

"Not quite all, I hope. Did he tell you what the man he

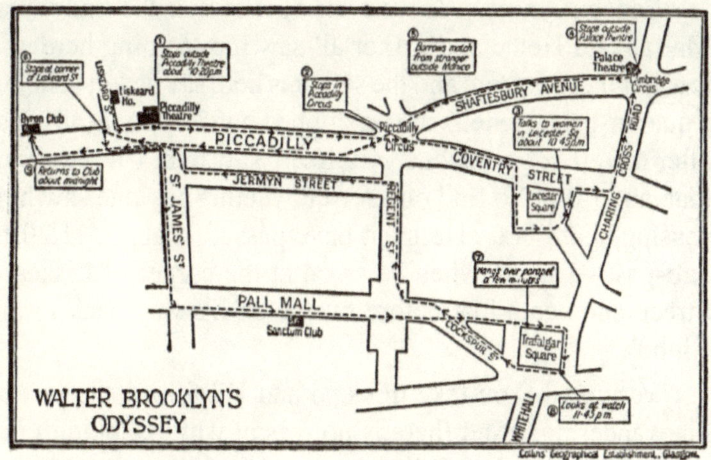

spoke to looked like—I mean the chap who gave him a match outside the Monico?"

"Yes, he was a tall, dark man, clean-shaven and very blue in the chin, wearing a long black overcoat and a squash hat. And he almost certainly had some trouble of the eyes. He wore glasses; but he kept blinking all the time behind them."

"That ought to help. Now what about this woman, Kitty? What is she like?"

"He says she is about forty, but dresses—and paints—to look younger. She's getting fat, has bright golden hair—certainly dyed—and wears a great many rings. She's fairly tall, and walks with a bit of a waddle. Her eyes are dark and piercing, he says, and she has a smile that looks as if it was switched on and off like an electric light."

"I must say she doesn't sound attractive."

"But he says she is—extraordinarily; and, what is more, she's very well known. He has heard her other name, but he can't remember it. He thinks she has had several surnames."

"That seems to be all we can get to start with. What I propose to do is to follow your stepfather's route, trying to find some one who saw him at each point where he stopped."

"Yes, but you can leave a bit of it to me. We know that Marian and Helen and Carter all saw him coming here at a few minutes past ten, and the servants here say he left at about a quarter-past. He tells me he stopped outside the theatre just after that. If so, some one very likely saw him. I'll see about that, and I'll try to find out as well whether any one saw him passing again later. He must have passed at about 11.20 to half-past—I mean when he stood at the corner of Liskeard Street, and again just before twelve on his way back to the Club."

"Very well. You take this end and I'll follow the rest of his wanderings. And there is no reason why I shouldn't get to work at once. It will be best to go over the ground in the evening, just as he did."

They sat and talked of the case for a while longer; and then they sat for a time without talking at all, happy in each other's presence despite the tragedy in which they were involved. At length Ellery started up, saying that he must go out and get some dinner, and then go to work seriously.

"And by the way, Joan," he added, "why shouldn't you come out and have dinner with me? I'm sure Mary would look after Sir Vernon."

"My dear boy, does it occur to you that I've left him to himself for a good long time already—or rather left poor Mary alone to look after him? I couldn't have done it if Marian had not promised to come in and help."

"I'm sure Mary wouldn't mind," Ellery began, pleading with her to come.

"Oh, of course, Mary's an angel. She never minds anything. But that's no reason why she should be put upon. No, my boy, you go and have your bachelor dinner, and I'll get Winter to send me up an egg."

"Mayn't I share the egg?"

"Certainly not. Get along with you." And Joan sped her lover on his way with the taste of her kiss fresh on his mouth. It seemed a profanation to eat anything after that; but all the same, while Joan ate her egg and then took her turn in watching over Sir Vernon, Ellery, seated alone in the grill room at Hatchett's was making a very solid and satisfactory meal. Somehow, love seemed to give one an appetite, he reflected, as he lighted a cigar. Then he set forth upon his quest, walking slowly down Piccadilly towards the Circus. He had no fixed plan of action. As he put it to himself, he was following the route Walter Brooklyn had taken and just keeping his eyes open, in the hope that something might turn up. Nothing did turn up till he reached Piccadilly Circus. There, as he knew, Walter Brooklyn had hung about for a few minutes, but had spoken to no one.

The quest certainly did not seem to be hopeful. Piccadilly Circus was crowded with people, some hurrying this way or that in pursuit of some definite object, others standing or strolling about as if they had nothing to do and nowhere in particular to go. The flower-women who sit on the island in the middle of the Circus in the daytime had already left their posts, and would presumably have done so on Tuesday before Walter Brooklyn took that disastrous walk. But before long Ellery picked out two persons who remained at fixed spots while the rest of the crowd changed from minute to minute. The one was a policeman regulating the traffic and the queues at the point where the buses stopped by the island: the other was a night-watchman in his little hut, keeping guard over a piece of the roadway which was under repair. These were the most likely of all the crowd to have been there on Tuesday night, and with them he determined to begin his inquiries.

The policeman was quickly disposed of. He had not been on duty on Tuesday; but a little persuasion in tangible form soon secured the name of the constable who had, and the news that he had only been kept away that night by a misadventure, and would be on duty again the following night. Ellery made a note of the name, and said to himself that he must see the other policeman later. For the present he strolled over towards the watchman, whom he found reading a tattered book in his little cabin, by the light partly of the lamps and sky signs, and partly, though it was a warm summer evening, of a blazing fire in a pail. He was a little, old man with a pair of steel spectacles, which had carved a deep rut in his nose, and he seemed to be reading with extraordinarily concentrated attention. Ellery managed to see what the book was. It was Sartor Resartus. The man was clearly a "scholar," and probably a homely philosopher of the working-class.

It seemed best to use the opening which providence had provided. "That's a fine book you've got there," said Ellery, casting his mind back to the days at school, when he had first and last read his Sartor, only to forget all about it and Carlyle as he reached years of discretion.

The little old man peered up at him over his glasses. "It is the book for me," he said. "That Carlyle, sir, he was a man."

"I dare say you manage to read a great deal at your job."

"I do that. You see, I had a accident ten years ago. 'Fore that, I was a navvy; but that finished me—for heavy work, I mean. At first, I was wretched at this job; the company gave it me, when doctor said I was fit for light work. And then it came to me I'd take up reading, like. I hadn't hardly ever opened a book till then—not since school. I can tell you, it's been a revelation to me. I don't ask nothing better than to sit here with a good book now. But it isn't often one of you gentlemen seems to notice what I'm reading."

The old man spoke slowly, and rather as if he was thinking aloud. He seemed almost to have forgotten that Ellery was there.

"Perhaps I shouldn't have noticed, unless there had been something I wanted to ask you. A man's life may depend on it, and I wanted your help."

The old man peered up at him again, and a little gleam of excitement came into his eyes; but he only nodded to Ellery to go on.

Ellery handed him a photograph of Walter Brooklyn. "On Tuesday night, at about half-past ten, that man stopped for some minutes on the island in the middle of the Circus here. He is accused of having been somewhere else, and his life may depend on our finding some one who saw him here. What I want to ask is whether you happened to notice him."

The old man thought for a minute before answering. "I can't say I did; but I seem to know his face somehow. Half-past ten, you said?"

"Then or then abouts, it must have been."

"No, I didn't see him. At half-past ten I was in here reading, and I didn't notice much. But I know I've seen that chap somewhere. Wait a minute while I think."

Ellery waited. It seemed a long while before the old man went on.

"Now, if you'd have said half-past eleven, or maybe a quarter-past, I should have said I saw him."

"Yes. Why, he did cross the Circus again at about that time."

"Then I saw him. It was like this, you see. About a quarter-past eleven on Tuesday I gets up to walk round the works here and see if all's right. Up there at the corner by Shaftesbury Avenue I saw a gentleman—very like your gentleman he was and smoking a big cigar—come strolling across the road. Very slow, he was walking. Seemed as if he was annoyed about something—waving his stick in the air, he was, as if he was making believe to hit somebody. I only noticed him because a big motor-car came round suddenly from Regent Street as he was crossing, and he had to skip. Came straight into the ropes round the work up there. I hurried to see if he was all right; but before I got there he dusted himself down and walked on. I'm almost sure he was your man. I've got a memory for faces, and I noticed him particularly because he seemed that ratty, if I may say so."

"Can you tell me again what time that was?"

"Not far short of half-past eleven—leastways it was after the quarter, twenty to twenty-five past, maybe."

Ellery congratulated himself on an extraordinary stroke of luck. It was, of course, far more important to establish Walter Brooklyn's presence in Piccadilly Circus between 11.15 and 11.30 than at 10.30; but it had seemed impossible to do so. Some one might have noticed him when he hung about there for several minutes; but it seemed very unlikely that his mere walking across the Circus at the later time could have been confirmed. By a lucky chance it had been, and the first link in the alibi had been successfully joined.

The next thing was to get the watchman's name and address, and to arrange for his appearance if he were called upon. The old man readily gave the particulars; but when Ellery talked of payment for his services, he refused. "I don't want money for it," he said; "not unless I have to appear in court. Then I'll want my expenses same as another. But I'll tell you what. If I've done you a good turn, you come here again some night and talk to me about books. That'll be a lot more to me than what you'd give me. There ain't no one I've got to talk to about what I read. It'll be a treat to have a talk to a gent like you, what knows all about books and what's inside 'em."

"I'm afraid," said Ellery, "you do me too much credit. It's years since I read Carlyle, and I've forgotten most about him. But I'll come back, and lend you some more of him if you want it. But I expect you know a lot more about him than I do."

It turned out that what the old man wanted above all else

was a copy of Carlyle's Cromwell. Ellery promised to bring it, and after a few words more they parted on the best of terms, and Ellery walked on slowly along Coventry Street and into Leicester Square. He felt that luck was on his side.

Chapter XVII
The Lovely Lady

To walk round Leicester Square in search of the mysterious Kitty gave Ellery an uncomfortable feeling. Kitty appeared to belong to a type of lovely lady which had not come much in his way, and his first sensation was one of strong distaste. Moreover, he very soon realised that the description given to him was not likely to be of much value. There seemed to be a whole tribe of Kittys in the neighbourhood of Leicester Square, and Ellery liked each one he set eyes on less than the last. He came speedily to two conclusions—first, that he would never spot the right one by means of the description which Walter Brooklyn had given, and secondly, that it would be quite out of his power to address one of these ladies, or to do anything but seek refuge in flight if, as seemed most probable, one of them attempted to address him. He tried to overcome this feeling; but it was no use. Even though no one had yet spoken to him, he turned tail, and took refuge in Orange Street for a few minutes' reflection.

He knew that he could not do it. Moreover, to walk round Leicester Square addressing strange females by a Christian name which might or might not belong to them was probably an excellent prelude to adventures of a sort, but hardly to the gaining of the particular information of which he was in search. The way to find Kitty was not to hunt for a hypothetical needle in a very unpleasant haystack, but to go straight to some one who was likely to know. And who would be more likely than Will Jaxon, who was celebrated as the devil of a fellow with the women, and lived, moreover, in bachelor chambers hardly more than round the corner in Panton Street? Ellery set off there to find his man.

Jaxon had been with Ellery at Oxford, and, dissimilar as many of their tastes were, they had kept up the acquaintance. They had in common an intense absorption in the technique of the theatre, in which Ellery was interested as a young and promising writer of plays, and Jaxon as an equally promising producer. But Jaxon's way of living was very different from his friend's. He was not a vicious man; but he said that vice, and still more the shoddy imitation of it which passes current in the London demi-monde, attracted him as a study. He liked watching the game, and making little bets with himself as to its fortunes. It was, he said, a harmless amusement, and, if the professors of psychology based their views largely on a study of the "diseases of personality," why should not he, a mere amateur, follow their example? So he passed much of his time among persons whose ways of living were, to say the least, not in conformity with the dictates of the Nonconformist conscience. It was his pride to know the Society underworld; and, in particular, he was wont to boast that he knew the "points" of all the important "lovely ladies" of London. It was ten to one that he would know where to find Kitty.

Jaxon, fortunately, was in, and Ellery was soon able to explain his business. He wanted a woman, none too young, and getting fat, whose name was Kitty something-or-other. She was, he believed, often to be found round about Leicester Square.

"You're the very last man I ever expected to come to me on a quest like that," said Jaxon with a laugh. "Now, if it had been Lorimer or Wentworth—but you of all men. Oh, I know it's all right, and your intentions are strictly honourable. But do you know that there are at least a dozen Kittys, all of them celebrated in their way, who conform fully to the description you have given me? How am I to know which one you want?"

Ellery repeated his description, giving every detail that had been told him—the golden, dyed hair, the smile that switched on and off like an electric light—"That's not much help. It's part of the professional equipment," said Jaxon—the dark eyes, the slovenly walk.

"The golden hair and the dark eyes help to narrow the field; but there are still half a dozen it might be—all of the fat and forty brigade, and all of them no better than they should be according to the world's reckoning. Five of the six are just the ordinary thing; but the other is something quite out of the common run. She's not what you would call an honest woman; but she's a very remarkable person for all that. I wonder if it is she you are after."

"Tell me about her first."

"Well her name—or at least the name she's known by—is Kitty Frensham. Kitty Lessing it used to be when I first knew her. In those days she was more or less the property of a Russian Archduke, or something of the sort. Or rather, he used to be altogether her property. Then, a year or so ago, he died, and since then she has been rather at a loose end. She's fat and forty; but she's a most fascinating woman. Awfully clever, too."

"Can you get hold of her for me?"

"Yes, I think I know where to find her; but you'd better understand that she's not at all the ordinary sort of street-crawler. If she's your woman, the description you gave was a bit misleading. She is most often about with Horace Mandleham, the painter chap, nowadays. Come round to Duke's with me, and I dare say we shall find her."

Ellery knew about Duke's, of course; but he had never been

there. Just at the moment, it was the latest thing in night clubs in London, and everybody who fancied himself or herself as a bit in advance of other folk was keen to go there. Ellery was not advanced, and it took some persuasion to carry him along. He seemed to think that Jaxon ought to cut out his prize for him from under the guns of Duke's and bring her home in tow. But Jaxon said he could find her, but he couldn't possibly bring her. Finally, Ellery agreed to go. After all, he reflected, it was all in the day's work. He had known what sort of man Walter Brooklyn was; and he must not complain if the task of clearing up his character meant going into some queer places.

Duke's certainly did not rely for its popularity on external display. It was approached by three flights of narrow and rickety stairs, and the visitors had to satisfy two rather seedy-looking janitors, not in uniform, at top and bottom. And, when they entered the Club itself, Ellery had a still greater surprise. The famous Duke's consisted of one very long low room—or rather of three long, low attics which had been amateurishly knocked into one. The decorations were old and faded, and the places where the partitions had been were still marked by patches of new paper pasted on to hide the rents in the old. The ventilation was abominable, and what windows there were did not seem to have been cleaned for months. The furniture—a few seedy divans and a large number of common Windsor chairs and kitchen tables—seemed to have been picked up at second-hand from some very inferior dealer. Tables and floor were stained with countless spillings of food and drink, and a thick cloud of tobacco smoke made it quite impossible to see any distance along the room. There was only one redeeming feature, and Ellery's eye fell upon it almost as soon as he entered the place. Near the door was a magnificent grand piano, on which some one was playing really well an arrangement from Borodine's Prince Igor.

Jaxon drew Ellery to a vacant table. "We'll sit down here and order something, and then in a moment or two, I'll go round and spy out the land," he said. "From here we shall see any one who goes out. And, by Jove, there's one of the six Kittys—not the one I told you about. I shouldn't be surprised if we found the whole half-dozen before the evening's out. Everybody looks in here just now."

Ellery felt very uncomfortable when he was left alone to sip his gin and water while Jaxon went round the room, exchanging a few words with friends at several of the tables. But soon his friend came back to report. "No, she's not here now; but I've spotted another Kitty for you. I forgot her: she makes the seventh on our list, and you'd better have a word with the two who are here. Bring your drink across, and I'll introduce you to that one over there. She's Kitty Turner, and the chap she's with is a fellow from Bloomsbury way called Parkinson—a civil servant, I believe. I'll do the talking, or most of it. You just ask her if she knows Walter Brooklyn when you get a chance."

They drew a blank at the conversation. Kitty Turner was certainly a very bright lady, laughing immoderately both at her own and at Jaxon's jokes, and, it seemed to Ellery, a good deal relieved to get a rest from her tête-à-tête with the gloomy fellow who was sitting by her side. He, at any rate, seemed to take his pleasures sadly. Indeed, it struck Ellery, as he looked round the room, that very few of the people there seemed to be really enjoying themselves. The women were cheerful, but there was something forced about the gaiety of many of them; and some of the men seemed to need a deal of cheering up. Ellery found himself wondering why on earth so many people came to this sort of place, if they did not even find it amusing. He at any rate was not amused, even as Jaxon seemed to be, by regarding the place as a sort of psychological study. He had come there for a definite purpose; and, as soon as he had satisfied himself that Kitty Turner knew nothing of Walter Brooklyn, he was ready to move on. A signal soon brought Jaxon to his feet, and they strolled across the room to try the next Kitty on the list.

Kitty Laurenson did know Walter Brooklyn, but not to any degree of intimacy. She had met him a few times, and Ellery rather gathered that, in her opinion, he had been less attentive than he should have been to her charms. She had certainly not seen him on Tuesday, or indeed for weeks past. Ellery liked her even less than the other; for her attitude towards him seemed to be strictly professional, and, as soon as she was sure that he could not be fascinated, she showed him plainly that the sooner he went away the better he would please her. Ellery again gave Jaxon the signal, and they left her table. They were just discussing whether it was worth while to wait a time in the hope that some more Kittys might turn up, when Jaxon said suddenly, "By Jove, here she comes, and alone too. We're in luck."

Ellery turned, and saw entering the room a stout, rather coarse-looking woman of about forty or forty-five, so far as he could judge through the intervening smoke, and despite the artificial obstructions which the lady herself had placed in the way of those who might be minded to inspect her too closely. He saw at once that she was a person to be reckoned with. The face was powerful, and the pair of keen black eyes which were glancing penetratingly round the room, as if in search of some one, were not easily to be forgotten. The figure was without dignity; but the woman's expression gave it the lie. Certainly she was more likely to have owned the Russian Archduke than to have been owned by him.

Jaxon left Ellery standing by himself and went up to her. She greeted him pleasantly. "Oh, Will, I was looking for Horace. Do you know if he is here?"

Jaxon replied that he had not seen him and asked her to join him and his friend while she was waiting. She agreed, and Jaxon led her across and made the introduction.

From the moment when he was introduced to Kitty

Frensham Ellery had a feeling that he had found what he wanted. She was very gracious; but, as Jaxon introduced her, she smiled, and the coming of her smile was for all the world as if she had suddenly pressed the switch and turned it on like the electric light. Both the other Kittys had smiles which they turned on and off at will; but their smiles came into being gradually, whereas this woman smiled, and stopped smiling, with quite extraordinary suddenness. Ellery was so sure that she was the right woman, and also, as he told Jaxon afterwards, so sure of her common sense, that he plunged straight into his story.

"There's something I want to ask you," he said, "indeed, I got Jaxon to introduce me on purpose. You know Walter Brooklyn, don't you?"

Her face at once became serious. "Yes, I do. I have just seen the terrible news in the evening paper. Do you think he can have done it, Mr. Ellery? I suppose you know him too."

"Yes, I know him, and I am quite sure he had nothing to do with it. I want you to help prove that I am right. You saw him on Tuesday night, did you not?"

"I had quite forgotten it; but I did. I spoke to him for a minute or two. I was coming out of the Alhambra with Horace—Mr. Mandleham, that is—and Horace had left me for a minute to look for a taxi. The Old 'un came up and spoke to me, I remember."

"The Old 'un? Is that a name for Walter Brooklyn?"

"Yes, we used to call him 'The Old Rip'; but it got shortened to 'the Old 'un.' He goes the pace rather, even now, you know."

"I dare say he does; and of course that is likely to make it all the worse for him with the jury—if it's the usual sort."

"But if he didn't do it, surely he's all right, isn't he?"

"The fact that you remember meeting him may be the

means of saving his life. Can you tell me at what time that was?"

"Oh, Lord, Mr. Ellery, I never know the time. It was some time in the evening, fairly early. We left before the show was over. Horace would probably know."

"Did Mr. Mandleham see Mr. Brooklyn?"

"Yes, he did. When he came back he asked me who it was I had been talking to."

At this point a new voice struck into the conversation. "Hallo, Kitty, you seem very deep in something. Haven't you even a word for me?"

"Why, here is Horace," said Kitty. "I've been waiting for you for hours, Horace. It's really too bad. But now you come over here, and make yourself really useful for a minute. It's not a thing you do often."

Horace Mandleham was fortunately quite precise about the time. They had left the Alhambra a few minutes after half-past ten, and he had come back with the taxi just about a quarter to eleven. Walter Brooklyn had at that moment taken his leave of Kitty Frensham. Yes, that was the man. He recognised at once the photograph which Ellery passed across to him. He was quite ready to swear to it, if it was of any importance. He had seen the evening paper, and knew the chap was in trouble.

A good deal to his surprise, Ellery found that he definitely liked Kitty Frensham, and before he left he had even promised to go and see her soon in her flat in Chelsea, which, as she told him, was hardly more than round the corner from his own rooms. She had promised, and had made Mandleham promise as well, to give every help that could possibly be given in clearing Walter Brooklyn, although she had made it plain that she did not like him, and although her reluctance to find herself in a court of law was evident enough. Still, she had recognised that she ought to do what she could; and Ellery half-believed that a part of her willingness was due to the fact that he had impressed her favourably. He had come prepared to spend money in securing the evidence of a "lovely lady" of unlovely repute: he had secured the willing testimony of an exceedingly clever and, even to his temperament, fascinating woman. Kitty Frensham was certainly not the sort of person to whom money could be offered for such a service. It puzzled Ellery that such a woman should have, as he put it to himself, "gone to the bad." She was worthy of something better than that anæmic specimen, Mandleham.

It was by this time too late to do more; but, before going home, Ellery 'phoned through to Joan, who was waiting up for a message from him and told her briefly what he had accomplished. The quest, he said, had taken him to some strange places; he would tell her all about it on the morrow. Joan, too, had news of a sort; but she said that it would keep. Both of them retired for the night well pleased with the results of their first evening's experience of practical detective work. It had been easy going so far; but, Ellery said to himself, fortune had a most encouraging way of smiling on the beginner. Probably their troubles were still to come.

Chapter XVIII
The Case for the Defence

The more Fred Thomas thought over the case which he had to handle, the less he liked it. He was certainly not accustomed to be squeamish; and considerably more than his share of rather shady business came his way. But he did not like these cases of what he called "serious crime." Sharp practice was well enough; but a lawyer engaged in it regularly had best abstain from the defence of murderers. Thomas had by this time gone into the whole case, and was fully aware of the force of the evidence against his client held by the police. In his mind, there was not much doubt of Walter Brooklyn's guilt. He had obviously been in the house; the stick and the telephone message showed that; and what were you to do with a man who would not make a clean breast of it to his own lawyer? What was the use of his client's reiterated assertions that he had not been near the place, and that he knew nothing at all about the murders? Indeed, was not the refusal to speak the clearest indication of guilt? If Brooklyn, though he had been present in the house, had not been guilty, surely he would have told what he knew. Still, unsatisfactory as his client was, he would have to do his best for him. He could not very well throw up the case after he had once agreed to take charge of it. But he was not hopeful, and, for the moment, it seemed the best course to go and talk the whole thing over with Carter

Woodman.

But, when one came to think of it, was there not yet another indication of the man's guilt? If the man had been innocent, he would surely have gone first of all to the family lawyer.

Thomas knew Woodman only slightly, and was not quite sure of his reception. But, when he rang up, Woodman readily agreed to see him and to give all possible help. "After all," he had said, "the man's a sort of relation of mine, whatever he may have done"—a way of putting the position which did not strengthen Thomas's belief in the innocence of his client.

When Thomas was shown into Woodman's office, he was surprised at the cordiality of his reception. Woodman was "so glad" he had come, and they must work together to do what they could for the poor fellow—"a bit of a bad hat, between ourselves, but—for the sake of the family, you know."

Thomas went straight to the point. "Mr. Brooklyn positively assures me that he was not in Liskeard House on Tuesday night, and that he knows absolutely nothing of the murders."

Woodman said nothing; but he drummed on the table with his fingers, and the action conveyed a perfectly clear message. What were you to do for a fellow who would not tell his own lawyer the truth?

"He says that he simply strolled about all the time between ten o'clock and midnight."

"Alone?" asked Woodman.

"Yes, quite alone. Judging from his story, it would be impossible to obtain confirmation—even if it were all true."

"Then what line of defence do you propose to adopt?"

"It was on that point I wanted your advice. In the circumstances, and assuming that they remain unchanged, what can we do but deny the story and trust to a blustering counsel to get him off?"

"H'm, surely more than that is needed?"

"Certainly; but what more can be done, unless there is something else that Mr. Brooklyn can tell us?"

"Look here, Thomas. You can be quite frank with me. I'm quite sure Brooklyn was in the house and that he knows all about the murders, even if he didn't actually commit them. But, like you, I want to get him off."

"Can't you help me to make him speak?"

"He doesn't like me, and nothing I could say would have any influence. If he had been inclined to trust me, he would have sent for me in the first instance. You'll have to make him talk somehow. But I can tell you what will weigh most heavily against him. He stands to gain a fortune by these murders—not by either of them singly, but by both together. It's hard to get over a fact like that as well as the other evidence; the suggestion of motive is so clear—and, to put it bluntly, his personal character doesn't help matters."

"Do you happen to know whether Mr. Brooklyn was pressed for money?"

"He was always pressed for money, and just lately he has been even harder pressed than usual. He was round here on Tuesday trying all he could to get money from me, and he left me with the expressed intention of seeing Prinsep, and having another attempt to raise the wind through him. I know Prinsep was determined to refuse, and he wasn't a man to refuse gently, either."

"What you say makes me feel more than ever like throwing up the case. I'm not bound to go on if he won't be frank with me."

"Don't throw it up. We must give the fellow every chance. It's difficult for you, I know, but do the best you can. I expect your idea of a good hectoring counsel is the best that can be managed. After all, they have no direct evidence."

"I'm afraid what they have is good enough."

"Oh, you never know, with a jury."

"What came into my head was that the best possible line of defence, if it can be arranged, would be to throw suspicion on some one else. Not enough to do the other person any real damage, but just enough to create a reasonable doubt."

Woodman made no reply for a moment. Then he said, "That's all very well; but where do you propose to find the person and the evidence?"

"First of all, it is surely very probable that George Brooklyn was actually killed by Prinsep. There is good evidence for that, you'll agree."

"Good enough to make a case, and it may even be true, though I don't think it is."

"Well, I propose to argue strongly that it is true, and I think we can create enough doubt to make it impossible to convict Mr. Brooklyn on that head. That leaves the murder of Prinsep."

"Unfortunately, that is just where the evidence against Walter Brooklyn is strongest."

"I know it is; and I want you to help me to find some one else who could reasonably be suspected of killing Prinsep. Never mind the evidence. I'll find that if you'll help me to the person, It won't need to be enough to do the suspected person any real damage. It isn't as if we wanted to get any one convicted: I only want to throw dust in the jury's eyes."

"I'm sorry; but I can't help you there," said Woodman shortly.

"What about the servants?"

"Out of the question. They're as innocent as you are."

"What does it matter if they are innocent? Can they be proved so?"

Carter Woodman brought his fist down on the table with a bang. Then he said very deliberately, "I am anxious to use all legitimate means of getting Mr. Walter Brooklyn acquitted; but I must tell you once and for all, Thomas, that I decline to be a party to attempt to throw the guilt on any innocent persons."

"My dear fellow, what is the use of talking about legitimate means in a case like this? You know as well as I do that only illegitimate means can give my client a dog's chance."

"Then I'm sorry I can't help you."

With that the interview ended. Thomas left Woodman's office more firmly than ever convinced of Walter Brooklyn's guilt, but also determined to follow up his stratagem of shifting the suspicion, or at least some part of it, elsewhere. The more he thought of the plan, the more it appealed to him. It wasn't much of a dodge in itself; but it seemed to offer more hope than anything else in this case. If the fellow did get hanged after all, he would have only himself to blame. Thomas would have done his best.

Following up this line of thought, Thomas made up his mind that the first thing to do was to get full information about the servants.

Thus, Walter Brooklyn's legal adviser, though with a very different idea in his mind, set to work upon an aspect of the case which had already been considered and investigated by the police. It will be remembered that Inspector Blaikie had cross-examined the two men-servants, and that subsequently he and Superintendent Wilson had agreed to have the two men watched—not that they were much disposed to believe that either of them had anything directly to do with the murders, but because their complicity or knowledge, or even their guilt, was just barely conceivable. Morgan's presence at the house of his friends at Hammersmith on the Tuesday night, and his return to Liskeard House at about a quarter to eleven, had been duly verified; but his statement that he had gone straight to bed, and remained there until the morning, rested wholly on Winter's evidence. There was no reason to suspect this, unless it should turn out that Winter was himself involved. The police had, therefore, directed most of their attention to the butler, who had certainly gone up to his room with Morgan at a quarter to twelve. Had he stayed there, or had he come down again and played some part in the night's doings? On this point the police could find no evidence at all. Morgan stated that Winter was in his room in the morning, that his bed had been slept in, and that he rose at his usual hour. But Morgan had slept heavily, and he could not positively say that Winter had remained in his room all night. This fact, however, was clearly no evidence at all against Winter, and there had been nothing in his demeanour to suggest that he was in any way concerned. His past history, too, seemed to make him a most unlikely criminal. Accordingly, now that the evidence seemed to point conclusively to the guilt of Walter Brooklyn, the police, while they still kept some perfunctory watch on the two servants, practically dismissed them from their minds.

Thomas, when he had ascertained the main facts about the two men-servants, did not for a moment suspect that either of them was guilty, or think it likely that either had any knowledge of the crimes. His first step was to ask Walter Brooklyn himself whether he supposed that either of the servants could throw any light on the matter. Supposing his client to be at the least fully cognisant of the night's events, he thought that the question could hardly fail to give him some guidance. But Walter Brooklyn displayed little interest, and by doing so confirmed the lawyer's opinion that the servants had nothing at all to do with it. "Go and see them by all means," Brooklyn had said, "but I don't suppose they know anything about it." That was all he would say, and he still stuck to the story he had first told Thomas, and maintained that he himself was equally ignorant of what had taken place. A marked coolness, which did not increase Thomas's zest for the case, had sprung up between him and his client, and although certain questions had to be asked and answered, it was clear enough that Walter Brooklyn greatly preferred the solitude of his cell to his lawyer's society.

It was on his own initiative, therefore, that Thomas went to see both Winter and Morgan, and received from them a repetition of what they had told the police. From them he learnt nothing new. But from one of the maid-servants he picked up a fact which had escaped Inspector Blaikie's attention. A few days before the murders the butler, Winter, had quarrelled violently with John Prinsep, and, in the heat of the quarrel, Prinsep had practically given the man notice to leave. The notice had not been quite definite, and the maid had heard Winter confide to Morgan that he intended to hang on and see what happened, and to get the matter cleared up with Prinsep the one way or the other before the month expired. She did not know what the quarrel had been about; and Thomas did not think it politic to push his inquiries further, or to ask either Morgan or Winter himself for an explanation. He, therefore, cautioned the girl against telling any one at all that there had been a quarrel. "It would only make further trouble," he said; "and we have trouble enough on our hands already."

Thomas had thus found the first essential for building up a case on suspicion against Winter—an actual quarrel and therefore a possible motive for murder. But he recognised that the argument was very thin, and that he must, if possible, get something more definite. Inquiries, however, failed to give him anything at all that could be used to defame either Winter's or Morgan's character. They appeared to be persons of unblemished respectability, and Winter's long service in the Brooklyn household seemed never to have been marred before by such an incident as his quarrel with Prinsep. The position did not look promising for Thomas's client; but he determined to persist.

His persistence was at length rewarded. He discovered what had been the cause of the quarrel between Winter and

Prinsep. And it was Morgan who told him, quite unconscious that he was providing a link in the chain which Thomas was attempting to forge. Thomas had turned his attention to a further study of the character and circumstances of the murdered men, and had gone to Morgan for light on the ways of his late master. It was easy to see that Morgan had disliked Prinsep, though he had always behaved to him in life as a perfectly suave and well-drilled servant knows how to behave—with a deadly politeness that conceals all human feeling behind an impenetrable mask. But, now that Prinsep was dead, Morgan no longer concealed his opinion of him. He had neither prospect nor intention of remaining with the Brooklyns, and he did not care whether they liked or disliked what he said. Accordingly, he told Thomas without any hesitation that, shortly before his death, Prinsep had been engaged in a peculiarly unpleasant intrigue with a girl down at Sir Vernon's country place at Fittleworth, in Sussex—the daughter, in fact, of Sir Vernon's head gardener there—and what made it worse was that the girl was engaged to be married at the time to a decent fellow who had only found out at the last moment how things were going. He would marry her all the same; but that did not make Prinsep's part in the affair less dishonourable.

It did not take Thomas long to extract the information that the "decent fellow" whom Prinsep had wronged was actually no other than this very man, Winter, against whom he had been trying to build up a case. Winter was twenty years older than the girl; but he seemed to be very much in love with her, and naturally enraged by Prinsep's misuse of her. Here at last were all the elements of a crime of passion, and Thomas began to see his way clear to throw upon Winter quite enough suspicion to make it very difficult for a jury to convict Walter Brooklyn. Indeed, might he not even have stumbled accidentally on the truth, or a part of it? Perhaps after all Walter Brooklyn was not the murderer, although he knew all about it. But, on the whole, he was still inclined to believe that his client was guilty, and that nevertheless fortune had presented him with an excellent chance of shifting the suspicion elsewhere. Certainly he would say not a word of his discoveries to any one until the time came to adopt an actual line of defence at the coming trial.

Chapter XIX
The Police Have Their Doubts

While the representatives of the defence—official and unofficial—were pursuing their separate lines of investigation, the police had not been altogether idle. Inspector Blaikie had not been long in finding out that Thomas had been making inquiries among the servants at Liskeard House, or in drawing the conclusion that the defence would make an attempt to shift some part at least of the suspicion to other shoulders with the object of creating enough doubt to make it difficult for a jury to convict their client. He was not surprised at this, and it did not at all alarm him; for, among other things, he regarded it as sure proof that the lawyer held his own case to be weak. The inspector was quite unable to take seriously the idea that Winter was in any way implicated in the murders; and Morgan's complicity, owing to the position of their bedrooms, was practically impossible without Winter's. Blaikie therefore treated Thomas's moves as being merely the necessary preparation for an attempt to throw dust into the eyes of the jury, and not in the least an endeavour to find the real murderer. There could be no doubt about it—Thomas's tactics were, from the inspector's standpoint, the final and conclusive proof—Walter Brooklyn had murdered Prinsep, and either he or Prinsep had murdered George Brooklyn. They had the right man under lock and key.

But it is one thing to be sure that you have the right man in custody, and quite another to be sure of getting him convicted by a jury. The inspector admitted that the case against Walter Brooklyn was not conclusive. His complicity was practically proved; but there was no direct evidence that he had actually struck the blows. The evidence was circumstantial; and, in these circumstances, the inspector did not disguise from himself the fact that any attempt to shift the suspicion might at least create enough doubt to make a conviction improbable. Accordingly, while Joan and Ellery were doing their best to prove Walter Brooklyn's innocence, Inspector Blaikie was searching, with equal vigour, for further proofs of his guilt.

But he found nothing that was of material importance, so far as he could see. The sole addition to his case was the evidence of a taxi-driver, who, from his accustomed post on the rank outside the Piccadilly Theatre, had seen Walter Brooklyn pass at somewhere about half-past eleven or so; but the man could not be sure to a few minutes. This was all very well in its way, the inspector thought; but as Walter Brooklyn's presence inside Liskeard House at about 11.30 was proved already, it could not be of much importance to prove his presence just outside at about the same time. There was, however, this to be said for the new piece of evidence. Walter Brooklyn denied the telephone message, and maintained that he had not been at Liskeard House at all. Direct evidence that he had been at the time in question within a minute's walk of the house was certainly better than nothing.

Nothing further had come to light when, on Saturday morning, Inspector Blaikie went to Superintendent Wilson with his daily report on the case, telling him first about the taxi-man's evidence. The superintendent seemed to attach some importance to this. "Where you have to rely on circumstantial evidence," he said, "the accumulation of details is all-important. Every little helps. Your taxi-driver may yet be an important link in the chain."

The inspector confided to his superior that the result of his reflections on the case was to make him far more doubtful than he had been of securing a conviction.

"Quite so," said the superintendent. "I thought you would realise that when you had thought it over."

The inspector replied that he saw it now, and went on to explain what he believed to be the strategy of the defence—throwing suspicion on the servants. "The trouble of it is," he said, "that although I'm absolutely sure in my own mind that Winter had nothing whatever to do with the affair, there's no way of proving the thing one way or the other. So far as the evidence goes, he might have done it. Of course, there's absolutely no shred of evidence that he did; but that is not enough to prevent a clever counsel from arousing suspicion in the mind of a jury."

"Are you so sure," said the superintendent, "that there is no shred of evidence? I mean, of course, of what the other side may be able to dress up to look like evidence. I should say that fellow Thomas is clever enough to find something that he can make serve as a cause for suspicion, if there is anything at all that will serve. For example, this Prinsep seems to have been a bit of a beast. Is there anything to show whether Winter was on good or bad terms with him? If they had quarrelled or anything of the sort, that is just the kind of fact Thomas, or his counsel, would use to good effect."

"You're right there; but I've come across nothing that would suggest a quarrel. Morgan—that's the valet chap—made no secret of disliking Prinsep very cordially; but Winter seems to be just the good, faithful family servant."

"I dare say there's nothing to be found out in that way: but you might make a note of it, and get a few inquiries made. We want to know exactly how strong the defence is likely to be. And, by the way, I suppose you still have no doubts in your own mind that Walter Brooklyn is the murderer?" The superintendent opened his eyes, and looked at the inspector as he spoke.

"None at all—at least, it seems to me practically certain. Quite as certain as the case against most men who get hanged. Do you mean that you are in doubt about it?"

The superintendent made no direct reply to this. "At any rate," he said, "the evidence is certainly not conclusive. I suppose you have no idea whether the defence will try to prove an alibi."

"I don't see how they can. According to his own story, Brooklyn was just strolling about alone all the evening. He can't prove that, surely."

"Oh, I don't know about that. If it were true, he might have been seen by a dozen people. And, even if it weren't true, Thomas might be able to produce witnesses who would swear they had seen him. Thomas wouldn't stick at that. Any alibi he tries to produce will need very careful scrutiny."

"But we know Brooklyn was in the house at 11.30."

The superintendent smiled, and leant back in his chair. "No," he said, "that is just where you go wrong. We don't know it. It rests on the evidence about the telephone message. But have you considered all the possibilities about that message? The defence clearly will not admit that Walter Brooklyn sent it. We believe he did; but is it not quite possible for the defence to argue that somebody else sent that message with the deliberate intention of misleading us? And is it not also possible that Brooklyn sent it, but not from Liskeard House?"

"But why should he say he was at Liskeard House if he wasn't?"

"I don't say he wasn't. But he may maintain that the man who took the message down made a mistake. After all, such mishaps are common enough. Or he may have been meaning to go to Liskeard House before the messenger arrived."

"I think that is ruled out any way. We have proved from inquiries at the telephone exchange that Liskeard House did ring up Brooklyn's club at about the time stated. There was some trouble about the connection, and the operator remembers making it."

"Well, take the other possibility. May not the defence argue that some one else must have impersonated Brooklyn at the telephone, with the deliberate object of throwing suspicion upon him? The murderer, supposing him not to be Walter Brooklyn, would obviously want to get some one else suspected if he could. On that theory, all the circumstantial evidence would be false clues left by the real murderer."

"That doesn't seem to me at all likely, if I may say so. The evidence that was left on the spot where Prinsep was killed was obviously meant to incriminate George Brooklyn. That seems to show that, when the murder was done, the murderer had no idea that George Brooklyn was dead already, if indeed he was. A criminal would hardly lay two distinct and actually inconsistent sets of clues, leading to quite different suspects."

"Not unless he was a quite exceptionally clever criminal, I grant you. But tell me this. Why should a man, who otherwise covered his traces so well, give himself away like an utter fool by that telephone conversation?"

"Obviously, I should say, because the 'phone message was sent before the murder, and the murder was not premeditated. Having killed his man, Brooklyn took the only possible course by denying the conversation."

"Yes, that theory hangs together; but I'm not satisfied with it. There seems to me to be every reason to believe that the murders were most carefully thought out beforehand, and in that case the sending of the telephone message needs a lot of explanation. Then, again, we have still no indication at all of how Walter Brooklyn, or for that matter George Brooklyn, got into or out of the house."

"On that point I have absolutely failed to get any light. My first idea, of course, was duplicate keys, and the stable yard. But the yard was quite definitely bolted as well as locked by eleven o'clock. The wall could not be scaled without a long ladder, which is out of the question. The front door is quite impossible, unless three or four servants were in the plot. I suppose they must have slipped in through the theatre, although it beats me how they got in without being seen."

"May not Walter Brooklyn have come in through the stable yard before it was closed, and been in the house some time before the murders? He may have been going away when your taxi-man saw him at about 11.30."

"Even so, that doesn't explain how he let himself out and bolted the place after him from the inside. And, in any case, George Brooklyn was still alive at 11.30, when he was seen leaving the building by the front door. He had to get back, and Prinsep, if he killed him, must have been alive too until well after 11.30."

"And you can add to that the difficulty that George Brooklyn seems to have got back into the garden after 11.30, and that, where one man could enter unseen, so could two."

The inspector scratched his chin. "The whole thing is a puzzle," he said. "But there's one thing I'm sure of. It's a much worse puzzle if you don't assume that Walter Brooklyn was the murderer."

"Still, there's nothing so dangerous as to simplify your problem by assuming what you cannot conclusively prove to be true. If I were a juryman, I certainly could not vote for a conviction on the evidence we have at present."

"But there's no one else who could have done it."

"Oh, yes, there is. There's all the population of London. I grant you we have at present no reason for suspecting any one else in particular. But that may be because we don't know enough."

"Then what do you want me to do?"

"Hunt, for all you're worth, for further evidence. Don't shut your eyes to the possibility that Walter Brooklyn may not be the murderer. Hunt for evidence of any kind, as if you were starting the case afresh."

"And, meanwhile, Walter Brooklyn remains in custody?"

"Most certainly. There is presumptive evidence that he is the guilty party. But it's nothing like a certainty. Remember that."

The above conversation serves to show that the police, on their side, were becoming seriously worried. They had hoped that the strong presumptive evidence against Walter Brooklyn would speedily have been reinforced by further discoveries; but so far they had been disappointed. Inspector Blaikie at least was still strongly of opinion that he was guilty; but a strong opinion is not enough to convince a jury, and the inspector did not like to see the acquittal of a man he had arrested, especially as he had no other evidence pointing to some different person as the guilty person. Superintendent Wilson at least, while he could not blame the inspector for his conduct of the investigation, was growing more and more dissatisfied with the progress of the case. He had an uneasy and a growing feeling, which he had at first been unwilling to admit even to himself, that they were on the wrong tack.

Chapter XX
Superintendent Wilson Thinks It Out

When the inspector had left him, Superintendent Wilson gave himself up for a time to his thoughts. Leaning back in his chair, with his long legs stretched out before him, and the tips of his fingers pressed together before his face, he concentrated his faculties upon the Brooklyn affair. A heavy frown settled on his brow, and he gave every now and then an impatient twist of his body, eloquent of his mind's discomfort. At length he sighed, looked at the clock, rose, put on his hat, and started for home. He had made up his mind, as he did when difficulties beset him, to talk the case over with his wife.

Superintendent Wilson never mentioned business to his wife when things were going well; but whenever his usually clear brain seemed to be working amiss, it was his way to unload on her all his trouble. Not that Mrs. Wilson had a powerful intellect—far from it. She was a comfortable, motherly woman, inclined to stoutness, and completely wrapped up in her children and her home. For her husband she had a profound admiration. He was, to her mind, not merely the finest detective in Europe, but the cleverest man in the world. But she was quite content to admire his cleverness without understanding it; and her husband made no attempt, as a rule, to discuss his cases with her.

He had found, however, that on the rare occasions on which his thinking got into a blind alley, her very passivity was the best possible help he could have. As he talked to her, and as she assented unquestioningly to everything that he said, new ideas somehow arose in his mind. Doubts were dispelled, new courses of action suggested, the weak spots in the armour of crime became apparent. He would tell her that she had been the source of his most brilliant inspirations; and she would placidly accept the rôle, without bothering to inquire in what way she contributed to his flashes of insight into the most abstruse mysteries that came under the notice of the Criminal Investigation Department.

It was a sign of deep dissatisfaction with the progress of the Brooklyn case that the superintendent now took his troubles home to his wife. He found her, in the pleasant sitting-room of their house facing Clapham Common, placidly knitting woollies for the children in anticipation of the coming winter. From the garden came the noise of the children themselves, playing a game which involved repeated shouts of "Bang, bang, bang!" as the rival armies engaged.

"My dear. I want to consult you," he said, coming up and kissing her.

Mrs. Wilson laid down her knitting on the table beside her, and composed herself to listen.

"It's about this Brooklyn case. I suppose you've read about it in the papers. I'm working on it, you know."

Mrs. Wilson, who confined her newspaper reading to a glance at the pictures and headlines in the Daily Graphic, had barely heard of the case, and knew none of the details. Her husband therefore began by giving her a brief, but perfectly clear, account of the circumstances of the crimes. It helped to clear his own mind, and to put the essential facts in their proper focus.

"How dreadful!" was Mrs. Wilson's appropriate comment

at various points in the story. "And who did it?" she asked when her husband had done, smiling at him as if he were certain to know.

"My dear, if I knew that, I shouldn't need to consult you. Blaikie feels quite certain it was Walter Brooklyn, old Sir Vernon's brother. I'd better tell you just what there is against him." And the superintendent gave an account of the evidence leading to the presumption of Walter Brooklyn's guilt—the walking-stick, his failure to explain his movements on the night of the murders, his very strong motive for the crimes, and finally, the telephone message sent from Liskeard House on the fatal evening.

"But you say he didn't do it. Then who did?" asked his wife.

"No, my dear, I didn't say he didn't do it. All I say is that I'm not satisfied that he did."

"But you say he sent the telephone message——"

"Even if he did send the message, that doesn't prove that he committed the murders. He may have been there, and yet some one else may be the murderer. But I'm not even sure that he ever did send the message."

"If he didn't send it, some one else did."

"Yes, my dear, that's the very point. But if it was some one else, then that some one was deliberately trying to incriminate Walter Brooklyn."

"That is what you call laying a false clue, isn't it?"

"Yes, but the trouble is that, if the telephone and the walking-stick are false clues, we have to deal with two quite different sets of false clues, both deliberately laid, and pointing to quite different conclusions as to the murderer. Is that possible?" The superintendent paused, and looked at his wife. But instead of answering, she got up and went to the window. "Georgie," she said, "you mustn't pull the cat's tail.

If you're not good I shall send you to bed." Then she came back to her seat. "Yes, dear, you were saying——"

"I was asking whether it was credible that some one should have laid two sets of quite inconsistent false clues for the purpose of misleading us."

"Two sets of clues, dear. And both to mislead you. It must be very difficult to see through them both."

"By George," exclaimed the superintendent, leaping from his chair and beginning to pace up and down the room. "By George, you've given me just the idea I wanted. Yes, that must be it."

"What must be what, dear? I had no idea I'd said anything clever."

"Why, both sets of clues weren't meant to mislead us. That's it. The criminal laid two sets of false clues. He meant us to see through one set; but he thought we should never see through the other. He reckoned it would never occur to us that both sets of clues were false. Oh, yes. We were to feel awfully bucked up about seeing through the first set of clues—the obviously false ones—and then we were meant to go on and hang the wrong man gaily on the strength of the others. It was a clever idea, too, by Jove."

"Do you mean——" Mrs. Wilson began; but her husband was now in full flow, and he cut her short.

"What I mean is that the criminal deliberately laid the set of clues which pointed to the two men having murdered each other. We were bound to see through these, because the conclusion to which they pointed was just physically impossible. Then he laid the clues pointing to Walter Brooklyn, really meaning this time to get Walter Brooklyn hanged for the murders. My word, yes, this does throw a new light on the case. My dear, you've done it again. There's lots to find out yet; but I'm sure it will come out right now that I know where to begin."

"Then who was the murderer, dear? Have I told you somehow? I'm sure I don't know who it was."

"Neither do I, my dear. But I think I do know now how to begin looking for him. When I've found him I'll tell you who he is. And half the credit of finding him will be yours." The superintendent was so moved that he went up and kissed his wife as he kissed her only on occasions of rare exaltation. Then he got back to business with a sigh.

"If both sets of clues are false, my dear, you see that doesn't make them valueless. They may still be used to point to the real murderer. Yes, I begin to see light already. If Walter Brooklyn did not send that telephone message, who did? Not much help there, I'm afraid, except that it was a very daring criminal indeed, and probably one who knew intimately both Walter Brooklyn and Liskeard House. Ringing up Brooklyn's club shows that—he knew the man's habits. There is something to go upon at all events. But there's the walking-stick too—yes, that may be the point on which the whole case turns."

By this time Superintendent Wilson was talking to himself, almost oblivious of his listener. His wife knew too well to interrupt him. She resumed her knitting, only looking up at him from time to time as he paced up and down the room.

"The stick. H'm. If Walter Brooklyn didn't leave it in Prinsep's room, who did? It was a very remarkable stick, and quite certain to be recognised. Just the thing, in facet, for a false clue. Let me see. Brooklyn said he lost it on the Tuesday afternoon—the day of the murders. That means that somehow or other the murderer got hold of it. H'm, h'm. We're getting warm, my dear. When we know for certain who got hold of that stick we shall have found the murderer. Yes, we must certainly find out all about that stick. Left in a taxi, was it? I think not. I'm beginning to have a very shrewd idea of where it was left." The superintendent paused.

"Where was it left, dear?"

"Wait till I know for certain, darling. I'll find out, never fear. And then I shall know who the murderer was. But even then I shall be a long way off getting a conviction." The superintendent laughed.

"But surely, if you know——"

"Knowing is one thing, and proving a case to a jury quite another. But that's enough for the present. I want to sleep on this." And with these words Superintendent Wilson went out into the garden to play with the children.

Chapter XXI
Don Quixote

While Fred Thomas was trying to make a shield for Walter Brooklyn's guilt by throwing the suspicion upon others whom he himself believed to be innocent, Joan and Ellery were following up their attempt to prove her stepfather's alibi. Two points they had already established, thanks to Ellery's mingled sagacity and good fortune. Walter Brooklyn had definitely been in Leicester Square at a quarter to eleven, and in Piccadilly Circus at about twenty past eleven. So far his story was confirmed. Moreover, if he had been seen in the Circus at 11.20, it was difficult to believe that he had rung up his club from Prinsep's room at Liskeard House, after making his way unseen into the building, less than ten minutes later. It was true that the evidence was not absolutely conclusive, as neither time could be fixed, quite certainly, to within a few minutes. But at least the evidence against him was severely shaken, and there seemed to be good reason for urging that the telephone message, round which the case had practically been built up, was a fake. Find out who sent it, the defence could argue, and you would find the real criminal.

Still, even if the telephone message could be discredited—and Ellery realised that this would take some doing—there remained the walking-stick, and the undoubted fact that Walter Brooklyn had expressed the intention of seeing Prinsep that evening. They could not feel that the evidence which they had so far gathered made his acquittal even probable, much less secure, especially as there was still no evidence that seemed to point in any other direction. Joan and Ellery felt that they must get further confirmation of the alibi. It was a question of accounting, not for a few minutes here and there, but for every minute of Walter Brooklyn's time. Clearly, what now mattered most was where he had been between the time when the old night-watchman saw him in Piccadilly Circus and his return to his Club at about midnight. George Brooklyn had been seen alive as late as 11.30, and Prinsep only a few minutes before. If Walter Brooklyn had murdered either, it must have been done between 11.30 and midnight; for it seemed clear enough that he had not left his Club again during the night. Of this the night porter was positive. At the same time, it was desirable, though less important, to confirm also his story of his movements during the earlier part of the evening. After they had talked the situation over, Joan and Ellery determined to pursue the hunt together, and once more to follow Walter Brooklyn's route in search of further confirmation.

For what it was worth, Joan had already been able to confirm her stepfather's first statement about his movements. A door porter at the Piccadilly Theatre had seen him standing for a minute or two outside the main entrance "a bit before half-past ten," and had noticed him walking off along Piccadilly towards the Circus. Thereafter, although Joan and Ellery hunted high and low, they could get no further trace of him until his meeting with Kitty Frensham in Leicester Square at a quarter to eleven. They found and interrogated without success the policeman who had been on duty in Piccadilly Circus. They even inquired of the porter outside the Monico and the Criterion and of a few street sellers who were standing at the corners. There was no information to be obtained; but they agreed that this did not greatly matter, if only they could get evidence bearing on Walter Brooklyn's movements after half-past eleven, or still better, from 10.45 onwards. They would begin at the other end, and try to trace his movements between 11.30 and midnight. Accordingly, they walked down together to Trafalgar Square. Here there were two possible lines of investigation. Walter Brooklyn had first leaned for some moments over the parapet opposite the National Gallery: he had then walked down to the top of Whitehall, and had there paused to set his watch by a clock standing out over one of the shops. There was a slender chance that some one might have noticed him on one or other of these occasions.

"How shall we make a start here?" asked Ellery, rather forlornly, as they stood at the corner of Cockspur Street, overlooking Trafalgar Square. At the foot of the Nelson Column stood the usual curious—and incurious—crowd listening to some orator descanting on the rights—or wrongs—of labour.

"Follow the old precept, of course," said Joan promptly. "Ask a policeman. There seem to be plenty about."

Ellery went up to the nearest and began to explain his business. He was speedily referred to the sergeant, who was standing at the edge of the crowd, eyeing the little knot of speakers on the plinth, as if he was meditating a possible arrest. "He'll know who was on duty on Tuesday night. I wasn't," said the constable.

The sergeant was communicative. First, he bade them wait a few minutes while he listened to what the speaker, then on her feet—for it was a woman—was saying. What she said appeared to give him satisfaction; for he smiled happily, as he entered a note in his book. Then the speech became more commonplace, and the sergeant, bidding a constable take notes while he was busy, signified his willingness to attend to Joan and Ellery. But, before they could tell him of their concerns, they had to listen awhile to his, which related mainly to the iniquity of allowing seditious meetings to be held openly in Trafalgar Square. "They tell us to take it all down, they do—every word; and then they do nothing. They shove it away in some pigeon-hole or other."

"They" were presumably the powers that ruled, at the Home Office, over the doings of the Metropolitan Police.

"What I say is, What's the police for, if it isn't to stop this kind of thing?" He jerked his thumb in the direction of the plinth.

"But you make an arrest sometimes, don't you?" Joan asked.

"Once in a blue moon, maybe. But even then, more often than not the Home Secretary lets 'em go. Disgusting, I call it, and demoralising for the country. If I had my way . . ."

He had his way for a few minutes, as far as words went, and then, as the reward of patient listening, he let Ellery have his say. But he was not helpful.

"Yes, I know who was on duty here that night. There was Bill Adams and Tom Short down by Whitehall, and there was George Mulligan patrolling up there by the Gallery. But it's a hundred to one against any of them having noticed your man. Adams is on duty here, and the other two will be along at the station. You can have a word with Adams now, and I'll take you along to the station myself in a few minutes. They're just finishing up there." He jerked a thumb in the direction of the plinth.

Adams, a tall, fat policeman, who kept patting himself on the stomach while he talked, had seen nothing of Walter Brooklyn, whose photograph Ellery showed him. "Lord bless you, if I was to notice everybody I should have a job on," was his comment, clearly showing his view of the hopelessness of their search. Discouraged, they left him, and went to the station with the sergeant.

Here, the same fate befell them. Neither of the two constables had noticed Walter Brooklyn; and both of them seemed to think the quest quite hopeless. Ellery did not give the name of the man he was looking for, lest the police, intent on building up their own case, might refuse him information. Only an unrecognisable snapshot had appeared in the Press.

"Well, sir," said the sergeant. "I've done my best for you, and I'm sorry it's no use. But it's what I told you to expect." Ellery distributed suitable rewards in the appropriately furtive manner, and prepared to take his leave. But Joan stopped him.

"I have an idea," she said. "It may come to nothing; but it's worth trying." Then she turned to Mulligan, a short, humorous, and very obviously Irish constable.

"Tell me, is there any tramp, or person of that sort, who is often to be found at night in Trafalgar Square? I mean some one you're always having to move on."

"Lord, miss, there's a dozen or so. Move 'em on night after night; but they come back just the same."

"Well, I want you to find me a man like that—one who's always hanging about the Square, and is likely to know others who do the same. Can you find me a man of that sort?"

"Certainly, miss, I can. I see what you're after, and I should say the chap we call 'the Spaniard' is about what you want. He's a bloke who goes about in a long cloak and a broad-brimmed felt hat—often not much else, I should say, barring the remains of a pair of trousers—he's pretty nearly always about in the Square, and he's always talking to any one he can find to listen."

Ellery broke in. "Can you find him for us now?"

The constable looked at the sergeant. "If the sergeant here will let me leave the station for half an hour, I expect I can," he said.

The sergeant was duly placated, and the two set off with Constable Mulligan. He led them, not into the Square, but into the little alley behind St. Martin's-in-the-Fields. There he pointed to the bar of a rather disreputable-looking public-house. "You go in there," he said to Ellery, "and ask if 'the Spaniard' is there. They'd know him. If I were to go in, they'd shut up like a knife when you aren't looking."

Ellery went in and ordered a drink. A glance round the bar showed him that "the Spaniard" was not in the bar at the moment. He turned to the woman behind the bar counter and asked her if she knew where to find "the Spaniard." The woman looked at him with an air of surprise; but she made no reply. Then she turned to a curtained door behind her, and spoke through it. "Alf," she said, "come here a minute."

Alf speedily appeared in his shirt-sleeves—a portly, middle-aged man, rather stolid to look at, but with a pair of cunning little eyes that looked at you, not steadily, but with a succession of keen, quick glances. Ellery heard the woman whisper to him, "This gent here's asking for 'the Spaniard.'"

"And what might you be wanting with 'the Spaniard,' mister?" asked Alf, leaning across the bar, and speaking confidentially almost into Ellery's ear.

"Certainly nothing to his disadvantage. But I want to know something, and I think he may be able to tell me."

The publican looked at him a trifle suspiciously. "Is the gentleman known to you, maybe?" he asked.

"No; or I could probably find him for myself. I thought you might know him."

"Well, he ain't here," said Alf, apparently making up his mind to Ellery's disadvantage. Ellery began to expostulate; but at that moment, through the same curtained door through which mine host had come, walked a quite unmistakable figure—a very tall, thin man, with perfectly white hair and beard, the latter cut to a fine point. The new-comer wore a long and very threadbare black cloak, now green with age, and he seemed just about to place upon his head a very wide-brimmed black—or rather greenish—felt hat, which Ellery thought of instinctively as a "sombrero." In a fine, high-pitched voice, perfectly cultivated but a good deal affected, and with a curious intonation that seemed like the affectation of a foreign accent, he addressed the woman behind the bar. "Did I hear my name spoken among you?" he asked.

The woman turned to Alf, who shrugged his shoulders.

"Here he is," he said to Ellery. "I suppose you'd better ask him what you want."

Ellery put on his best manners. "Sir," said he to the man called "the Spaniard," "may I have the honour of a few words with you on a matter which concerns me very deeply, and you, I must admit, scarcely at all?"

"The Spaniard" bowed low. "The honour, sir," he replied, "is with me. For, as the poet says, 'Honoured is he to whom man speaks the things of his heart.'"

"We will call the honours easy, if you please. But I shall be very much obliged for a few words with you."

"If it please you, then, let us take the air together. I can speak and listen better under the sky."

"With pleasure; but just a word before we go. My friend, Miss Cowper, and the—gentleman who brought me to you are waiting outside. You will not mind if they accompany us?"

Ellery had some misgiving that, suddenly confronted with a policeman, the old "Spaniard" might reach the conclusion that he had been led into a trap, and refuse to speak.

"And to whom do I owe the honour of this introduction?"

"Well, to be frank, he is a policeman; but he is acting quite in a non-professional capacity."

The old man hesitated a moment. Then he said only, "Let us go."

Outside, Ellery's fears were speedily removed. He saw Joan and the policeman waiting a few doors off. "The Spaniard" saw them too, and, at sight of Mulligan, his face lighted up with pleasure. He greeted Joan with a low bow, and then turned to Mulligan with another.

"Ah, my friend, it is you. As the poet says, 'Even among the thorns the rose is sweet.' You are not, I thank God, as others of your cloth." Then he turned to Ellery. "Mr. Mulligan and I are old friends," he said: "but it is not always so between me and the guardians of law and order, as you quaintly term them."

"Yes," said Mulligan, smiling. "'The Spaniard' and I have had many a good talk together. But you didn't know, did you, father, that I'd tracked you here. I wouldn't go in because I thought there might be others who wouldn't be so pleased to see me."

"As always, the soul of consideration. The mark, gentlemen, of true chivalry. I will requite you as best I can by any service that I can do to your friends." And again he lifted his hat, and made a sweeping bow.

When Joan and Ellery talked the thing over afterwards, they remembered that their eyes had met at this moment, and they had much ado not to laugh outright. They discovered that the same thought had come into their heads. This was not merely "The Spaniard": it was Don Quixote himself come to life again. But where was Rosinante?

Constable Mulligan excused himself. "I mustn't be away from the station any longer. Now you've been introduced you can get along without me. You know where to find me if you want me again." And, thanked and rewarded by Ellery, the constable returned to his duty, after putting a hand affectionately on the old man's shoulder by way of farewell.

Joan and Ellery between them told "the Spaniard" the full story of their quest, first as they walked towards Trafalgar Square, and then leaning over the very parapet over which Walter Brooklyn had leaned. "The Spaniard" heard them through, only inclining his head every now and then to show that he fully appreciated some particular point in the narrative.

Finally, Ellery produced the photograph of Walter Brooklyn, and asked the old man whether he had seen the original on Tuesday night.

"A fine figure of a gentleman," said "the Spaniard," "and, indeed, I know him well by sight, though hitherto I have been denied the honour of knowing his name. Often have I seen him in Pall Mall."

"Yes, but did you see him on Tuesday?" Joan could not help interrupting.

"The Spaniard's" way of continuing was in itself a mild and courteous reproof. "Often, my friends, have I seen him, little deeming that one day my memory of him might be of service to others." And then he added, "Yes, I saw him here on Tuesday—here, on this very spot to which I have led you. Here he stopped and lighted a cigar. I noted that he lighted it from the stump of another."

"That was because he had no matches," said Joan excitedly. "That bears out what he said."

"Madam, if it would not incommode you, might I crave your permission to smoke even now?" Joan readily gave it, and the old man deftly rolled a cigarette with strong black tobacco from a battered metal case.

"Can you tell us at what time you saw him?" said Ellery.

"Ah, time. Why should I mark the hours? What need have I to know? It was evening."

"But what you tell us is of no use unless you can say what time it was."

"Alas, if I had but known, my watch should never have gone—the way of all watches." A faint flicker of a smile, and an extraordinarily expressive gesture, accompanied the phrase. It was as if all watches had a mysterious knack of vanishing into infinite space. "But, nevertheless, another's memory may serve where mine fails. For I was not alone."

"Who was with you? Can we find him?"

"I will find him for you; but not till evening. And meantime, I will seek for those who may have seen Mr. Brooklyn in Whitehall. If any can find such a man, I can find him. There is a fraternity among us who wander under the sky. We remark what passes around us; for we have no affairs of our own to disturb our minds." He turned to Ellery. "It would be well that you should leave the photograph with me until evening. Then we will meet again."

An appointment was made for Trafalgar Square at eleven o'clock that same night. The old man would not meet them sooner, or elsewhere. Joan could not leave Sir Vernon at that hour; but Ellery would come. In parting, she thanked "the Spaniard" for all that he had done.

"What can a man do better than come to the aid of ladies in distress? Truly, as the poet says, 'He enlargeth his heart who doeth his neighbour a kindness.' The word I have rendered 'neighbour' is feminine in the Spanish," he added, half to himself.

"What a queer old bird!" said Ellery, as they walked away. "It was difficult to keep it up while we were talking to him; but it was well worth while."

"I think he's a dear," said Joan. "A bit queer, of course; but see how he's helping us. We could never have done anything without him."

"He's quite off his chump, that's clear. But he seems to be quite all there when it's a question of getting something done. We're meeting some queer people on this job."

"Who do you suppose he is?" asked Joan.

"Nothing on earth, if you mean how does he get his living. I should say he was just what they call a character, picking up somehow barely enough to exist on, and drifting about with nothing in particular to do. He probably drinks, or has been in trouble somehow."

"I don't care what trouble he's been in. He fascinates me. And he's obviously an educated man."

"Yes, I dare say he was quite the gentleman—in the orthodox sense—years ago. Now he is one of the bottom dogs, keeping up his self-respect by playing the hidalgo."

"Don't you suppose he's really a Spaniard?"

"No more than you or I. He's probably been in Spain. That's all. But, whoever he is, he seems likely to get us just the information we want, and that's what we really care about. Only I feel inclined to introduce him to my night watchman at Piccadilly. They would make a pretty pair. They are both hero-worshippers."

Chapter XXII
"The Spaniard" Does His Bit

Ellery met "the Spaniard" in accordance with his appointment in Trafalgar Square that evening. As he approached, he saw the old man pacing up and down the pavement in front of the National Gallery, walking slowly with a dignity and grace worthy of some grandee of the olden times. He was curiously like the Lavery portrait of Cunninghame Graham. "The Spaniard" made Ellery a low bow, accompanied by a sweeping gesture with his broad-brimmed hat; and Ellery, doing his best to live up to the occasion, returned the salutation with a very inferior grace.

"You have news for me?" he asked.

"If you will do me the honour of accompanying me in my promenade, I think I may be able to impart certain facts of interest to your fair lady."

"The Spaniard," as Ellery told Joan afterwards, took the devil of a time to come down to brass tacks. But what he had to tell was quite conclusive. He had found, and could produce, conclusive evidence that Walter Brooklyn had been in Trafalgar Square at the time he had stated. He had discovered two men who had seen him leaning over the parapet opposite the National Gallery, and one of them had definitely noticed the time by the clock of St. Martin's Church. This had been at 11.40. Moreover, the second man, perhaps, "the Spaniard" hinted—oh, so delicately that his way of saying it seemed to make petty larceny a fine art—in the hope of picking a few trifles out of Mr. Brooklyn's pockets, had actually followed him round the Square, and seen him take out his watch and look at the time. He had shadowed Brooklyn up Cockspur Street and the Haymarket, actually as far as the corner of Jermyn Street, where some object of greater immediate interest had served to distract him from the chase. Moreover, in return for suitable rewards, both these men were prepared to give evidence. "The Spaniard" had arranged for them both to meet Ellery, if he so desired, and, in a few minutes' time, they would be in the bar of the little public-house in which Ellery had originally met with "the Spaniard" himself.

This was more than satisfactory, and Ellery at once went to meet the two men and hear their stories. They fully bore out what "the Spaniard" had said, and Ellery took their names and addresses, and then arranged to see them again on the following morning at the same place, and to take them, with the other witnesses he and Joan had collected, to Thomas's office, where they would be able to consider the steps that had best be taken towards securing Walter Brooklyn's absolution. He could get hold of the remaining witnesses later in the evening; but first he had to thank "the Spaniard" and to settle with him for what he had done.

Ellery had no doubt that "the Spaniard" both needed and expected payment for the very real service he had rendered; but it was, he found, by no means easy to come to the point. The old man, despite his seedy garments, was very much the fine gentleman in his manners; it was easy enough to thank him handsomely, and to receive his still more handsome acknowledgments. But it was not at all easy to offer him money. Still, it had to be done; and, awkwardly and stammeringly, Ellery at last did it.

He was met with a refusal. "The Spaniard" was only

too glad to have been of some service—to a lady. Thanks were more than enough: pecuniary reward would degrade a charming episode to the level of a commercial transaction. Perhaps, some day, Ellery, or Miss Cowper might be in a position to do him a service. He would accept it gladly; but he begged that, until the occasion arose, no more might be said upon the matter. Ellery had to leave it at that, making a resolution to seek at once an occasion for being of service to the man who had helped so greatly in their quest. Meanwhile, he could only thank him again, and exchange, in taking his leave, the fine courtesies which gave "the Spaniard" such manifest pleasure.

Ellery's first action, on leaving Trafalgar Square, was to take steps to summon his other witnesses to meet him at Thomas's office the following morning. Kitty Frensham he secured by a telephone message to Mandleham's flat. Mandleham at once promised to come himself, and to bring Kitty with him, at half-past ten. Ellery then walked on to Piccadilly Circus, where he found his friend, the night-watchman, deep this time in Carlyle's Oliver Cromwell, which Ellery had lent him. He, too, promised to be in attendance. Ellery then walked along Piccadilly to the theatre, and secured the attendant who had seen Walter Brooklyn standing outside at "a bit before half-past ten." This completed his preparations; and he rang at the bell of Liskeard House, and asked for Joan.

"What news?" she asked anxiously, coming forward to greet him as he was announced.

"The best," he replied. "The alibi is proved."

"Oh, I am so glad. And now I can tell you a secret. I wasn't absolutely sure my stepfather had told us the truth. At least, I was sure; but I couldn't help having a doubt every now and then. And I simply couldn't bear the thought that he might have been implicated. I knew, of course, that he hadn't killed any one; but I wasn't quite sure he didn't know all about it.

And everybody else seemed to believe the worst, and at times I couldn't help being a little shaken. Now you must tell me all about what you've found out."

Ellery did tell her all about it, and also of the steps he had taken to arrange a meeting at Thomas's office for the following morning. Joan said at once that she would go; and Ellery thereupon rang up Thomas, to whom he had so far said nothing, at his home, and demanded an interview. Joan and he must, he said, see Thomas on urgent business. They would be bringing several witnesses who could throw valuable light on the case, and they would be at his office at 10.30 on the following morning. Would Thomas be sure to keep the time free?

Thomas was plainly surprised, and also curious; and he tried to make Ellery tell him over the 'phone what it was all about. This Ellery would not do, merely saying that the matter was of vital importance, but he would rather explain it all in the morning. Thomas thereupon agreed to cancel a previous engagement, and to be ready for them at the hour arranged. "Now, at last," said Ellery, as he hung up the receiver, "I think we are entitled to a good night's rest."

"I'm afraid there won't be much sleep for me, darling," said Joan. "Sir Vernon was told to-day about poor George. He kept asking for him, and in the end Marian had to tell him all about it. Of course it has made him worse. Now, he keeps asking to see the police, and insisting that they must find the murderers. But he knows nothing at all about it—he has no idea who did it. Some one must be with him all the time, of course. Mary is with him now, and I have to take her place at midnight. She is tired out, poor thing."

"And what about you, poor thing?" said Ellery; for he could see that she was almost at the end of her strength. He drew her head down on to his shoulder, and tried to persuade her to give up the idea of coming to Thomas's office in the morning. But Joan was firm: she must see the thing through. She would be all right: she could get plenty of sleep later in the day. Ellery had to consent to her coming, and the lovers sat together till midnight, when they bade each other farewell, as lovers do, for all the world as if their parting were, not for a few hours, but for an eternity.

It was getting on for one o'clock when Ellery reached home; and he was surprised as he went up the steps, to see a light in his sitting-room. He let himself in with his key, and found his landlady sitting bolt upright on the hall chair. "Lord, Mr. Ellery," she said, "how late you are. There's a person in your room been waiting for you more than an hour. I wouldn't go to bed with him there—not for worlds, I wouldn't. He said he must see you, and would wait."

"What sort of a man?"

"Oh, not a nice man. He looks to me more like a tramp, sir, than anything else. I was afraid he might steal something if I left him."

Ellery opened the door and went in. He at once recognised the man who had followed Walter Brooklyn on Tuesday from Trafalgar Square to Jermyn Street—one of the witnesses whom "the Spaniard" had found. The visitor lost no time.

"Look 'ere, mister," he said, "it's off."

"What's off? What do you mean?"

"What I mean is you don't catch me givin' hevidence in this 'ere case. You treated me like a gent, and I thought I'd let you know. But to-morrow I shan't be there. You gotter understand that."

"Do you mean you won't help to clear Mr. Brooklyn? Why, what's the matter?"

"Well, mister, I may not be what I oughter be—leastways, some folks says I ain't. But I got views o' my own as to what's right, same as others. And I've found out a thing or two about this Mr. Brooklyn of yours. He can swing, s'far as I'm concerned."

"My good fellow, the man's innocent of this crime, whatever you may know about him. You must say what you know."

"Not so much 'good fellow,' and there's no 'must' about it, mister. That chap deserves hangin' for things he's done, and I don't care if they hangs 'im on the right charge or the wrong 'un. I know a girl what . . ."

"I don't mind telling you that I don't like Mr. Brooklyn any better than you do. But I want to see him cleared. He didn't commit these murders, I know that."

"Come, come, mister, why not let 'im hang? What's it matter to you, anyway? He'd be a good riddance, from what I 'ear of 'im."

"But you can't see a man condemned when you know he's innocent."

"Why not, mister? I says, Why not? It's not as if you had any personal interest in the fellow, so to speak."

"But I have. He's the stepfather of the girl I'm engaged to marry. She would never get over it if he were convicted."

The pickpocket's manner changed from sullenness to interest. "Eh, what's that you say?" he said. "Nah, if you'd told me that at onct, I'm not one to stand between a man and his girl."

"You'll come, won't you?"

The man hesitated. "I don't say as I won't," he said. "But, if I do come, 'twon't be for any love of your Mr. Brooklyn. I'd see 'im hanged, and glad too, along of what I know."

"I don't care why you come, as long as you do come."

"Well, mister, I'll come. If yer want to know why, it's because I've took a bit of a fancy to yer. But I'll 'ave a bit of me own back on that Brooklyn gent, if he gets off bein' 'ung. I didn't lift 'is watch off 'im that night; but I will when 'e gets out."

"Oh, you're welcome there. Pick his pockets as much as you like."

"In course yer won't let on ter the police what I've been sayin'. I've bin treatin' yer as if yer was a pal, yer know."

Ellery promised that his visitor's calling should be kept a dead secret. Then he gave him a drink and showed him out, after obtaining a renewal of the promise that he would attend in the morning. The man slouched out into the night.

Love did not keep Ellery awake. He was tired, and he slept soundly, only waking in time to snatch a hasty breakfast, and to call for Joan early enough to take her straight round with him to their appointment at Thomas's office.

Chapter XXIII
Walter Brooklyn Goes Free

The business transacted at Thomas's office that morning was protracted; but the result of it was never in doubt. Thomas had before long to admit that he had been suspecting an innocent man, and that man his own client. At first he was inclined to be incredulous; but, when witness after witness was produced, he had to admit absolutely that Joan and Ellery had proved their case. The testimony of one, or even two, witnesses might have been doubted; but the cumulative effect of the evidence, given by the old night-watchman, Kitty Frensham, and Horace Mandleham, and the men whom "the Spaniard" had found, was irresistible. It was true that the evidence of the stick and the telephone message which Walter Brooklyn was supposed to have sent were unaffected by the case which Joan and Ellery had prepared; but Thomas, though he knew nothing of Superintendent Wilson's new view of the case, agreed that any charge based on these would certainly collapse in face of a conclusive alibi. Thomas confidently stated that it was only a matter of a short time before Walter Brooklyn would be released "without a stain on his character."

There were stains enough on it already, Joan said to herself, even if this last disgrace were removed. Walter Brooklyn was not guilty of murder, and had been, in this case, unjustly accused. But no amount of sympathy with him in his present misfortune could wipe out the recollection of what she had suffered while she had still felt it her duty to live with him. She had done her best to absolve him of the charge of murder, because she was fully assured of his innocence; but, that once accomplished, she desired to have no more to do with him. When, therefore, Thomas suggested that she should go at once to the prison and tell her stepfather the good news, while he and Ellery saw the police and endeavoured to make arrangements for his release, Joan refused and said that she would prefer Thomas to see his client himself. To the rest of the suggested programme she agreed, and Thomas at once got through on the 'phone to Superintendent Wilson, and arranged an immediate appointment. Joan and Ellery agreed with him that the best course was to tell the police the whole story at once, and, instead of waiting for the trial, to endeavour to secure Walter Brooklyn's release as soon as the necessary formalities could be carried through.

Taking their witnesses with them, therefore, Joan, Ellery, and Thomas set out for Scotland Yard. There they left the witnesses in a waiting-room, and were at once shown in to the superintendent. Inspector Blaikie, who had been sent for when Thomas's message was received, was also present, and the two police officers now heard from Joan and Ellery what they had done. The superintendent listened very quietly to their story, in one of his favourite attitudes, with his eyes closed most of the time, his legs thrust out before him, and his hands buried deep in his trousers pockets. The inspector once or twice tried to interrupt, and was at first obviously incredulous. But, before they had done, the strength of their case was evident, even to him, and the testimony of the witnesses, who were then called in and examined one by one, was quite conclusive in its cumulative effect. Walter Brooklyn had been seen by no less than seven persons, and it was quite inconceivable, in view of the times and places at which they had seen him, that he could have made his way into and out of Liskeard House and committed even a single murder, in the time available. The superintendent jotted down a list of the independent testimonies which went to the making of the alibi.

10.15 or so. Shown out of Liskeard House by Winter.

10.20 or so. Seen by porter at Piccadilly Theatre walking up Piccadilly towards the Circus.

10.45. Seen in Leicester Square by Kitty Frensham and Horace Mandleham.

11.20 or so. Seen in Piccadilly Circus by night-watchman.

11.30 or so. Seen by taxi-driver near Liskeard Street in Piccadilly (exact time uncertain).

11.35 (about). Seen, at time not precisely fixed, but it must have been at this time, by "the Spaniard," leaning on the parapet and then walking along the top of Trafalgar Square.

11.45. Seen by witness of unknown occupation at the top of Whitehall and followed by him up Cockspur Street and Regent Street, as far as the corner of Jermyn Street.

12 midnight. Seen by night-porter entering the Byron Club (the porter is positive he did not go out again).

When the last witness had withdrawn the superintendent looked at his notes.

"What do you make of it now?" asked Thomas. The reply, unhesitatingly given, was that the alibi seemed to be conclusive.

"I admit," said the superintendent, "that for a time we were barking up the wrong tree. There remain, of course, to be explained the telephone message and the presence of your client's stick. I don't say that we shan't have to test even the alibi further—some of your witnesses are of rather doubtful character. But personally I admit that I have no doubt about it; indeed, quite apart from the alibi, I had already made up my mind on other grounds that your client was innocent. Your discoveries merely confirm my opinion."

"Then you agree," said Thomas, "that my client ought to be released."

"Before you answer that question, sir," put in Inspector Blaikie, "may I have a word? I admit that what we have just heard is very powerful testimony; but surely the telephone message proves that Mr. Brooklyn was in the house, and therefore that there is something wrong with the alibi. To say nothing of the stick. I hope you won't agree to a release at least until there has been time to look into the matter further."

The superintendent rose from his chair. "You will excuse us for a moment," he said to the others, and he beckoned to the inspector to follow him into the adjoining room. "My dear inspector," he said, when he had shut the door, "you will kindly leave me to manage this affair."

The inspector replied, "Certainly, sir"; but he added, half to himself, "All the same, I believe he did it."

"I shall order release—I mean I shall announce that the prosecution is withdrawn, and get the man released as soon as possible. To my mind the alibi is quite convincing. But, even apart from it, I was going to tell you this morning that I proposed to recommend Walter Brooklyn's release. I will explain my reasons when the others have gone. You leave it to me."

The inspector said nothing, but followed his superior officer back into the other room.

"Well, Mr. Thomas," said the superintendent, "I shall certainly offer no opposition to your client's release. Will you take the necessary steps on your side?"

Thomas said that he would, and the superintendent added that, in that case, there should be neither difficulty nor delay. Only formal evidence of arrest had been offered before the magistrate, and they might now consider the charge as definitely dropped.

Joan began to thank him; but he stopped her.

"It is not a matter for thanks," he said. "We appear to have arrested the wrong man, and the need for apologies, if it exists, is on our side. You will, however, agree that appearances were strongly against Mr. Brooklyn, and that we could hardly have taken any other course. Indeed, it seems clear that whoever did commit the murder, or murders, must have deliberately planned to throw suspicion on your stepfather. That, I think, furnishes an important clue."

"But I suppose you have now no idea at all who the murderer was?"

"It is hardly fair to ask me that question, Miss Cowper," said the superintendent, smiling. "You come here, and knock the police theory into smithereens, and then you ask us if we have another theory ready-made. No. We have not a theory, but we do possess certain very important clues."

At this point Thomas had a word to say. "It is just possible that I may be able to help you there. In preparing for the defence of my client, I had, of course, to consider who the criminal, or criminals, might be, and to make certain inquiries. I lighted on certain information which you may find useful. I am not likely to need it now; but I will gladly make you a present of it for what it is worth."

"What is your information?"

"I believe you have been watching certain of the servants at Liskeard House—Morgan, I mean, and the butler, Winter."

The superintendent glanced at Inspector Blaikie, who nodded.

"You may, or may not, have discovered that the man Winter had a very strong personal cause of quarrel with Mr. Prinsep; quite enough, I think, to be the motive of a serious crime."

The superintendent again looked towards Inspector Blaikie, who very slightly shook his head. Then he said to Thomas, "I think you had better tell us all you know."

"Well, to begin with, the butler had a violent quarrel with Mr. Prinsep a few days before the murder, and was practically given notice to leave. That can be proved by the evidence of the maidservants and of Morgan."

"This is the first I've heard of it," said Joan, "and what's more, I don't believe it. Winter is a very old and trusted family servant. I am sure Mr. Prinsep would not have given him notice."

"The maids say that the notice was not quite definite, and that Winter was not sure whether he would have to go or not. He spoke to Morgan about it. But the evidence as to the quarrel is quite decisive."

"I think it's horrible," said Joan. "I'm every bit as sure that Winter had nothing to do with it as I am about my stepfather. And what if they did have a quarrel? John—Mr. Prinsep, I mean—was always hot-tempered."

"I have not yet told the inspector what the quarrel was about. It was about the girl Winter was engaged to—a girl down at Fittleworth—the head gardener's daughter, I believe. I understand that Mr. Prinsep had some relations with her, and Winter objected."

At this Joan suddenly went red all over; but she said nothing. The superintendent, who was watching her, said very quietly, "Do you know this girl, Miss Cowper, and can you throw any light on the incident? I am sorry to ask; but—" he paused for her answer.

"Of course I know the girl well; but I would rather not speak of it. I had no idea that she was to be married to Winter."

"Very well, Miss Cowper. I see that you do know, and that there is some truth in the story. Can you say that there is not?"

"I prefer not to say anything."

"That will do. I see your point, Mr. Thomas. This certainly

provides what we have been seeking—a possible motive for Mr. Prinsep's murder. But, of course, it is merely a possible indication. There is no evidence against Winter, as far as I am aware."

"That, Mr. Superintendent, is entirely your business. I merely gave you what information I had gathered. Tracking down the criminal is fortunately no concern of mine."

"Quite so. And that is the whole of your information?"

"Yes. Apart from that I know no more than you know already."

"Then I can only thank you for the help you have given; and assure you that everything possible shall be done to expedite your client's release. And, by the way, you had better say nothing to any one else of what you have just told me." And thereupon, with the skill born of long practice, the superintendent bowed his visitors out of the room. To Inspector Blaikie he spoke a word, asking him to remain for a few minutes' discussion.

Joan's indignation burst forth as soon as she was outside the building. She was particularly angry with Thomas.

"I call it abominable. We have just succeeded in clearing one innocent man, whom an hour or two ago you believed to be guilty: and now you are wantonly throwing suspicion on some one else. What business is it of yours? I know Winter had nothing to do with it."

"That is all very well, Miss Cowper; but it was my duty to tell the police, and, moreover, by doing so, I probably speeded up Mr. Brooklyn's release by at least twenty-four hours. It is always wise to have the police on your side—when you can."

"If it was your duty, why didn't you tell the police when you first found it out?"

"I will be quite frank with you, Miss Cowper. I did not, because, until your very smart work in proving Mr. Brooklyn's alibi, my best chance of getting him off was to be able to throw unexpected suspicion on some one else at the trial."

"I call it beastly—even to think of using methods like that."

Thomas was very suave. "But I suppose, Miss Cowper, you would not have liked to see your stepfather condemned. I had to do the best I could."

"I don't care. It can't be right to throw suspicion on an innocent man like that. Do you—yourself—believe Winter did it? Why didn't you do what he did—clear my stepfather by proving the truth of what he said?"

"Perhaps, Miss Cowper, it was because I am not so clever as you are. I have already congratulated you on the way you have managed this affair."

"I don't want your congratulations. Do you believe Winter did it?"

"As to that, Miss Cowper, I do not pretend to know. It is for the police, and not for me, to find out."

Joan, on hearing this, simply turned her back on him, and walked away. Thomas very politely raised his hat to her back, told Ellery that he must be off, and hailed a passing taxi. Ellery hurried after Joan.

For a minute after he came up with her, she strode on fast, saying nothing. Then, "Don't you think it's beastly?" she said.

"I agree with you that Thomas is a cad, and I don't believe old Winter had anything to do with it. And I don't think there was any need for him to tell the police. But he probably did it, as he said, in order to get the police on our side."

"And now they'll all be off full cry after Winter. I suppose they will want to arrest him next."

Ellery shook his head. "Hardly, without more evidence than they possess. But they will probably have him watched."

There was a further silence, during which Joan continued to walk fast, staring straight in front of her. At last she said,

"I've been thinking, and I'm sure I see what we ought to do. So far we have only been trying to prove that my stepfather did not do it. We've succeeded. But at this rate we shall all of us be suspected in turn. There's only one thing for it. There will be no peace and quietness till some one finds the criminal. I don't believe the police will ever find him. Why shouldn't you and I find him ourselves? We haven't done badly so far."

Ellery whistled. "That's a much taller order than proving your stepfather's alibi," he said. "But I'm game. There certainly won't be much peace for any of us till somebody finds out who did do it. But I'm dashed if I know how to begin."

"Neither do I, at present. We have to think it all out, and make a fresh start. Come home with me, and we'll start planning it at once."

"They say two heads are better than one, and I'm prepared to be your very faithful follower. But you'll have to be Sherlock Holmes, I'm afraid."

"Come along then, Watson. But try not to be as stupid as your namesake."

Chapter XXIV
A Fresh Start

"Well, where do we stand now?" said Superintendent Wilson, as he turned back into the room after showing his visitors out.

"Nowhere at all, sir, I should say," was the inspector's discontented reply. "You have let the bird in the hand go, and all the other birds are safer than ever in the bush. Are you so sure there's no doubt about that alibi?"

"Still harping on that, are you, inspector? Come, put the idea of Walter Brooklyn's guilt out of your head. It's not often I take much stock in alibis; but this one is absolutely convincing."

"I'm not so sure, sir, all the same. At least, I'd have kept hold of the man we had got till we could lay some one else by the heels."

The superintendent shrugged his shoulders impatiently. "That's the worst of you, inspector," he said, "you are impervious to evidence. You never will give up an idea when you've once been at the trouble of forming it. And therefore you don't see how this morning's business really helps us."

"Helps us? No, I'm jiggered if I see that. If you're in the right we are in a worse hole than ever."

"No, my dear inspector, it does help us." And the

superintendent rubbed his hands with satisfaction. He smiled to himself as he reflected that he could see further than most people through a brick wall.

"How do you mean?" asked the inspector.

"Well, if Walter Brooklyn was not in the house, it is clear that he did not send that telephone message. But some one did send it. Who was that some one? Find him, and you find the murderer. It was clearly sent with the deliberate intention of throwing suspicion on Walter Brooklyn."

"Yes, if you're right about the alibi, I see that. But I don't see that we're any nearer to finding out who did send it."

"Well, at least," said the superintendent, "there are certain things to go upon. First, there is no doubt at all that the message was sent, and sent from Liskeard House. The inquiries at the Exchange prove that."

The inspector nodded.

"That being so, is it not safe to conclude that it was sent by one of the inmates, or by the murderer, before making his escape? If the murderer was an inmate of the house, the two possibilities are reduced to one. Probably he was at any rate some one familiar with the house and the family."

"I see," said the inspector, and his face brightened up for the first time. "That is certainly a point. You mean that Winter could without difficulty have sent the message?"

"Doubtless he could; and so could others. Don't jump to conclusions. I agree that it would fit in with the theory your mind is now forming that Winter is guilty. But remember that we have really nothing against him. Even if the story about the quarrel and his engagement turns out to be true, that doesn't carry us very far. It is not enough to prove motive. If everybody who had a motive for murder killed his man there would be nobody left alive. Direct evidence is what counts."

"But direct evidence isn't easy to get."

"Nothing that is worth while is easy to get. Our job is to do things that are difficult."

"That's all very well, but——"

"But me no buts, inspector. So far from being depressed by this morning's events, I am greatly encouraged. They fit in exactly with my own view."

"But, if you don't believe Winter did it, who do you think did?"

"Come now, inspector. That is a question for the end of the argument, not the beginning. I had at least fully made up my mind, before I knew anything at all of this alibi, that Walter Brooklyn did not do it."

"What on earth made you think that? Had you some fresh evidence?"

"No, inspector, merely some fresh use of the old evidence. The more I thought about it, the plainer it became that both those sets of clues were deliberately laid by the same person—I mean the murderer. Don't you see my point?"

"But why did the murderer lay two inconsistent sets of false clues?"

"That, my dear inspector, is the point. He laid them both in the hope that we should see through the one set, and not through the other. Which is just what you have done. He is a clever scoundrel. He meant us to hang Walter Brooklyn."

"He's too clever for me, if that's so. But, supposing you're right, I don't see that we are much nearer to finding out who he is."

The superintendent assumed the air of one instructing a little child, and, as he spoke, ticked off the points on his fingers. "My dear Blaikie, we have to trace the murderer through the false clues which he left. Point number one. Walter Brooklyn's stick was found in Prinsep's room. If Walter Brooklyn did not put it there, who did?"

"Dashed if I know," said the inspector.

"Who could have put it there? Some one must have got it from Walter Brooklyn."

"He said he left it in a taxi, didn't he?"

"No, he said he didn't know where he had left it. It might have been in a taxi, or it might have been in any of the places he visited that afternoon—in Woodman's office, for example, or in the Piccadilly Theatre. You must find out again exactly where he went, and, if possible, where he did leave the stick. There is just the chance that Prinsep found it and took it up to his room. But I don't think so. I think it was clearly left on the floor of Prinsep's room in order that it might serve as a clue to mislead us."

"I see your point. I'll find out what I can."

"Then there's the telephone message. It is not very difficult to imitate a man's voice over the telephone; but I doubt if the murderer would have risked it unless he had known the man he was imitating pretty well. He may even have been something of a mimic. The idea of imitating the voice would have occurred to such a man. Find out if there is any one connected with the Brooklyns who is much of a mimic."

"Why, old Sir Vernon Brooklyn used to be the finest impersonator in England in his younger days, before he took to serious acting."

"I was not thinking of him. There may be others. That sort of talent often runs in families."

"I'll make inquiries."

"Now I come to a much more important point. When one man takes elaborate measures to get another hanged, it usually means he has either some violent grudge, or some strong reason for securing the removal of that particular person. If the murderer tried to get Walter Brooklyn hanged, when he might apparently have got away without leaving any clue at all, he must have had either a violent hatred, or, more probably, a very strong motive for wishing Walter Brooklyn out of the way. We have to find out who had such a motive."

"Motive seems a dangerous line to go on. You remember that Walter Brooklyn had the strongest financial motive for killing his nephews. He gets a pot of the money when Sir Vernon dies."

"I know he does; but what I want you to find out is who would get the money if Walter Brooklyn were removed. When you found out about the will, did you discover that?"

"No. It seemed quite enough to find out that Brooklyn stood to get it by killing his nephews. So far as I remember, there was nothing in the will to say who would get the money if they all died."

"That's a point you must make quite sure of—not merely what is in the will, but who is the next of kin after Walter Brooklyn. It may be the decisive clue."

"I believe you have some definite suspicion in your mind."

"My dear inspector, if I have I'm not going to say any more about it just now. You go and find out what I have asked; and then we can talk."

"I'm to do nothing, then, about Winter?"

"I certainly did not say that. That man Thomas seems to have found out something you had missed. It is your turn to pick up something that has escaped him. Watch the servants at Liskeard House—the maids as well as Winter and Morgan. Keep an eye on the whole household. And meanwhile I will find out all about that girl at Fittleworth. I can have inquiries made locally on the spot."

"Then you're inclined to think Winter may have done it?"

"Not at all. There you are jumping to conclusions again. I'm not at all disposed to say anything definite just at present. What we need is further information, and all we can do for the present is to follow up every hint we get."

"I'll do my best, sir. But it doesn't look to me very hopeful."

"Oh, never say die. Even if we could not find out the whole truth for ourselves—and I believe we can—there is plenty of chance still for the murderer to give himself away. In my experience that is how ninety-nine out of a hundred murderers get caught—I mean of those who do get caught at all. You watch Winter carefully, but don't jump to the conclusion that he's guilty. Watch them all: keep your eyes and your mind wide open. We'll pull it through yet."

"But," said the inspector, unable any longer to keep back the question, "if you think neither Walter Brooklyn nor Winter did it, who do you think did?"

"If I knew that, my dear inspector, I shouldn't be giving you these instructions. The real criminal may be some one quite outside our previous range of suspicion. Indeed, I shan't be at all surprised if he is."

"But you mean that the immediate thing is to go fully into these new aspects of the case?"

"Quite so. Do that, and report progress. And remember to keep your eyes wide open for anything that may turn up. We must trust largely to luck."

As Inspector Blaikie left Superintendent Wilson's room, he was in a curiously divided state of mind. At one moment he still said to himself that all his good labour could not have been wasted, and that Walter Brooklyn must really be guilty after all. The next he found himself assuming, with greater assurance, that Winter was the murderer. He was one of those men who can only keep their minds open by entertaining two contrary opinions at the same time. He shook his head over what seemed to him the weakness of his superior in letting Walter Brooklyn go without arresting some one else.

Meanwhile, in the lounge at Liskeard House, Joan and

Ellery were sitting very close to each other on a sofa making their plans for the discovery of the criminal.

"How had we better begin?" he asked, running his hand despairingly through his hair.

"I can see only one way," Joan replied. "We have nothing to go upon—nothing, I mean, that would make us suspect any particular person. So the only thing to do is to suspect everybody—to find out exactly where everybody was when the crime was committed, and what they were doing that evening."

"That's something of an undertaking."

"I don't mean all the world. I mean everybody who was, or was likely to have been, in this house. Of course, it may have been some one quite different; but I think that's the best way to start. And we mustn't rule out anybody—even ourselves—however sure we are they had nothing to do with it. Even if that doesn't find the criminal, it may help us to light on a clue."

"But it is still a tall order. We don't even know at what time the murders were committed."

"Isn't that a good point to begin upon? Let me see. When were George and John last seen alive?"

"Both at some time after eleven. George was seen leaving the house at half-past, and Prinsep was seen rather before that time in the garden. Isn't that so?"

"Then that," said Joan, "definitely fixes the time of both the murders as being later than say 11.15, and one of them definitely after 11.30. That is something to go upon."

"Ah, but stop a minute. May not either the people who thought they saw George, or the others who thought they saw John, have been mistaken? Neither of them was seen close to."

"It doesn't seem very likely. Winter would hardly have mistaken some one else for George when he saw him going out by the front door."

"Still, my dear, it's possible. Winter was at the other end of the hall and only noticed him by accident. He probably caught no more than a glimpse."

"Yes, Bob; but the other man saw him from quite close. You remember he said he went to open the door for him; but George slipped out before he could get there."

"Yes, I know; but did the other man know George by sight? He was only a hired waiter, in for the evening. Winter probably told him afterwards it was George, and he took it for granted."

"I think you're romancing, my dear. If it wasn't George, who was it?"

"Surely, Joan, in that case it was the murderer, whoever he may have been."

Joan sighed. "Follow up that idea of yours by all means," she said, "but it doesn't sound to me very hopeful. The people who said they saw John are much more likely to have been mistaken. They only saw him from a window some way off; and it was half dark."

"Do you know, Joan, I'm half inclined to believe that neither of them was really seen then at all. What I mean is, they may both have been dead by half-past eleven. Suppose they were neither of them seen. Yes, and by Jove, that would get rid of one difficulty. I've never been able to see how George got back into the grounds after the place was all locked up. But suppose he didn't have to get back at all, because he never went out. Then the man who went out, and was mistaken for George, would be the murderer. Joan, aren't you listening?"

"Yes, Bob, I heard what you said, and I half think you're right. I was thinking of that telephone message."

"Why, what about it?"

"What I mean is, if that message was sent with the object of shifting the suspicion on to some one else, isn't it more likely to have been sent after, than before, the murders?"

"You're right. At least, it was probably sent after one of them. There's no necessary reason to suppose that they were both done at the same time. We don't even know that the same man did them."

"Oh, I don't know about that. Two murders in one night is bad enough; but to ask me to believe in two different murderers is too much of a strain on my credulity."

"Then you don't think Prinsep killed George?" Ellery asked.

"No, I'm nearly sure he didn't. It isn't, I'm afraid, dear, that I don't think he was morally capable of it. I simply feel sure he wouldn't have been such a fool."

"Not even if George had told what he thought of him about Charis Lang? They'd both probably have lost their tempers pretty badly."

"No, Bob, not even then. At least I'm nearly sure. I'm convinced there was only one murderer. Remember they were both killed the same way."

"Well, let's assume you're right. Then if what you said about the 'phone message was right, it was probably sent after one of the murders—I mean immediately after. The murderer wouldn't have wasted time on the premises."

"Yes, that means that 11.30, or thereabouts, is the critical time. Then half-past ten is the earliest possible. Winter went up to get John's letters then, and everything was all right."

"Oh, but George was seen long after that. Winter let him in by the front door at a quarter to eleven."

"Yes, it was certainly George he let in. They spoke, and he couldn't have made a mistake. That narrows it a bit."

"Then probably it all happened after a quarter to eleven—unless George found Prinsep dead when he got upstairs, and chased the murderer down the private stairs into the garden, and got killed by him out there. How does that strike you, Joan?"

"It's possible, Bob; but it looks as if we couldn't fix the time very nearly. It was somewhere between a quarter to eleven and half-past; but that's as near as we can get."

"Let it stand there: and now let's follow out our original plan, and see what we know about everybody who might have been mixed up in it. Let's write it down. I'll write."

Losing no time, they got to work. First, they made a list of every one who had been present at the dinner on the evening of the tragedy—Sir Vernon. John Prinsep, George Brooklyn and his wife, Carter and Mrs. Woodman, Lucas, Mary Woodman—and themselves. Next came the servants—Winter, Morgan, Agnes Dutch, the two other maids, the hired waiters. These were the only persons who, as far as they knew, had been in the house that night. Next, they wrote down exactly what they knew of the doings of every one of these people, leaving spaces in which they could fill in further particulars as they discovered more. When it was finished the list and comments took this form:—

Persons	Movements	Evidence for Movements
Sir Vernon	Went to bed 10.15	Joan, Mary
	Remained in room	Woodman
Joan	With Sir Vernon 10.15 to 10.30	Joan, Mary Woodman
		Sir Vernon
	With Mary Woodman, 10.30 to 10.40	Mary Woodman
		Self
	Then bed	

"That 'self' looks very suspicious," said Joan, as Ellery wrote it down.

"Yes, we are suspecting ourselves as well as others. I strongly suspect you."

"And I you. But get on."

Persons	Movements	Evidence for Movements
Mary Woodman	In landing-lounge till after 11	Joan to 10.40
	Then bed	Self

"Another suspect," said Ellery.

"Poor Mary," said Joan. "She couldn't hurt a fly."

"Then I suspect her all the more."

Persons	Movements	Evidence for Movements
Winter	Downstairs with servants till after 11.30	Other servants
	Lets in Morgan soon after 11.30	Morgan
	Then bed	Self

"He went to bed. But did he stay there? That's the point."

"Put down 'Did he stay there? No clear evidence.' After all, Morgan says he did."

"Yes, but Morgan isn't sure."

"We come to him next."

Persons	Movements	Evidence for Movements
Morgan	At Hammersmith till 11	Unconfirmed, but may be capable of confirmation
	Arrived at Liskeard House soon after 11.30	Winter
	Went to bed	Winter
	Stayed there	Winter

"I say, there wouldn't be much evidence of what Morgan

did, if it wasn't for Winter. Suppose they were both in it. Winter's story depends on Morgan's almost as much as Morgan's on his."

"We suspect them both. At least I don't, but I mean to pretend to do so. Who's next?"

"Agnes Dutch."

"Put her down."

Persons	Movements	Evidence for Movements
Agnes Dutch	Dismissed by Joan for night 10.30	Joan
	Went to bed	

"Next, please."

"The maid-servants."

"They're all in the same position. Put them down."

Persons	Movements	Evidence for Movements
Maid-servants	Downstairs till after 11	Winter and waiters
	Then bed	One another

"More collusion."

"Don't be silly. Now we come to the people who weren't sleeping in the house."

Persons	Movements	Evidence for Movements
Marian Brooklyn	Back to hotel 10.20	Carter and Helen Woodman
	Talked with Helen till 11.30 in Helen's room	Helen Woodman
	Then bed	No confirmation

"But she's out of it anyway."

"Yes, poor Marian."

Persons	Movements	Evidence for Movements

Carter Woodman	Back to hotel 10.20	Marian and Helen
	In hotel writing-room till 11.45	Told above had letters to write
	Gave letters to porter to post 11.45	Porter and liftman

"That seems all right."

"Yes. Helen's next."

Persons	Movements	Evidence for Movements
Helen Woodman	Back to hotel 10.20	Marian and Carter
	With Marian till 11.30	Marian
	Then bed	Carter Woodman after 11.45

"And now we come to you, Bob."

"Oh, I'm no use. I have a proved alibi already. I'm in the same position as your revered stepfather."

"Put yourself down all the same."

Persons	Movements	Evidence for Movements
Lucas	Left Liskeard House by car 10.15	All of us
	rrived home 10.45 and stayed there	Police satisfied

"And that's everybody."

"Yes, and I don't know that we're much further. There is no one on this list you can possibly suspect, except perhaps Morgan, and he can hardly have done it unless Winter was in it too."

"I don't know about that."

"Then whom do you suspect."

"No one and every one. I want time to think that list over. Leave it with me, and I'll put on my considering cap, and tell you to-morrow."

"Don't you go suspecting poor Winter, like the police."

"My dear Joan, this is most undetective-like advice. You ought to make a point of suspecting everybody."

"I make an exception of Winter."

"I'm afraid you want to make an exception of everybody. I have a far more suspicious nature."

"Is there anything I can do while you're thinking it over?"

"Yes. Go and see Carter Woodman and find out all you can about John's circumstances at the time of the murder. Carter may know something about this Winter story, or be able at any rate to tell you something useful we don't know. Then come here to-morrow morning, and I'll tell you if I've had a brain-wave."

Then at last Ellery said good-bye, and Joan went to get the sleep she badly needed.

Chapter XXV
Raising the Wind

Walter Brooklyn's release was arranged more quickly than any one had expected, and, while Ellery and Joan were still engaged in the conversation just reported, he came out of Brixton Jail a free man. At the gate he said good-bye to Thomas, and, hailing a taxi, ordered the man to drive to his Club. The porter at the Byron met him as he entered with an incredulous stare; for he was a firm believer in the theory that Brooklyn was guilty, and had for days past been telling all his friends, and those of the Club members who would listen to him, of the important part which, he himself had played in bringing the murderer to justice. Walter Brooklyn was not popular in the Club; and, by members and servants alike, the assumption of his guilt had been readily accepted.

Brooklyn passed the porter without a word, and went straight up to his room. As he passed by the door leading to the kitchen stairs, a discreetly faint smell of cooking floated up to him, and he thought how pleasant it would be to see a good dinner before him again in the comfortable Club dining-room. But a second thought gave him pause. Could he face his fellow-members just yet? He could pretty accurately guess what they had been saying about him; and he was not at all sure what his reception would be. It would be better to give time for the news of his release, and the convincing evidence of his innocence, to get round the club before he made a public reappearance. But a good dinner was indispensable. His first act on regaining the privacy of his apartment was to take up the house 'phone which connected with the kitchens, and to order dinner to be sent up to his room. The start of surprise which the chef gave on hearing who was speaking to him he could visualize over the 'phone as clearly as if the man had been standing before him in the same room. He was all the more careful for that reason in ordering his dinner, discussing the merits of one course after another at length with the chef. He meant to do himself well, and he meant the servants to understand that he was back quite on the old footing.

But Walter Brooklyn had other things to consider besides his reinstatement as a more or less respectable member of society. He was literally almost penniless, and he knew that his release from prison would merely reopen in a more insistent form the long struggle with his creditors. He must have money, and he must have it at once. His attempt to get money from Prinsep had completely failed, and Woodman had very decisively refused to give him an advance. But a great deal had happened since then. Now both Prinsep and George Brooklyn were dead; and, in more ways than one, that meant a change in his own situation. Prinsep had been the main obstacle between him and Sir Vernon, and there was at least a chance that, if he could see his brother, he would be able to get a substantial loan. He knew that Sir Vernon was very ill; but, if only he was not too ill to be approached, that might make the job all the easier. Could he not persuade the sick man to back a bill for him, or better still, write a cheque in his favour? That was one possibility. But there was another. Now that George and Prinsep were out of the way, who was there to whom Sir Vernon could leave his wealth? Only Joan and himself. Marian Brooklyn would doubtless get something, and Mary Woodman; but the bulk of the property would hardly go to them. Walter knew well enough Sir Vernon's strong sense of family loyalty; and he was fairly sure that, in the changed circumstances, he would profit heavily when his brother died. Might it not be better, instead of risking the giving of offence to Sir Vernon by asking for a loan, to try to raise the money on the strength of his expectations? From that point of view, Sir Vernon's illness would make the chances of success all the greater.

Walter Brooklyn had no positive knowledge of Sir Vernon's will. Some time back, however, Sir Vernon had written to him, enclosing one of the many "last cheques" which he had given to his brother, to tell him that, "except in a very remote contingency," he could expect no further assistance, "whether I am dead or alive." Sir Vernon had added, "I may as well tell you that I have left the bulk of my property to my two nephews; and, as long as they live, you will receive only a comparatively small legacy. You have forfeited all claim to my esteem, and, as long as I have other near relatives to whom I can leave my property, I feel under no obligations to place any of it in your hands. I know too well what you would do with it. I tell you this in order that you may not deceive yourself by any false expectations."

Little had Sir Vernon, expected, when he wrote his letter, that the time would come when it would positively encourage his brother to look forward to a big legacy. Walter had seen Sir Vernon after receiving that letter; and, while his brother had told him nothing positive, he had come away with a shrewd idea that he could expect nothing except in the unlikely event of both nephews dying before Sir Vernon, but that, in that event, he would get the bulk of the money. The question was whether Sir Vernon had altered his will, or whether he would do so now, when the money was likely actually to pass to his brother. Even if he wished to alter it, was he well enough to do so? That must be discovered.

He could find out easily enough about Sir Vernon's health.

Joan would tell him that, even if she had a good suspicion of his reasons for wishing to know. But would Joan be in a position to tell him what was in the will, and would it even be wise to ask her? He was under no illusions. Joan would not want him to have the money, and, even if he stood to benefit now, she would be just the person to persuade Sir Vernon to make a new will. Moreover, there was only one person who would be certain to know what the will contained, and that was Carter Woodman.

Walter Brooklyn's first idea, when he got thus far, was to see Woodman, find out about the will, and try to arrange for a loan on the strength of his expectations. But would this do either? Woodman was no friend of his; and, if his attention were called to the matter, he might easily induce Sir Vernon to make a fresh will. Yet Woodman was the only person through whom he could hope to arrange for an advance; for Woodman alone would know whether or not Walter was now Sir Vernon's heir. And somehow an advance must be got, and got quickly.

There must surely, he thought, be some way round the difficulty. Walter Brooklyn was no fool; and he set himself deliberately to devise some method of raising the wind with Woodman's aid. He came speedily to the conclusion that there was only one way in which it could be done. He must somehow get Woodman on to his side. That was not altogether impossible, much as the two men disliked each other. It was, Walter told himself, merely a matter of money.

Woodman, he considered, would certainly receive a legacy under any will Sir Vernon might make. Probably a few thousands, in return for his services. But he supposed that Woodman could entertain no hope of being one of the principal beneficiaries.

Woodman's expectations were probably small. But Walter Brooklyn had good reason to believe that, despite his apparent prosperity, Woodman was hard pressed for money. Left alone in Woodman's office for a few minutes the week before, he had hurriedly turned over certain private papers on the desk, and had gathered enough information to be sure that Woodman, like himself, would do a good deal for a supply of ready money. Might not this fact, he wondered, open up the possibility of a bargain? If, as he believed, the will was now in his favour, he could offer Woodman very favourable terms for negotiating an advance on his behalf. He would offer Woodman a share—a substantial share—as a loan—of whatever he could raise on the strength of Walter's expectations.

Why waste time? He would at least see at once whether Woodman was at his office, and try to arrange an appointment. The telephone was at his elbow, and he rang up. Woodman was there, and Walter got straight through to him. His clerks had already gone home for the night.

"Who is speaking?" came the voice from the other end.

"Walter Brooklyn this end. I want to see you as soon as possible."

As he gave his name, Walter heard a gasp from the man at the other end of the wire. Then, "Where are you speaking from?" came the voice.

"Not from Brixton, if that is what you mean. I'm speaking from the Byron Club."

"Good God, man! How on earth——"

"The police released me this afternoon. I am completely cleared of this charge, although I understand you were good enough to believe me guilty."

To this there came no answer.

"I must see you privately at once."

"What about?"

"I'll tell you that when we meet. Will you come round here?"

"When?"

"To-night, if you can. I shall be in my room all the evening."

"Not to-night. I have an engagement."

"Then to-morrow morning."

"Very well. At about eleven."

"I'll be here. Good-night."

Each man as he hung up the receiver had plenty to think about. Brooklyn was perfecting his scheme for raising a loan with Woodman's aid, and reflecting upon the various ways in which he might approach the subject. Carter Woodman also stood silent with a heavy frown on his face.

The fact that Walter Brooklyn had been released, although the evidence against him seemed overwhelming, came as a great surprise to Woodman. Something curious must have happened, When Brooklyn rang off, he had been on the point of asking for further details. He would get them somehow elsewhere. He would try to see the inspector. He rang up Scotland Yard.

"Hallo. Is that Inspector Blaikie? Carter Woodman speaking."

"Is that you, Mr. Woodman? I was just trying to get through to you myself. Are you at your office? Then may I come around and see you for a few minutes? Will what you wanted to say to me keep till I get round? Very well, I'll be with you in half a jiffy."

This was a piece of luck. Woodman would get the full story from the inspector, and he would also be able to give in return a piece of information which, he thought, would make Scotland Yard sit up. How on earth had they come to release Walter Brooklyn? Well, there was such a thing as re-arrest. After all, the man had not been acquitted.

The inspector arrived in less than a quarter of an hour. He explained that he wished to ask Woodman a few questions relating to Prinsep's private affairs, and also involving, he believed, certain of the servants at Liskeard House. Had Woodman heard anything of some trouble with a girl down at Fittleworth—the head gardener's daughter—a Miriam Smith?

Yes, Woodman did know about it; but he had not mentioned it before, as it was confidential, and there was no reason to believe it had anything to do with the murders. Prinsep had commissioned him to settle with the girl for a lump sum payment, in consideration of which she was to leave the district. Woodman understood there would be a child. Undoubtedly, Prinsep had behaved badly to the girl; but it was not the first time. Was there any reason to connect the incident with the murders?

"There may be, or there may not, Mr. Woodman. Are you aware that the girl was engaged to be married to the butler at Liskeard House? Winter, his name is."

"Oh, I know Winter. A most trusted old family servant. I had no idea that he was engaged to the girl. But I feel quite sure you are wrong if you connect him in any way with the murders. He is the last man to be mixed up in such a thing. Besides, between ourselves, I haven't a doubt that it was Walter Brooklyn who killed Prinsep. He may have killed George Brooklyn, too, or Prinsep may. But surely there is not much doubt he killed Prinsep."

"I see you have not heard the news, Mr. Woodman. Walter Brooklyn was released this afternoon."

Woodman thought that he would get fuller information if he simulated ignorance and astonishment.

"Released? Whatever for?" he said.

"Because our evidence seems to show that he had nothing to do with it."

"But, good heavens! there was his stick, and the telephone message, and his quarrel with Prinsep. What more do you want?"

"I can't go into the details, Mr. Woodman. But we have been convinced that he didn't do it."

"Of course, if you have made up your mind, it is no good my telling you what I was going to tell you. But, when I last saw you, you were sure enough he was guilty. What on earth has made you change your opinion?"

"If you have further information, you should certainly tell me, Mr. Woodman. We ought to know everything that has a possible bearing on the case."

"I will tell you; but it must be between ourselves. You know Thomas, who is Walter Brooklyn's present solicitor. The man knows his client is guilty, and he had the effrontery to come here and ask me to help him in arranging a collusive defence."

"Indeed, what was it he proposed?"

"That I should help him in an attempt to shift the suspicion to the men-servants. Of course, I refused to have anything to do with such dishonourable tactics. Thomas admitted to me that his client was guilty. I am only surprised that he seems to have succeeded so well in deceiving the police."

"You say that Thomas admitted Brooklyn's guilt to you?" asked the inspector, half-incredulously, but with a note of excitement in his voice.

"Undoubtedly, he did. Of course, I should not have told you if he had not made me that dishonourable proposal. I am telling you now in order to save an innocent man from suspicion."

"This is very strange, Mr. Woodman. The proofs of Mr. Brooklyn's innocence were considered to be conclusive. Superintendent Wilson very strongly holds that they are conclusive. He appears to have a perfect alibi."

"Alibis can be faked, and usually are."

"This one has been pretty thoroughly tested. But, in view of what you say, I must certainly take up the matter again at once. Of course, my first step will be to have a talk with Mr. Thomas."

"Pardon me, inspector, but I hope you will not do that. I have told you this in strict confidence, and it would endanger my professional position if it were known that I had done so."

"Surely not. The fact that the man made you a dishonourable proposal absolves you."

"He would deny it, and it would be only my word against his. He would merely deny, too, that he ever considered his client to be guilty. What else could he do? And we could not prove it."

The inspector stood silent for a moment, biting his lip, while he thought the position over. Then he said,—

"Very well, Mr. Woodman. Perhaps you are right. But I think I can get at the truth in another way. I will let you know the result. Rest assured that what you say will be given full weight."

"All I want is to prevent you from going on a wild goose chase after poor old Winter. I've known him since I was a baby, and he is quite incapable of doing what you suggest."

"That is as may be, Mr. Woodman. We are not inclined to suspect him seriously without further evidence. But I will certainly look into what you tell me about Mr. Walter Brooklyn. And now, there is another matter about which I want to ask you one or two questions."

"Ask away."

"You were good enough to give me very full particulars about the contents of Sir Vernon Brooklyn's will; but there were one or two points about which I omitted to ask you. Perhaps you will not mind clearing them up now. In the first place, as matters stand now, who did you say were the principal beneficiaries? I have the facts here in my notebook, but I want to check them."

"Let me see. Mrs. George Brooklyn gets one half of the sum which would have gone to George Brooklyn, and Miss Cowper half of what would have gone to John Prinsep. Mr. Walter Brooklyn is the residuary legatee, and stands, I suppose, to inherit about half a million, unless the will is altered."

"Thank you. The further point I want to know is what the position would be if Mr. Walter Brooklyn were to die before Sir Vernon. Who would be the residuary legatee in that case?"

Woodman paused for a moment before replying. Then he said, "The residue would go, of course, to the next of kin."

"Who is that? I think you have not mentioned any other relatives."

"To the best of my belief, inspector, I myself am the next of kin after Walter Brooklyn."

The inspector whistled. "Then you would inherit the bulk of the money if Sir Vernon Brooklyn died after Walter Brooklyn."

"Yes, that is, unless a new will were made. I should, of course, have to inform Sir Vernon fully as to the circumstances."

"Quite so. And now there is just one further point. Sir Vernon has not, I suppose, shown any desire so far to amend his will."

"He is far too ill to be troubled at present with matters of business."

"I see. Then, so far as you know, the old will stands."

"Yes. Mr. Walter Brooklyn is at present the principal heir."

"Thank you, Mr. Woodman," said the inspector, holding out his hand.

When Inspector Blaikie had gone, Woodman sat down again at his desk to think things over. What was the purpose of the questions just addressed to him? Clearly, the police had some new idea in their minds. They had come to the conclusion, on grounds adequate or inadequate, that Walter

Brooklyn was not the murderer, and they were clearly trying to find out afresh who else could have had a reasonable motive. That was the only possible reason for the careful inquiries into the terms of the will. Was it possible that the police had a real new clue—possibly even a definite suspicion? Would they even begin suspecting him, now they had discovered that he was next of kin? As long as Walter Brooklyn lived, he stood to gain nothing. It was ridiculous to think that he could be suspected.

The inspector also had a good deal to think about when he left Woodman's office. His first thought was to see his superior officer; but he found that the superintendent was out, and was not expected back for an hour or so. He made up his mind to fill in the interval by clearing up the new question, relating to Walter Brooklyn's guilt, which Carter Woodman had raised. He took a taxi, and drove to Liskeard House, where he asked to see Miss Cowper. She received him at once, and he came straight to the point.

"Miss Cowper, I have a question to ask you. You may think it a very peculiar one, and you need not answer it if you would rather not. I shall not tell any one that you refused, or that I asked it. I want to know whether, so far as you are aware, Mr. Thomas, your stepfather's solicitor, at any time believed in his client's guilt. I should not ask you, of course, if your stepfather had not been released. But I have a reason for asking."

Joan showed that the question startled her; but she answered without hesitation. "Yes," she said, "Mr. Thomas did believe what you say until we undeceived him with the evidence you also found convincing; indeed, that was why Mr. Ellery and I determined to go to work on our own. We felt that Mr. Thomas, believing what was not true, would never find out what was true. My stepfather told me that he was sure Thomas believed him guilty; but he said, 'I dare say he'll make as good a defence as another would when it comes to the point.' "

"I will tell you, Miss Cowper, exactly why I asked the question. It is being stated that Mr. Brooklyn actually confessed his guilt to his solicitor, and that Mr. Thomas told a third person that he was guilty. I should not, of course, tell you this if I believed it to be true. Your answer quite satisfies me that it is based on a misunderstanding."

"It is preposterous," said Joan indignantly. "My stepfather told Mr. Thomas the absolute truth; but the man would not believe it, until we proved it to him."

"That is just what I imagined, Miss Cowper. Thank you very much for speaking to me so frankly. It has saved a world of trouble. Let me assure you that no suspicion at all now rests on Mr. Brooklyn."

"I should hope not," said Joan. "But who put this abominable story about?"

"I cannot tell you that, Miss Cowper. But you may rest secure that no more will be heard of it. May I use your telephone for a moment on my way out?"

The permission was readily given, and, in the hall, the inspector stepped into the little closed lobby, in which the telephone was kept, and rang up Carter Woodman.

"Hallo, is that Mr. Woodman? Inspector Blaikie speaking. I have looked into that matter about which you spoke to me. About Walter Brooklyn, I mean—his having told Thomas that he was guilty. There's nothing in it. No, nothing in it. You made a mistake. You must have misinterpreted what Thomas said. He did believe Mr. Brooklyn to be guilty, but Mr. Brooklyn never told him so. It was merely his personal opinion. What? Am I sure? Yes, quite certain. No, I have not seen Thomas; but I am sure all the same. Yes, f now regard Mr. Brooklyn's innocence as quite established. Yes, quite certain. No doubt at all about it. We made a very natural mistake when we arrested him; but that's all done with now. I think we are getting on the right track. Thanks all the same. You were quite right to tell me, though there proved to be nothing in it. Good-night."

The inspector hung up the receiver, and went on his way.

Chapter XXVI
Two Men Strike a Bargain

Walter Brooklyn dined alone in his rooms. As a rule, a single Club waiter would have been deputed to attend upon him; but this evening he noticed that no less than four found an excuse for coming to help. Each course was brought to table by a different hand; for the whole Club staff were curious to get a good look at the member who had been miraculously delivered from jail and the gallows. That very afternoon, when they had discussed the case, they had all been taking his guilt for granted, picturing him in his lonely cell devouring the skilly of adversity; and now here he was back again amongst them, eating an excellent dinner as if nothing out of the way had occurred. If Carter Woodman had been there to express his continued confidence that Walter Brooklyn was guilty, he would, despite the release, not have lacked supporters among the Club servants; for Walter Brooklyn was not an easy man to like, especially for his social inferiors. But this evening those who were most convinced of his guilt were also anxious to take part in waiting upon him. There is a thrill to be got by close personal contact with a real murderer.

Downstairs, Walter Brooklyn had no doubt, the dining-room and the smoking-rooms, as well as the servants' quarters, were busy with the news of his release. Among the Club members, as among the servants, there would be differences of opinion; and he felt he could name certain members who would be vigorously affirming their belief that the police made a mistake, not when they arrested him, but when they let him go. The spiteful old johnnies, he said to himself, would gladly see him hanged. Their disappointment added to the pleasure of being a free man. And this was really a first-rate dinner. The Byron had its faults; but they did know how to cook.

Indeed, the more Walter thought about the new situation, the better he was pleased. His two inconvenient nephews were safely out of the way; and he had an excellent chance of becoming an exceedingly rich man. He smiled to himself as he counted his chickens. True, there were immediate troubles to be faced. He must have money now. But he was sure Woodman couldn't be fool enough to refuse the terms he was in a position to offer. Supposing even that he did refuse, there was still the way of going direct to old Vernon.

By the way, how was old Vernon? That dinner had been so good that the idea of telephoning to Liskeard House to inquire had gone clean out of his head. He would do it now. It would be the very devil if the old chap were to go and alter his will. The chances were he wasn't well enough to do it. He would ring up at once and inquire after him. It would be only decent. After all, the man was his brother.

Winter's voice over the telephone informed him that Sir Vernon had taken an alarming turn for the worse. His condition was said to be critical, but not hopeless. The doctor was with him now. Sir Vernon had been unconscious for some time. Winter promised to ring up and give the doctor's further report later in the evening.

Walter Brooklyn was duly sympathetic; and there was in him indeed some real feeling for his brother. But the thought uppermost in his mind was that, if old Vernon would only be obliging enough to die, it would be from his brother's point of view a very happy release. If only the will had not been altered already without his knowing about it. A horrible thought: not likely, perhaps, but disquieting all the same. How badly he wanted to see Carter Woodman in order to make sure. Poor old Vernon would never live to alter his will now. Everything depended on the terms of the will now in force. It was probably all right; but he would give something to know for certain. And, if Sir Vernon would only die now and get it over, there would be no need to bribe Woodman for an advance. The money would be his then. Should he wait and risk it? No; old men often took so unconscionably long a-dying. If things came right, he would never miss what he would have to give Woodman for the sake of immediate security. The telephone rang. It was Winter. The doctor had just left. Sir Vernon's condition was very critical, but the doctor said it was still not hopeless. He might rally and get well. But any shock would certainly be fatal. The doctor was coming again later. Should he 'phone up again? Brooklyn asked him to do so, and rang off. Yes, he must certainly see Woodman, unless old Vernon was obliging enough to die in the night.

Turning these things over in his mind, Walter Brooklyn sat, until a pleasant drowsiness came over him. He woke with a start. It was after eleven. Was not that a knock at the door? "Come in," he said.

When he saw who his visitor was, he greeted him warmly. "This is quite unexpected," he said, "but I am very glad you have come. Have a whisky." Carter Woodman nodded. "I found I could get here after all this evening," he said. Then he mixed himself a good stiff whisky, silently refilled Brooklyn's glass for him, and sank into a chair.

"What was it you wanted to see me about?" he asked. "Money, as usual, I suppose."

Brooklyn nodded. "A man must live, you know," he said.

"Your idea of living has always been one that runs away with the money, my dear chap," said Woodman, with a laugh.

"Never mind that. I want some now."

"But you know that Sir Vernon, through Prinsep, gave me positive instructions that I should only give you money on one condition."

"Isn't the position a bit different now, Woodman? I mean since what happened last week."

Woodman paused a moment. "There is a difference," he said, "but clearly I cannot advance you money without authority from Sir Vernon, and he is far too ill to be troubled about such things at present."

"I don't want you to trouble him. But I should have thought that, in the new circumstances, you would make no difficulty about advancing me a loan. I want £10,000 to clear off debts, and a few thousands to get along with for the present."

"My dear fellow, do you think I carry ten thousand pounds loose in my pocket?"

"I think you could get me an advance of more than that amount if you chose."

"But Sir Vernon may alter his will."

These words of Woodman's brought great comfort to Walter Brooklyn's heart. They proved at least that, as the will stood, he would come in for a considerable sum on his brother's death. He was emboldened to make a definite proposal.

"Look here, Woodman, you know what is in the will. I want you to advance me twenty thousand pounds at once on the strength of my expectations under it. There's no risk, practically; what there is, I'm prepared to pay for. If you let me have twenty thousand now, you shall have thirty thousand when Sir Vernon dies."

"Good heavens, do you think I'm rolling in money? If I had twenty thousand to spare I couldn't risk it on a pure gamble like that. The odds are that Sir Vernon will alter his will, or you may die before he does. Where should I be then?"

"I should imagine in that case you would get a big slice of the money yourself."

"But, really, that's no reason why I should give it to you. What you propose is absurd."

"You know very well, Woodman, that it is not absurd. But, if you don't like my proposal, make one of your own. What I want is twenty thousand pounds and a regular income assured until old Vernon dies."

"My word, you don't want much," was Woodman's comment; but his brain was working actively. He was, in fact, in quite as dire straits for money as Walter Brooklyn himself. Lately, his position was worse; for heavy stock exchange speculation had brought him to the point of certain bankruptcy unless he could raise a considerable sum at once. His mind went to work on a definite scheme, which indeed he had conceived before ever he came to visit Walter Brooklyn. While he perfected his plan, he continued to protest the impossibility of doing what Walter suggested. Before making his proposal he wanted to be sure how far the man to whom he was speaking knew what Sir Vernon Brooklyn's will contained. Twenty thousand pounds, he suggested, was a big sum to ask for on the strength of expectations under the will. He saw at once that this line of argument made Walter Brooklyn anxious, and before long he had convinced himself that Sir Vernon's brother had no certain knowledge of the provisions of the will. Then he was ready to spring his audacious proposal.

"Look here, Brooklyn, I've been thinking it over, and we may be able to manage something. I'll try to get you that twenty thousand pounds on condition that you make over to me one-half of your expectation under the will."

"You're asking me to buy a pig in a poke," was Walter Brooklyn's answer. "You know the details of the will, and I'm willing to tell you that I don't. I can't accept your terms; but I'm willing to pay you forty thousand pounds when I get the money if you let me have twenty down. Isn't that a fair proportion?"

"Considering the risk, certainly not. But I'm willing to make an alternative suggestion. Under the will, Joan and Mrs. George Brooklyn are both amply provided for. The inheritance of the rest of Sir Vernon's money probably lies between you and me, whether the will is altered or not. I suggest that we make an agreement to go equal shares in whatever is left to either of us. I add one condition, that you should draw up a new will, making me the heir to your estate."

"You stand to get the lot that way, whatever happens. I can see that it is very nice indeed from your point of view. And what, may I ask, do you offer me in exchange?"

"Twenty thousand pounds down, which I can borrow on the strength of our joint expectations, and I'm willing to add two thousand a year until Sir Vernon dies. And in addition, I offer you the security that, even if Sir Vernon cuts you out of his will, you will still get your share of the money."

"But, if Sir Vernon dies now—he's pretty bad, they tell me—the effect of it will be that I shall be making you a pretty handsome present."

"And I shall be presenting you with twenty thousand pounds in hard cash."

They wrangled for some time longer; but Walter Brooklyn, in ignorance of the precise terms of the will, was at a serious disadvantage. Finally, he agreed to Carter Woodman's terms; and Woodman at once sat down and drafted out a written agreement putting their compact into definite terms. He also drew up, in a few lines, a will constituting himself Walter Brooklyn's heir.

"Now, we must get these documents signed and witnessed," he said.

"There will be some one about downstairs," said Brooklyn

heavily. He had an uneasy feeling that he was being badly swindled; but twenty thousand pounds down was the main thing. Besides, he might find ways, though Woodman was a cute lawyer, of repudiating the bargain later, if it proved to his interest to do so.

There were two documents to be witnessed—the will and the agreement. The I.O.U., which was Woodman's further security for the £20,000, would not, of course, be signed until the money was actually paid over. The two men went downstairs, found the night-porter and a waiter who had not yet gone to bed, and completed the two documents in their presence. Then, taking the will and his copy of the agreement, Woodman bade Walter Brooklyn good-night, receiving a not very cordial response. His first business on the morrow would be to use the two documents and the joint expectation of the two men under Sir Vernon's will, as a means of raising at once, not merely the £20,000 for Walter Brooklyn, but the much larger sum of which he himself stood immediately in need. He thought he knew a man who would let him have the money. If he failed, bankruptcy was inevitable. Woodman congratulated himself on a good night's work. Already his chestnuts were half out of the fire.

Walter Brooklyn, when Woodman had gone, sat down again in his chair with a heavy sigh. He was very conscious that he had been swindled. Carter Woodman knew the terms of Sir Vernon's will, and he did not; and it was certain that, with this knowledge to help him, Woodman had struck a hard bargain. Moreover, he not only knew the will: he was in a very strong position, as Sir Vernon's legal adviser, to prevent the making of a new one which would be disadvantageous to him. Woodman was almost safe to score, whatever might happen. But there was solid comfort in the thought that, under the compact they had just made, it was to Woodman's interest that Walter should get the largest possible slice of Sir Vernon's money. Whatever came to Walter was to become Woodman's in time. Woodman, therefore, would be bound to do his best to serve Walter's interests. Yes, there were compensations in being swindled on such terms. Walter stood a good chance of wealth for as long as he lived; and what did it matter to him who might get the money after his death?

"After me, the deluge," said Walter Brooklyn to himself, summing up the evening's transaction.

Chapter XXVII
Robert Ellery's Idea

Ellery woke up in the morning with the dim consciousness that he had a great idea. What had he been thinking out when he dropped off to sleep the night before? The murders, of course—they were always in his thoughts. But what was the shattering new idea that had come to him as he lay awake? That was how his best ideas often came—in the night just before he went to sleep they came to him half-formed, and the next morning, by the time he was fully awake, they had somehow taken on form and certainty. With an effort he stretched and roused himself, and, as he did so, the idea came back to him. He felt certain that he knew who was the murderer.

Who, he had asked himself the night before—who, of all the persons who figured on the list Joan and he had compiled, was most likely to have done the thing? He felt certain that it was not the work of a stranger: the whole of the circumstances seemed to point to some one familiar with the house and its ways. Yet, on the evidence, it seemed clear enough that no one among those they had put upon their list could be guilty. But their list included everybody. Very well—this had been his first inspiration—there must be something wrong with the evidence. It must point away from the guilty, as it had pointed towards the innocent. The murderer who had laid that clever trail to incriminate Walter Brooklyn would obviously have taken the precaution to lay a trail pointing away from himself. Indeed, whoever had the apparently clearest alibi was on this showing the most likely to be guilty. It would be safest, in the circumstances, to ignore for the moment all the evidence which seemed to prove innocence, and simply consider, in the light of the remaining conditions, who was most likely to have been the murderer.

This narrowed the field considerably. The women, except as possible accessories, could be ruled out of account in any case; for no woman could have struck the blows by which the two cousins had met their deaths. That left—whom? Walter Brooklyn was out of it; for his alibi had been not merely accepted, but tested beyond possible doubt. Ellery could hardly suspect himself, though he admitted that any one else, following out his line of thought, might still suspect him. His alibi was not conclusive: it depended on the word of one man. But he could rule himself out: he could say positively that he had not done the thing. Then who remained? Only Harry Lucas, Carter Woodman, and the two servants, Winter and Morgan. Among these, if he was right, the real murderer must be found.

It was ludicrous, Ellery felt, to suspect his guardian. Harry Lucas had no possible motive, and he was the very last man for such a deed. He was ruled out of consideration as soon as the thought was conceived. About Winter and Morgan Ellery could not feel the same full certainty; but he was very strongly of opinion that the murders were not the work of a servant, and that neither of these men had the qualities which the deed seemed to demand.

Then there was left only—Carter Woodman. It was on that thought that Ellery had fallen asleep, and that was the idea that now came back to him with added certainty. Carter Woodman was the murderer.

But was not the whole idea preposterous? Woodman not

merely had an alibi which had satisfied the police; he was a relative, an old personal friend, the tried and trusted business adviser of the Brooklyns. His wife was one of Joan's dearest friends, and he himself had been constantly about with the men of whose murder Ellery was now suspecting him. The idea seemed preposterous enough, when it was put in that way; but, though Ellery presented these difficulties to his mind in all their strength, they did not at all change his attitude. No one else was the murderer: therefore Carter Woodman was.

There entered, certainly, into Ellery's conviction his own strong dislike of Woodman. The suggestion of Woodman's guilt, once made, was plausible to him, because he had not at all the feeling that the deed was incongruous. It would have been utterly incongruous with what he knew of any other possible suspect, even Walter Brooklyn; but the cap seemed to fit Carter Woodman. Ellery said to himself that Woodman was just the sort of chap who would commit murder, if he had a strong enough motive.

Yes; but where was the motive in this case? What did Woodman stand to gain? Knowing the terms of the will, Ellery was aware that he gained nothing directly; for Sir Vernon's fortune would now pass mainly to Walter Brooklyn, and the rest to Joan and to Marian Brooklyn. Of course, Woodman might hope to get Sir Vernon to make a new will in his favour, and, in any case, he probably stood now a fine chance of becoming the managing director of the Brooklyn Corporation. But a man would hardly commit two desperate murders merely on such chances. The more Ellery considered the matter, the surer he felt that there must be something else behind—something of which he was unaware, that would make the whole case plain.

He must see Joan, and tell her what he suspected. She might well know some fact, of which he was ignorant, that would throw a clear light on the motive behind the crimes. But would she ever believe that Woodman had done it? Ellery realized that what to him seemed like certainty would seem to others only a guess, and that he had not merely no proof but actually no evidence to support his assumptions. What evidence there was told the other way. Still, this did not shake his assurance. He must make Joan see the case as he had come to see it. Then they could seek together for the proof.

As soon as Ellery had breakfasted, he set off for Liskeard House to find Joan. They must get to work at once.

Joan, too, had spent a good part of the night thinking; but her thoughts had brought her no nearer to a solution of the mystery surrounding the murders. There was literally not one, of all those who seemed to be concerned, who could, in her judgment, have been the murderer. She was reduced to the supposition that it must be some outsider—some one whom they had not even dreamed so far of connecting with the crimes.

But Joan's thoughts, unlike Ellery's, persistently wandered from the problem which she had set herself to solve. She kept thinking of the future—of the thing that was dearest to the heart of the old man lying at death's door. It was not the money: it was the direction of the great dramatic enterprise which he alone had built up. He had set his heart, she knew, on passing on, not merely his fortune, but the headship of the Brooklyn Corporation to one of his own blood, one who could carry on the work he had set himself to do. Whom would he now put in the place which Prinsep had lately occupied? He might, indeed, die without the strength to make a change; but Joan did not believe that he would. It seemed to her inconceivable that he would leave matters so that the bulk of his fortune, and with it the control of the Brooklyn Corporation, would pass to her stepfather, who had manifestly neither the will nor the special capacity to carry on the work. She was convinced that Sir Vernon would change his will;

and she could see but one man whom he was now likely to make heir to his wealth and position. Carter Woodman had the talent and the knowledge to run the Corporation as a business, if not as an artistic success. Would Sir Vernon put Woodman in Prinsep's place? Joan hated the very idea; for she believed in the Brooklyn Corporation as an artistic venture, and she had always somehow both disliked and distrusted Carter Woodman. She would have found it difficult to give a definite reason for her dislike, and she admitted that she was perhaps unfair; but there it was. She hoped Carter would not get the job, and she was sure that, however successful he might be commercially, his accession to power would put an end to all hope of artistic success. Still, she told herself, it was no business of hers, and she would certainly not try to influence Sir Vernon in any way. She supposed he would make Woodman his heir; for there was no one else.

Against her will, the thought of Ellery came into her mind. He would be, would he not?—she seemed to be arguing with a non-existent adversary—just the man to carry on Sir Vernon's great artistic enterprises. Joan found herself building up quite a romance on the basis of Robert Ellery's succession to control of the great Brooklyn enterprise. How well he would do it! And then she reminded herself sharply that she had no right to entertain such ideas, and that, in any case, she certainly could not say a word on Bob's behalf to Sir Vernon. No, Carter Woodman would get the job. Joan sighed as she resigned herself to the inevitable. But despite her good resolutions, she was still thinking what an excellent successor to Sir Vernon Robert Ellery would make, when she was told that he was waiting to see her. She brushed the thought she had been entertaining out of her mind, and, dressing hastily—for she had breakfasted in bed—went down to see him.

"Well, my dear, what news?" he asked.

"My dear Bob, I've had a beastly night, and I feel utterly

washed out. And my thoughts keep on going round and round in a circle.”

“Poor darling,” said Ellery. “You are having a time.”

“And yet, Bob, it’s odd how little it all matters now I have you.”

“I must give you a kiss for saying that, my dear. And I must try to live up to it.”

“Dear boy,” said Joan, and then for a few minutes they managed to get along without the need for words. Joan was the first to rouse herself. “My dear Bob,” she said, “this is a fine way of wasting time. I thought our job was to find out who did it.”

“My dear child, I’ve been thinking all the time. It’s wonderful how putting my head on your shoulder clears my brain. Now I’m ready to behave like a real scientific detective.”

“I think you’ll do it better if you sit a little farther off. Now, my lad, what do you think about it?”

“I think just this, Joan. I think I know now who did it.”

Joan gave a gasp. “You know who did it!” she repeated.

“Well, I don’t know; but I think I have a very good idea.”

“Do you mean you’ve got some evidence at last. Who was it, Bob? Tell me.”

“No, I haven’t any fresh evidence yet. I’ve just been thinking. But I believe it was”—Ellery paused—“Carter Woodman.”

Joan gave a half-cry of surprise. “Bob, Bob, you can’t mean that. Whatever makes you say such a thing? My dear boy, it’s quite absurd.”

“Why is it absurd, Joan?”

“Well, Carter’s a member of the family, and one of our oldest friends, and—but what’s the use of discussing it? Why, he was here yesterday.”

"He may be here to-day, dear; but I don't see what that has to do with it."

"But Carter's been helping the police all through. He's——"

"Isn't that just what he would do if he were guilty?"

"My dear Bob, this is absurd. We know that Carter was in the Cunningham Hotel all the evening. He couldn't have done it. Really——"

"Do you think that the man who was clever enough to fasten all that suspicion on your stepfather wouldn't be clever enough to provide himself with a passable alibi?"

"Oh, yes. But all this doesn't tell me why you suspect Carter. Put it out of your mind, Bob. I know you don't like him, but that doesn't mean that he has committed murder."

"I've said to myself already everything that you are saying now. But I still believe that he did it."

"Why, Bob? Have you any reason—any proof at all, I mean?"

"No, I've no proof; but I've an idea. It's a question of elimination. If nobody else did it, then he did."

"But, my dear boy, what possible motive could he have had? People don't commit murders just for fun. Do be reasonable. Carter was on quite good terms with both George and John, and he had no reason for killing either of them."

"Do you mean that, Joan?" said Ellery, with a sense of disappointment. "I hoped you would be able to explain to me what motive he could have had. Come now, doesn't he really stand to gain something—I mean, don't you think Sir Vernon may make him his heir, or something of that sort?"

Joan paused. "Yes, Bob," she said, with a sigh. "There I think you're right. Sir Vernon will very likely put Carter in John's place, I should imagine. But——"

"Well, isn't that a motive?"

"No, my dear, it isn't. After all, we don't know that he will, and I'm quite sure people don't commit carefully planned murders just on a chance like that. Really, Bob, it's ridiculous."

Ellery said nothing, but got up and strode across the room. Then he turned and faced Joan. "Look here," he said, "supposing we hadn't cleared old Walter, and he had been put out of the way as well as Prinsep and George. Who'd have been the heir then—the next of kin, I mean?"

"Oh, Carter, I suppose. But you don't suggest——"

"My dear child, we've been a pair of fools. By George, I wasn't sure; but I'm sure now. What you've just said makes it clear as clear."

"Makes what clear?"

"Why, the motive. Of course, I ought to have seen it before."

"Ought to have seen it before? Ought to have seen what?"

"Why, whoever murdered John and George did his best to throw the suspicion on your stepfather, didn't he?"

"Yes, I suppose he did."

"And if your stepfather had been convicted, Woodman could have stepped into Sir Vernon's shoes without a word said as the next heir."

"When Sir Vernon died—yes. Probably, he could."

"And wasn't all this the surest way of hastening his end? But that is not my point. As long as Walter Brooklyn was likely to be convicted, the man I suspect stood to inherit Sir Vernon's money, and to step at once into Prinsep's shoes. He had murdered two of the people who stood in his way, and he did his best to murder the third judicially by faking up evidence against him. If Walter Brooklyn was convicted, he was quite safe to get both the money and the control of the theatres. That's what he was after when he tried to get your stepfather convicted of murder. Doesn't that theory fit the facts?”

“I suppose it does, Bob. But it would be a simply horrible thing to have to believe, and it doesn’t convince me in the least. I don’t like Carter; but we’ve treated him as almost one of the family all these years. Could he possibly have done such a thing?”

“I don’t like him either—in fact, I dislike him very strongly—and I believe he could—and did. But it won’t be easy to prove it.”

“But, Bob, it can’t be true. Carter was with the others at the Cunningham all the time on the night when John and George were killed.”

“I know he said he was; but was he? A thing like that needs to be proved. Why, he’s the only man who had any reason for killing these three people, and, unless he can prove conclusively that he didn’t kill two of them, and do his best to get the law to kill the third, I shall go on believing that he did. At any rate, I mean to look into it.”

“But you can’t possibly bring a charge of that sort without proof.”

“You and I are going to find the proof, and there are two things you can do to help. First, you must find out—from Marian will probably be best—where Woodman really was on Tuesday night, I mean whether he positively was with them in the hotel all the evening. I don’t believe he was.”

“My dear boy, it would be simply horrible to have to go and ask Marian things like that, when I can’t possibly tell her why we want to know them. To think that she is actually living with the Woodmans, without an idea that any one is suspecting Carter of having murdered her husband.”

“No, you mustn’t tell her a word. But you can easily find out what I want without letting her see what I suspect.”

“I suppose I must try to find out, just to prove that you’re all wrong. But I don't suspect Carter. It's just too horrible to think."

"My dear, whether we like it or not, we have to find the man who did this—more than ever now that your stepfather is cleared. A man who was capable of these things is capable of anything, and I can't bear the thought that you may be meeting him and regarding him as a friend."

"All right, Bob. I agree that we have to get to the bottom of this. I'll do my best. But I'm still sure you're wrong."

"That's right, Joan, I only hope I am. But, while you're seeing Marian, I will try to find out a few things about friend Woodman on my own."

At this moment Marian Brooklyn was shown in. She came across most mornings, and spent a part of the day at Liskeard House, taking her share in looking after Sir Vernon. It was a relief to her to have something to do. It stopped her from just thinking day and night of what she had lost. Ellery had not seen her since the tragedy, and he felt shy and awkward now in the presence of her grief. At the end of a few minutes he took his leave and left Joan to do what she had promised.

It was not easy to come to the point. How could she, without rousing suspicions, ask Marian about Carter Woodman's movements on the night of the murders? But, very soon, Marian gave her just the chance she needed, by saying that she and Helen had been alone together all the previous evening.

"Where was Carter?" she asked.

"He had to go out and see some one on business. He did not get back till we were just going to bed."

"Sitting up late as usual, I suppose?"

"It was about twelve o'clock—certainly not later. And you know I can't sleep if I go to bed early."

"I didn't know Carter did business in the evenings. He always used to boast of keeping his evenings clear for enjoying himself."

"Yes, and he had promised Helen to be in. But he said it was a very particular engagement. At some Club or other, I believe. He was seeing Sir John Bunnery about some legal business. When he came in he was dead tired, and went straight to bed."

"Marian, do you like Carter?" Joan asked suddenly. "It seems funny I never asked you that before. I hate him."

"My dear, you mustn't say that. Of course I like him. I don't mean I care for Carter like some other people; but of course I like him. Helen is a darling."

"That means you don't like him at all—only you're too nice to say so."

"I do like him, Joan. At least, I mean I don't dislike him."

"He seems to leave Helen alone a great deal."

"Far too much, and he's often out until all hours."

"He even went out again after the dinner here last Tuesday, didn't he?"

"No, he didn't that night. He went away to his room and wrote letters. But he didn't go out again. I stayed with Helen till he came up to bed—rather before twelve. But don't talk about that horrible night."

"I'm sorry, dear. I won't again."

And then they talked of other things, until Marian went in to sit a while with Sir Vernon. The doctor, who had been with him, saw Joan on his way out. Sir Vernon, he reported, was not yet out of immediate danger; but he was rallying wonderfully from the shock which he had sustained.

Chapter XXVIII
The Superintendent's Theory

When Inspector Blaikie reported to Superintendent Wilson the results of his conversation with Carter Woodman, he had formed no definite theory. He explained without comment the precise terms of the will, stating that, if Walter Brooklyn had been removed, Carter Woodman, as next of kin, would have became the principal beneficiary. He was not prepared for the conclusion which his superior immediately drew on hearing that this was the case.

"Then Carter Woodman is the murderer," said the superintendent, with an air of finality. "If we had known these facts before, it would have saved a world of trouble."

"But," said Inspector Blaikie, "Carter Woodman appears to have a perfect alibi. He was in the Cunningham Hotel at the time when the murders were committed—at least that seemed to be an undoubted fact when we investigated his movements."

"My dear inspector, it does not follow that, because Walter Brooklyn's alibi proved to be sound, all alibis are therefore equally sound. I do not need to remind you that alibis can be faked."

"Quite so, sir; but aren't you rather hasty in leaping to the conclusion that Woodman is guilty? We have really nothing against him, except a suggestion of motive. As matters stand now, he has gained absolutely nothing by the murders.”

“Perhaps not, though it is not safe to be too sure on that point. We may not know all the circumstances. But, if you are right, don’t you see that the very fact that, as matters stand now, he has gained nothing, is a very strong reason for suspecting him?”

The inspector failed to follow this reasoning. “Why do you say that?” he asked. “I can’t see it at all.”

“Well, it is clear that the murderer, whoever he was, did his level best to get Walter Brooklyn hanged. Who stood to gain by getting Walter Brooklyn out of the way?”

“I see. Carter Woodman. Yes, I follow now.”

“That is one strong point against him. Here is another. Do you remember where Walter Brooklyn thought he had left his stick on Tuesday afternoon? He went back to look for it, you remember.”

The inspector thought for a moment. “In Carter Woodman’s office,” he said at last.

“Well, then, isn’t it clear that he did leave his stick in Woodman’s office? Woodman found it, but denied the fact when Walter called to fetch it, and told him he must have left it in the taxi. Then Woodman deliberately planted the stick on the scene of Prinsep’s murder.”

“That’s pure hypothesis. I don’t say it isn’t true; but——”

“It’s more than hypothesis: it is divination. Surely you see that it must be what happened.”

“I expect, as usual, you are right,” said the inspector. “But will it convince a jury? I have tried all I know to get any evidence showing when the stick was left; but not a trace can I find. A jury will regard it as a pure hypothesis.”

The superintendent sighed. Juries are sadly lacking in appreciation of the subtleties of reasoning. “You’re quite right there,” he said. “My divination won’t hang Carter Woodman.

But it convinces you as it convinced me. We have to get faith in our own knowledge before we can make a case that will persuade others. You and I now have that faith. We know that Carter Woodman is guilty.”

“But even you can’t prove it.”

“Not yet; but it will be proved. And now I come to a third point. You remember that written message that was found in the garden near George Brooklyn’s body—the scrap of paper you picked up. It was in Prinsep’s writing.”

“Yes, I remember.”

“Have you thought any more about that scrap of paper, or have you just assumed that it was a request by Prinsep that George Brooklyn should meet him in the garden?”

“There didn’t seem to be much to be gleaned from it.”

“There I think you are wrong. I want to know exactly when that piece of paper was found, and by whom.”

“We found it in the garden that morning, when we were looking for clues after finding George Brooklyn’s body.”

“Who actually found it?”

“I suppose I did. No, I remember now, it was Carter Woodman who directed my attention to it. It was lying in a corner of the summer-house—the place they call ‘the temple.’ ”

“My dear inspector,” said the superintendent excitedly, “do you realise the significance of what you have just said. Woodman took good care that you should discover that piece of paper, because he had put it there for you to find.” The superintendent said these last words slowly, and with very great emphasis.

The inspector scratched his head thoughtfully. “I believe you are right,” he said. “It was after we had finished our first search that Woodman drew my attention to the scrap of paper.”

“He was afraid you would fail to notice it.”

"I can see that you are right, sir; but there again you have a thing which will not convince a jury for a moment. Your reasoning will seem to them fantastic. I only know you are right because you always are right when you make a long guess like that."

"But need it be only a guess? Look here." And Superintendent Wilson pushed the scrap of paper across to his subordinate. "Take a good look. Do you see anything curious about it?"

"It's written oddly near the edge of the paper."

"Yes, that is the point. The writing is right up at the top of the paper, and immediately above the writing is a torn edge. The paper, as we said before, is a sheet torn from the memorandum block found in Prinsep's room; but it is not a complete sheet. About an inch has been neatly torn off the top of the sheet. Is that a natural thing for Prinsep to have done, and does the writing look natural as it stands now on the sheet?"

The inspector looked again at the note. "No, it certainly does not," he said.

"Doesn't that suggest anything to you?"

"Do you mean that this is only part of the message?"

"That's exactly what I do mean. The message now says only, 'Meet me in the garden.—J.P.' Probably what it said originally was, 'Dear So and So—whatever the name may have been, and I don't believe it was 'George'—meet me in the garden.—J.P.' There may have been a date, too, at the top of the note."

"You mean that this note, though it was written by Prinsep, was not written with reference to the particular occasion we are concerned with."

"Precisely. Now, I suppose there is no hope of our finding the missing part of that memorandum slip; but I am convinced that is what happened."

The inspector made a sudden exclamation. "Good Lord! what a fool I have been," he said.

"How do you mean?" said the superintendent sharply.

"Why, I actually found what must have been the missing part of the slip when I was searching Prinsep's room. I thought nothing of it at the time."

"You have it now?"

The inspector shook his head ruefully. "No," he said, "it has gone west. When I searched the room, I naturally looked in the grate. There had been a fire, and on the hearth was a half-burnt scrap of paper."

"What was on it?"

"Nothing but the name of a day at the head—Monday, it was—and one word. The rest was burnt. It had evidently fallen out of the grate."

"The word was?"

"'Man.' Just 'man,' nothing else."

The superintendent gave an excited laugh. "Now I know what the note contained," he said. "'Monday, Dear Woodman, Meet me in the garden.—J.P.' How does that strike you? The note was from Prinsep to Woodman; but it was written on the day before the murders. Lord, what a pity you didn't keep the fragment. My dear inspector, never destroy anything. That is the only safe course for a man like you."

"I did show it to the sergeant, sir," said the inspector, considerably crestfallen at his superior's tone.

"Come, that's a bit better. The judge will probably accept your combined testimonies. It's a great pity, though, you didn't realise the importance of that scrap of charred paper. However, for our own purposes at least I think we can take it as proved that Woodman deliberately prepared and planted that note on the scene of the crime, believing that the other piece was safely burnt in the fire in Prinsep's room. Our case against

Woodman is mounting up. Come, inspector, you must follow up these new clues at once."

"Don't forget Woodman's alibi. That still holds unless we can shake it."

"It must be your next business to shake it. We now know that Woodman did leave the Cunningham Hotel that evening. It is your job to discover how he left it and how he got into Liskeard House. Make these the next points, inspector."

"I'll do my best, sir."

"And there is one other matter I should tell you about, though, in the light of our discoveries, it is now probably of quite minor importance, I think. Still, we must not be too cocksure, or neglect any fact that may possibly bear on the case. If we are right about Woodman, then he planned the whole affair very carefully; but he took a big risk all the same."

"Having you to reckon with, yes."

"Well, I doubt if a man would take a risk of that magnitude without some very urgent reason—such as grave and immediate financial embarrassment. I want you to look into Woodman's record, make inquiries about him in the city, and see if he appears to be in Queer Street, or anything of that sort."

"It wouldn't prove anything if he were."

"No; but it would greatly strengthen our case on the question of motive. It's worth looking into, at all events. And now, inspector, I won't keep you. There's work to do; and you had best be getting about it. And I want to do some more thinking in this case. It gets interesting."

Chapter XXIX
The Lie of the Land

When Joan and Ellery determined upon their course of action, Ellery's immediate part was to make a thorough investigation of Carter Woodman's movements. Apparently he had a perfect alibi—as good as Ellery's own—absolving him of all part in the events of the fatal Tuesday night. Indeed, in the eyes of the law he had scarcely needed an alibi, for nothing had occurred to throw any real suspicion upon him. Ellery suspected him nevertheless almost to certainty; but he admitted to himself that even now his suspicion was based on what others would regard as no more than a guess. Tuesday, therefore, seemed the best starting-point; for if Woodman's alibi for that occasion held good, that would finish the matter, and prove that the whole edifice of suppositions which Ellery had built up was founded on nothing.

It was easy enough for Ellery to walk into the Cunningham Hotel, where he was already known, under pretext of a visit to Marian Brooklyn. But, having made his entry, he did not proceed to the suite of rooms which she shared with the Woodmans. His object was to explore the hotel in order to discover whether there was in fact, as the porter and the manager had stated to Inspector Blaikie, only one possible exit. The porter, who had been at the door from ten o'clock onwards through the night had been quite certain that Woodman had not gone out that way. He had come in with his wife and Mrs. Brooklyn at about a quarter past ten, and he had not returned to the entrance hall until about a quarter to twelve, when he had given the porter his late letters for the post, and had gone straight upstairs again. That seemed clear enough; for the porter was very positive that Woodman had not gone out at any time during the evening.

There was, the manager had told the police, another exit, of course, for the hotel servants. But the only way to this from the club quarters lay through the great kitchen, and it would be quite impossible for a guest to leave by this way without being observed. Ellery had chosen eleven o'clock at night for his visit to the hotel, and meeting the manager, whom he knew, he asked to be shown into the kitchens. The management was excessively proud of these, and made a regular show of them to its guests. The manager readily agreed to take him round, and even a cursory inspection was enough to show Ellery that, even at that hour in the evening, no guest could possibly have left by the servant's exit without being seen by at least half a dozen persons. The preparation of theatre suppers was in full swing, and the kitchens were alive with chefs and waiters at least until midnight.

Leaving the manager, as if he were going up to the Woodmans' apartment, Ellery resumed his prowl. On the ground floor he speedily discovered there was no possible means of exit except the main door. There remained the basement, occupied mainly by a vast grill room which was closed at ten o'clock. Ellery descended the stairs, and pushed open the grill room door communicating with the hotel. The place was in darkness and, without turning on the light, he made a tour of the huge room. At the far end were cloak rooms and another flight of stairs communicating with the street. So far it would be fully possible for a guest to make his way without attracting attention. Ellery went up the far stairs, and approached the door leading from the grill room to the street. It was heavily barred and bolted, as well as locked. But the key was in the lock, and there seemed to be nothing to prevent the bolts from being withdrawn from the inside. As quietly as he could Ellery took down the bars, slid back the bolts, and unlocked the door. He stood, not in the street, but in a small outer hall with another locked door in front of him. This door also could be undone from the inside, and, opening it cautiously, Ellery found himself looking out into St. John's Street. He had established the fact that it was possible at night for a guest to leave the Cunningham Hotel unobserved. Quietly he re-locked the doors and slid back the well-oiled bolts and bars, surprised for the second time to find how little noise his operations made.

Woodman, then, could have both left and returned to the hotel without being seen. But had he? The very lack of possible observers seemed to make it impossible to prove the case either for or against him. If no one had seen Ellery make his investigations—and as he returned to the ground floor he was certain that no one had noticed him, at least until he reached the top of the basement stairs—why should any one have seen Carter Woodman when he had followed the same route? The effect of Ellery's investigations was to make Woodman's alibi insecure. But it afforded absolutely no positive evidence of his guilt.

Still, it was something to have shown that the alibi was not conclusive, and Ellery was fairly well pleased with the result of his visit. But he had not yet done. According to Woodman's story, he had written his letters in a small and little used writing-room on the first floor, at the opposite end of the hotel from his own rooms, but quite near the basement stairs, to which another small flight of stairs led directly from the first floor almost from the writing-room door. Ellery went into the writing-room and found it deserted. He remembered that Woodman had stated that he had had it to himself throughout the time he had spent there.

Ellery had no definite idea that the writing-room would yield a clue, but he thought that he might as well have a look round. He glanced at the blotting pads which lay on each table, only to see that the blotting paper was evidently changed very frequently. But, picking up one of the blotters he discovered that, while the top sheet was practically clean, the old used sheets of blotting paper had been left underneath. Rapidly he examined every sheet. On several he saw marks of Carter Woodman's writing, and of his large bold signature. This, however, showed only that Woodman often used the room. So far it bore out his story. The pads bore impressions of several other handwritings; but only one other recurred frequently. Ellery was able to make out the signature by holding the paper up to the light. The writing was curious and quite unmistakable. The name of the writer was Ba Pu—evidently an Oriental.

Ellery had an idea. It was a chance and no more; but he made up his mind to see Ba Pu, if he was still in the hotel, and to put a few questions. Returning to the hall he asked the porter the number of his room.

"Oh, you mean the Burmese gentleman," said the porter. "He has a suite on the first floor. His sitting-room is No. 17. He came in only a few minutes ago."

Ellery made his way to No. 17 and knocked. The Burmese—a small, dark-skinned man with curious twinkling little eyes and quick movements—was in his room and received him with ready courtesy. Ellery presented his card and apologised for intruding upon him.

"Oh, no," said the Burmese. "You not intrude. Very please."

"You may think it very strange of me," said Ellery, "but may I ask you a question without explaining fully why I ask it? It is on a matter of real importance."

"Ask. Yes," said the Burmese. "I help if I can." He spoke English quickly and jerkily, but he evidently understood the language well. "I very glad meet you, Mr. Ellery. I Burmese, come here study the British conditions. Go back Burma tell my people all about this country. You help me. I help you."

"Then that is a bargain, and I can ask you my question at once. Did you use the writing-room opposite here at any time on the evening of Tuesday, the 17th of this month?"

"Why, that the very day I come here. Yes, I use him that night. I came here study your conditions. I want meet all your famous men. I go there write letters ask them meet me. I write your Mr. Bernard Shaw, your Mr. Wells, your Mr. Arnold Bennett."

Ellery interrupted. "Can you tell me at what time that evening you were in the writing-room?"

"Yes, I tell you. I come here to stay. Evening I wish write letters. I wish at once to meet your famous men. I go to writing-room door. I peep in. I see gentleman there, writing. He not notice me; but I shy. I steal away."

"What time was that?"

"Eleven by the clock—no earlier. It was what you call eleven less a quarter."

"I see, about 10.45."

"Yes. I go back to my room and I wait. I leave door open and soon I see gentleman come out of writing-room and go downstairs. Then I go in. I write my letters."

"Do you know when that was?"

"I go back to writing-room a few minutes after I go back to my room. About eleven of the clock—it was then."

"And how long did you stay there?"

"I stay there long time—what you call the three-quarters of hour, perhaps."

"And then you came back to your room?"

"Yes. I come back here."

"You did not see the gentleman who was in the writing-room again."

"Yes, I see him. He come upstairs there, outside my door, just after I get back to my room."

"You left the door open then."

"Yes. There was no air. It is what you call stuffy here. I see him go into writing-room."

"And that was the last you saw of him?"

"Yes. But he stay in hotel. I see him later—days later—often times."

"Then you would recognise him if you saw him. Is this he?" and Ellery passed a photograph of Carter Woodman to the Burmese.

"Yes, that he." And then the Burmese smiled blandly and added, "And now you tell me why you wish know this."

"I would rather not tell you just yet, Mr. Pu, if you will forgive me. All I can say is that what you have told me affects a man's life."

"You not want to tell me, you not tell me. But you help me get interview with Mr. Bernard Shaw. I help you. You help me. See?"

Ellery promised his good offices—for what they were worth.

"And Mr. H. G. Wells?"

Ellery again promised with rather more hesitation, to do what he could.

"And Mr. Bennett?"

This time Ellery, foreseeing further additions to the list, suggested that he should come back and have another talk with Mr. Pu in a day or two. He would certainly do anything possible to help him.

"And Mr. Bertrand Russell?" the Burmese was saying, as

Ellery managed to talk himself out of the room.

Here at last, Ellery said to himself, as he left the hotel, was proof, proof positive, even all but certainty. Woodman had lied about his doings on Tuesday evening, and his alibi was a fake. At the time when he had said that he was writing letters in the small writing-room he was really somewhere else. He had left the writing-room at a few minutes before eleven, and he had only returned to it, by the stairs which led directly to the basement, about three-quarters of an hour later. The inference was obvious—to Ellery at least. But his new certainty that Woodman was the criminal was still of course very far from complete demonstration. A man might lie about his movements, and still not be a murderer. What should the next step be? He would see Joan, and convince her now that his suspicions had been rightly directed. She could hardly still doubt.

Chapter XXX
A Letter and Its Consequences

One of Joan's duties, during these troublous days, was to deal with Sir Vernon's private letters. The management of the Brooklyn Corporation had passed, for the time being, into the hands of a subordinate; but there were many private letters to be read and answered. Ill as he was, Sir Vernon liked to be consulted about some of these; and Joan always set aside a few to discuss with him each morning. On the day following Ellery's successful investigation at the Cunningham Hotel, Joan sat opening the letters at breakfast. Most of them contained little of interest; but there was one, marked Private, which was clearly of importance. As Joan read it, she felt that yet another of the clues leading to the discovery of the murderer had come unexpectedly into her hands.

The letter was from Sir John Bunnery, the successful solicitor, well-known in the sporting world as "the bookmaker's attorney," a nickname which he had earned by his long association with legal cases connected with the Turf. Sir John had been a friend of Sir Vernon's in earlier years; but the two men had quarrelled many years ago, and since then they had seen nothing of each other. Carter Woodman, however, was, as Joan knew, a friend of Sir John's, and she was not surprised when, glancing down the letter, she read his name.

Sir John Bunnery began by offering his sympathy to an old friend in the misfortunes which had come upon him, adding that he hoped their drifting apart of late years would not make the sympathy less welcome. Then, having said the proper thing, he came to business. On the previous day, he explained, a somewhat curious request had come to him from Mr. Carter Woodman, who had asked for his help in securing a large loan, stating that there could be no doubt about the repayment of the money, as full security could be given that far more than the sum asked for would be available under the will of Sir Vernon Brooklyn. He, Carter Woodman, was one of the beneficiaries under the will, and he was also in a position to offer, in return for the loan, the joint guarantee of Mr. Walter Brooklyn, who had now, in tragic circumstances, become the principal beneficiary under the will. Woodman stated that he was Walter Brooklyn's heir, and that he and Walter were prepared to make themselves jointly liable for the repayment of the sum asked for. Sir John said that he would, of course, be most pleased to assist Mr. Woodman, who was a personal friend; but although Woodman had approached him in confidence, and asked him not to mention the matter even to Sir Vernon, he had felt it necessary to write equally in confidence to Sir Vernon in order to ascertain whether Woodman and Walter Brooklyn were in fact the heirs. Sir Vernon would understand that he was asking for this information only in strict confidence, and he—Sir John—would quite accept the position if the answer was that Sir Vernon did not feel able to tell him how matters stood. In that case, however, he would feel compelled to decline to arrange the very large advance—£60,000—for which Woodman had asked. A hint would be enough to tell him how he ought to act. Sir John ended with a repetition of his condolences, and expressed the hope, that, when Sir Vernon was well enough, their old friendship might be renewed.

Joan read the letter right through with a feeling of bewilderment. What could it all mean? Were her stepfather and Carter Woodman really acting in collusion in an attempt to raise money in anticipation of Sir Vernon's death? And, if they were, what light did their extraordinary proceeding throw on the murders?

The letter gave Joan a good deal to think about. The information which Woodman had given to Sir John Bunnery might, of course, be technically correct. She realised that, under the existing will, Walter Brooklyn was, now that the two persons who had stood in his way had been removed, the principal beneficiary. But he had become so entirely by an accident, which was certainly no part of the testator's intention, and his chance of remaining so depended entirely on Sir Vernon's not making a new will in some one else's favour. Woodman, of course, might have a good reason for thinking that he would not do that, even if he were able; but Joan doubted this, and was more inclined to believe that he was relying on Sir Vernon's speedy death without making a new will. Walter had, in any case, only become the heir after the murders. That was but a few days ago; and he and Woodman had, Joan reflected, certainly been quite extraordinarily prompt in trying to take advantage of the new position. Either they must be in some terrible financial difficulty, or they must fear the making of a new will, and hope to raise the money before this could come about.

What surprised Joan far more were the statements that Walter had made Carter Woodman his heir. She knew well that Walter had no love for Woodman; and she at once realised that he could only have taken such a step in return for a pecuniary consideration. There was obviously, in Woodman's application to Sir John Bunnery, evidence of a very unpleasant bargain. The whole letter made Joan very angry indeed.

In any case the receipt of the letter could not but considerably strengthen Joan's suspicions of Carter Woodman. "Of course," she said to herself, "he hoped to raise this money without our hearing anything about it." And she could not help feeling that it looked very much as if he had deliberately planned the whole thing in order to lay hands on the money.

But, apart from the effect of the letter upon Joan, what was likely to be its effect on Sir Vernon? She felt that she must show it to him; and she did not conceal from herself that she positively wanted him to see it. For she hardly concealed from herself now her desire, her hope for Ellery's sake, that Sir Vernon would alter his will. The effect of Sir John Bunnery's letter, she thought, would certainly be to make him very angry with both Walter Brooklyn and Carter Woodman; and she felt sure that, ill as he was, Sir Vernon, under the circumstances, would lose no time in making a new will. Woodman, indeed, had, she felt, effectively destroyed his chances of getting the money for the sake of which, if her suspicions were correct, he had probably done two men to death. Sir John Bunnery's breach of confidence had hoisted the engineer with his own petard.

Taking this letter and one or two others from the heap which lay before her, Joan went up to Sir Vernon's room. She read him the others first, and received his instructions, or rather his permission to deal with them as she thought best. Then, without any previous comment, she read him Sir John Bunnery's letter, watching his face as she read.

The effect of the news upon him was exactly what she had expected. He was very angry, and while she was reading he interjected indignant comments. He was effectively roused; and, as soon as she had finished reading, he bade her write at once to Sir John Bunnery, not answering his question directly, but strongly advising him not to lend the money. "Write at once," he said, "and I will sign it myself. The answer must be sent immediately."

Joan needed no second invitation. She sat down at once, and having written the answer, read it through to Sir Vernon, who signed it. She then gave it to one of the servants, with instructions that it should be posted immediately. When she came back into the room, Sir Vernon was sitting up in bed. He had a pencil in his hand, and was trying to write on the fly-leaf of a book he had taken from the table beside his bed. As Joan came to him, he sank back, exhausted by the effort.

"Come here, my dear," he said. "I shan't rest now till I've made a new will, and I want you to write it for me. It can be put into proper legal form later, if there is time."

"Shall I send for Carter Woodman?" said Joan.

"No, my dear. No more Carter Woodman for me just now. I shall have to find a new lawyer. But never mind that now. You write what I tell you."

Then, slowly and painfully, the old man dictated a new will. "I have to make it simple," he said. The new will left Joan the whole of his fortune, with the request that she should pay to all persons mentioned in the previous will, and still living, the sums there left to them, except that no sum should be paid to Carter Woodman. A further clause appointed Joan and Henry Lucas joint executors, and a third, an after-thought, provided for the payment of a small annuity to Helen Woodman. "There is no need for her to suffer for what he has done," said Sir Vernon.

Two of the servants were then called in to witness the will, and Joan, at Sir Vernon's command, took it downstairs and had it placed at once in the office safe of the Brooklyn Corporation.

"I am easier now in my mind," said the old man, as Joan returned from her errand. "You will have to carry on the Brooklyn tradition now, Joan," he added. Joan took his hand, and sat by him, and, in a few minutes he fell asleep. Joan sat by his side for a while. Then she quietly disengaged her hand, and left him sleeping. He was tired out; but she believed the exertion had done him good.

In the lounge Joan found Ellery, in a high state of excitement. "News, darling," he said. "I have news for you, and it shows that I was right."

"I have some news for you, too, my boy. It's a most extraordinary thing that has happened. I'm not so sure as I was that you were wrong."

"I think my news makes it simply certain I was right."

"Bob, Sir Vernon has made a new will, cutting out Carter."

"My dear, you don't mean to say he suspects?"

"No, of course he doesn't; but this morning we found out that Carter and my stepfather are trying—the two of them—to raise money on the strength of the will."

"Good Lord, how did you find out that?"

"A letter came to Sir Vernon from Sir John Bunnery, saying Woodman had approached him in confidence for a loan of sixty thousand pounds, on the joint security of his and my stepfather's expectations. He said my stepfather had made him his heir."

"Made whom?"

"Why, Carter. So that he stood to get the money any way."

Ellery whistled. "My word, the plot thickens. And now let me tell you my news."

And so the two lovers exchanged their information. Joan, in her anger against Carter Woodman, was now a good deal easier to convince. She admitted at once the force of Ellery's evidence. If Woodman had lied, it was not likely that he had lied for nothing. Her anger for the time prevented her from realising the full horror of the position; but presently it came home to her. "Oh, poor Helen," she said, "what are we to do? It will break her heart."

"My dear we must clear this thing up now. We can't leave it where it stands. You see that."

Joan pulled herself together. "Yes, I suppose we have to go through with it."

"And find positive proof."

"I suppose we must go on."

"We can't prove it yet, you see," said Ellery. "But we've made a really good beginning on the job of bringing last Tuesday's business home to Woodman, and we mustn't lose any time in following up that trail to the end."

"But how do you propose to follow it up? Haven't you done all you can there?"

"No. Don't you see? We must prove that the man the servants took for George that night when he went out of this house was really Carter Woodman."

"That all sounds very well; but I don't see how you're going to do it."

"Neither do I; but I mean to have a shot."

"My dear Bob, let me try. It's my turn to do something. I have an idea, and I may be able to find out about it."

"You're very mysterious. Won't you tell me what the idea is?"

"No, Bob. It may come to nothing; and I'd rather try it myself first. It won't take long to find out. You've done all the clever things so far; and I think it's my turn for a change."

"Right you are, Joan. I only hope it's a good 'un."

"I hope it is; but it's only a chance. You come back here to-night and I'll tell you. Besides, I want an excuse for seeing you again."

"Darling," said Ellery, and their conversation for the next few minutes can be left to the experienced imagination of the reader.

Chapter XXXI
A Button in a Bag

As soon as Ellery had gone, Joan put on her things and walked across to the Cunningham Hotel, where she went straight upstairs to the rooms occupied by Carter Woodman and his wife. As she expected, there was no one at home. Woodman was at his office, and Marian Brooklyn and Mrs. Woodman were, she knew, away for the day. Joan locked the two doors opening on the corridor, and had the suite safely to herself.

It would have been awkward if any one had interrupted her, for what she did was to make a thorough search of the rooms, looking particularly at all the articles of male clothing and going very carefully through Carter Woodman's own belongings. Her search was entirely unsuccessful, and, having replaced everything neatly so that no one would notice that it had been disturbed, she unlocked the doors and gave it up as a bad job.

"So much for that little idea," she said to herself. "I could never really have hoped to find it there."

But was that the end of her idea? As Joan finished her tidying up she began to hope that it was not. Carter Woodman had not been foolish enough to leave what she was looking for in his own rooms; but he must, she said to herself, have left it somewhere. Where then would he have left it? Where would she, if she wanted to get safely rid of a rather bulky object, so as never to hear of it again, be likely to leave it?

A station cloak-room at once occurred to her as a likely place; but the prospect of searching all the cloak-rooms of London was not alluring. Moreover, there were a dozen other places in which he might have disposed of a compromising object with almost equal safety. At the bottom of the river—a stone was all that was needed. In a pawnshop—of course after removing all marks that would serve to identify the article. In a cab, or any of a hundred other places, merely by leaving them behind. The cabman would hardly ask questions, if he found something of obvious value. To hunt for what Woodman had hidden seemed far more hopeless, far worse than looking for a needle in a haystack. It would need an army of men to do the searching. The police might be able to do that sort of thing. She and Ellery certainly could not.

Yet, if their theory was right, Woodman had almost certainly returned to the hotel after murdering George and Prinsep, bearing with him at least one very comprising piece of property. He could hardly have got rid of it—or them— safely the same evening. Most likely he would have done them up in a bag or parcel and gone out to dispose of them the next morning, on his way to his office. A bag was the more likely, for, as Woodman habitually carried one, it would attract less notice than a parcel. Assume that he had gone out with the things in a bag. Had he taken them to his office, or had he got rid of them on the way? Either might be the case, and it would not be easy to follow up the clue.

Then Joan had a sudden thought; swiftly she got up and again locked the doors. Among the things she had searched there had been a large hand-bag. She had looked into it, and found it empty. As the objects she was seeking were bulky she had not studied it very carefully; but it was Just possible that it might repay further inspection.

But, before Joan could make her search she heard steps coming along the corridor. Hastily she unlocked the sitting-room door and hurried into the bedroom. Hardly had she done so when she saw Carter Woodman come into the room. Fortunately, the bedroom communicated directly with the corridor; and Joan, without pausing to make any further examination or to watch Woodman's movements, let herself out noiselessly into the corridor and sped down the stairs unobserved. A narrow shave, and all, it seemed, for nothing.

Then Woodman's presence in the hotel gave Joan another idea. If he was there, he was not at his office. Why should she not complete the task she had set herself by having a look round there as well? She took a taxi, and, in less than a quarter of an hour, she was in Woodman's outer office, and in talk with his confidential clerk. She was told that Woodman was not in, and would not be back until after lunch. She told Moorman that she could not wait, but that she would like to go into the inner office and write a note. Moorman at once showed her in, and withdrew to the outer room.

Joan saw that whatever she did she would have to do quickly. First, she scribbled a hasty note stating that she had come to see Woodman to inquire about her stepfather's affairs. As he was out, however, her business would keep. Having done this, she cast her eyes quickly round the room. In one corner was a hat and coat cupboard, and in it was hanging a coat of Woodman's. Very quickly she went through the pockets. The only papers were a number of restaurant bills, evidently stuffed in hastily and forgotten. Joan confiscated them, without much hope that they would be of use. Then, in the bottom of the cupboard, she noticed a hand-bag, twin brother of the one she had been on the point of examining at the hotel. Hastily she opened it. Apparently it was empty; but, feeling round the corners, Joan found a hard object—a coat button—which she quickly transferred to her purse. Then, putting back the bag and closing the cupboard, she returned to the outer room. A talk with the clerk might have its uses.

"Mr. Woodman has been looking rather ill just lately," Joan began. "Do you think he is really unwell?"

"I must say, miss, he's not well. Between you and me, miss, he's been badly worried."

"About these terrible murders, you mean?"

"About them, miss, and about other things. Mr. Woodman wouldn't like my saying so, but he has had terrible worries."

"Oh, dear, I hope nothing serious."

"Oh, probably not, miss, and you mustn't say a word about it to any one. I ought not to have said what I did say. But I'm worried too. You'll be sure not to mention it, miss, won't you?"

"All right, Moorman, don't you worry."

"But, miss, Mr. Woodman is such a short-tempered gentleman. And you don't know how angry he'd be if he knew what I have been saying to you."

"You'll have to look after him, Moorman. See that he doesn't worry too much. By the way, I suppose I couldn't catch him now at lunch. Where does he usually lunch?"

"Generally at the Blue Boar up Holborn, miss. He generally goes to the Blue Boar every day when he's in this part."

"If I try there, and don't find him, where else could I try? Does he ever go to any other restaurant?"

"I don't quite know where he'd be, miss. One day last week he went to the Avenue by Hatton Garden. But I don't think he's been there since. He's never been there but the once to my knowledge."

"When was that, Moorman?"

"As it happens, miss, I can tell you. It was the day we heard of those terrible murders. Last Wednesday, miss."

"Thank you, Moorman. I'll see if he's at either of those

places. If not, I may come back."

But Joan did not go to either of the places of which Moorman had told her. Instead, she went to the nearest telephone box, and 'phoned to Ellery, who was lunching at his club, to come at once and meet her outside Chancery Lane Station. Meanwhile, she went into an A. B. C. and ordered a cup of coffee. As she waited she took out the coat-button and had a good look at it.

She was not in much doubt. The button was of a quite peculiar kind—a bright brass button identical with those which George Brooklyn always wore on his summer evening coat. Here was luck indeed. According to her theory Carter Woodman had been mistaken for George Brooklyn because he had deliberately come out of Liskeard House wearing George's coat and opera hat. George was very particular with his dress, and the coat was quite unmistakable. With these, if not in them, he must have returned to the Cunningham Hotel, where he would have stowed them away somewhere safely for the night. But the next morning his first object would be to get rid of their incriminating presence. She had guessed that he would pack them away in the bag which he usually carried, and so leave for the office bearing them away without any risk of arousing suspicion. Then her first thought had been that he would leave them in some railway cloak-room, or drop them quietly into the river. But this would involve the risk that the bag might turn up, and be identified as his. What would be the safest way of disposing of the hat and coat without leaving the bag, or running any risk of identification? She thought she had guessed at least one way in which it might have been done, and it was to follow this up that she wanted Ellery's help. She had now proved definitely to her own satisfaction that the coat had been in Woodman's bag; but she was not sure whether the police would be willing to accept the evidence of a solitary coat-button.

They must find the coat, unless it had been put beyond reach of recovery. When Ellery arrived Joan told him that they were going to lunch together at the Avenue Restaurant opposite Hatton Garden. In a few words she told him what he was to do.

At the Avenue Joan remained at the table they had chosen, while Ellery went to the gentlemen's cloak room. There was no attendant in the room at the time, and Ellery made a quick survey of the two or three dozen hats and coats which were hanging there. What he was looking for was at any rate not among them. In a few minutes the attendant came in, and Ellery entered into talk.

"Do you get many hats and coats left behind here?" he asked.

"Not many, sir. Sometimes a gentleman leaves a coat or an umbrella; but he generally comes back for it. Gentlemen sometimes leave things when they're a bit on, sir, if I may put it so without taking a liberty. But not often, sir. Most of the customers here are very regular gents. When things is left we keep them here for a week or two and then we send them to the Lost Property Office. Have you lost something, sir?"

"No, but a friend of mine thinks he left a coat and opera hat here a week or so ago. Have you found anything of the sort?"

"Yes, I have," said the porter. "And what's more, I'm damned, sir—begging your pardon, sir, if I could make it out at all. Gentlemen don't usually walk about in opera hats at lunch time, or go away leaving their hats behind. But this lot was left at lunch-time. I know that, sir, because it weren't here in the morning, and I noticed it after lunch."

"Perhaps it had my friend's name in it."

"No, sir, that it hadn't. I searched that coat, and not a name nor a scrap of paper was there on it. A pair of gloves and a few coppers was all it had in it."

"Wasn't there a name in the hat either?"

"No, there wasn't, or we would probably have found the owner by now."

"Well," said Ellery. "I'm going to take you into my confidence. I believe that coat and hat did belong to my friend, and I want you to let me have a look at them. The matter is more important than it sounds, for if it is the coat I think it may be the clue to the discovery of a murderer."

"Lord, sir, you don't say so." The attendant's face brightened, and a new sense of importance came into his manner. "Lord, a real murderer." He rubbed his hands. Then he said, remembering that he had no idea who Ellery might be. "In that case, sir, oughtn't we to send for the police?"

"All in good time," said Ellery; "but before we do that you must let me see the coat and hat and find out if I am right. It wouldn't do to bring the police here on a wild goose chase. I don't want to take them away; but you must keep them safe and not give them up to any one until the police come."

The porter thereupon brought out the coat and hat. The coat was undoubtedly George Brooklyn's, or own fellow to his, and to make the proof complete there was a button missing, and the remaining buttons were the same as that which Joan had found in the handbag in Carter Woodman's office. Ellery turned to examine the hat. There was no name in it, but in the crown there was evidence no less valuable. At some time the adhesive gold initials which hatters use had been fastened inside. These had been removed, or fallen out; but their removal had left the spaces which they had covered cleaner than the rest of the white silk lining. The initials "G.B." stood out, not as plainly as if the gold letters had remained, but quite unmistakably when the lining was carefully examined. There could be no doubt that Joan's sagacity had resulted in bringing to light George Brooklyn's hat and coat, or that they had been left in a place which Woodman had visited on the day following the murder. Their theory that Woodman had masqueraded as George Brooklyn was confirmed, and the new evidence served to connect him, more closely than any previous discovery, with the murders at Liskeard House.

Ellery drew Woodman's photograph from his pocket. "Have you ever seen this gentleman?" he asked. But the porter did not remember. He might have, or he might not. So many gentlemen came to the Avenue, and he was not continuously in the cloak room. The lady at the cash desk would be more likely to remember. She was a rare one for faces.

Cautioning the man to take the greatest care of the hat and coat until the police came, Ellery rejoined Joan in the restaurant upstairs and told her of his success. They determined to see the manager, and take further precautions against the disappearance of George Brooklyn's clothes. Joan had selected a table in an alcove, at which it was possible to talk quietly without being overheard, and, through the head waiter, Ellery got the manager to come and join them there. They told him, in confidence, the greater part of the story, names and all, except that they did not give Carter Woodman's name. The manager promised that the coat and hat should be kept safely, and given up only to the police. He then sent for the cashier, to whom Woodman's photograph was shown; but she did not remember his face, and was inclined to be positive that he had not really lunched there on that day. The waiters were then called in turn and shown the photograph; but none of them remembered having seen Woodman. The manager seemed to regard this as conclusive evidence that he had not lunched in the restaurant.

"Of course," said Ellery, "he may have lunched here and not been noticed. But I'm inclined to believe he didn't lunch here at all. There was nothing to stop him from walking straight into the cloak room, and then going right away as if he had lunched without coming into the restaurant at all. I wonder how Moorman knew he lunched here that day?"

"We can't ask him that without putting him on his guard," said Joan. "But what we have is good enough. And we can make Moorman speak out later, if it becomes necessary."

The manager had by this time left them, and they were discussing the situation alone. Suddenly Ellery broke in on something that Joan was saying.

"By Jove," he said, "I've just remembered. What a fool I am not to have thought of it before."

"What is it this time?"

"Why, you remember those finger-prints of Prinsep's that were on the club George was killed with. I know how they got there. When we were in the garden before dinner I saw Prinsep take down that club from the statue, and swing it about. He was showing it to—whom do you think?"

"Not Carter Woodman?"

"Yes, Woodman. That must have given him the idea of using the club. He may have remembered that it would probably have Prinsep's finger-marks on it."

"Yes, but if he used it afterwards it would have his marks too."

"Not necessarily. Don't you remember the police saying at the inquest that some of the marks were blurred, as if the club had been handled afterwards? That inspector fellow said he was sure the murderer had worn gloves. That's it. Woodman must have worn gloves, and they blurred the marks. That shows that Woodman killed George as well as Prinsep."

"Of course it all helps to make it likely; and I never thought John had done it. But it's not proof, you know."

"It may not be proof, but, by George, with the rest of the facts we have I think it's good enough."

"No, Bob, I don't think it is good enough—for proof, I mean—unless we can prove that Carter was in Liskeard House that evening. If we could prove that, I agree that we could bring the whole thing home to him."

"But we know he went out of the Cunningham, and lied about where he had been."

"We know he lied, but we can't even prove that he went out of the hotel. We only showed that he could have got out, and in again, without being seen. It really isn't good enough—yet."

"But how are we to make it any better?"

"If Carter got back into Liskeard House I'm going to find out how he did it. He couldn't have come in by the front door—some one would have been certain to see him. And I'm fairly certain he couldn't have got in through the theatre without being seen."

"Then how on earth did he get in?"

"That's what I mean to find out. If he didn't come in the other ways, he must have come in through the coachyard."

"But surely the evidence at the inquest showed that it was all locked up, and no one could possibly have got in that way."

"My dear Bob, the evidence only showed that it was locked at eleven o'clock. The police theory was that the murders were somewhere about midnight. But we believe Carter got out of the Cunningham some time before eleven. He must have come through before it was locked. And we know now, thanks to that coat-button, how he got out."

"You may be right. But the chauffeur and his wife both said they didn't see any one come in before they locked up; so that, even if Woodman did come that way, I don't see how we can prove it."

"You are a Jeremiah. Of course I don't see either. But I haven't really tried yet, and I'm going to. And now, Bob, let's pay our bill, and get to work on it. It must be so, and I'm not going to believe it can't be proved."

Chapter XXXII
Sir John Bunnery

Before Joan and Ellery parted, they arranged what each should do next to clear up the remaining difficulties. Joan was to test her theory about the coachyard, while Ellery was to investigate the circumstances surrounding the extraordinary attempt of Woodman and Walter Brooklyn to raise a loan in anticipation of Sir Vernon's death. Woodman had approached Sir John Bunnery; and Sir John's subsequent letter to Sir Vernon seemed to make it worth while to find out what information he possessed. Ellery made up his mind to go and see Sir John; and Joan furnished him with a convenient pretext for doing so. Sir Vernon had determined to get his new will into proper legal form at the earliest possible moment, and had told Joan that Woodman must on no account be allowed to do the drafting of it. She had suggested that Sir John Bunnery might be called in, and Sir Vernon had readily agreed. Joan therefore commissioned Ellery to call on Sir John, and ask him to come to Liskeard House at his earliest convenience for the purpose of drawing up Sir Vernon's new will.

Ellery wrote on his card, "From Sir Vernon Brooklyn," and, aided by the name, was speedily shown into Sir John Bunnery's private office. Sir John was not at all the popular idea of what "the bookmaker's attorney" ought to be. He was a small, dried-up old man, with very sharp little eyes that darted to and fro with disconcerting suddenness. He had a way of sitting very still, and looking his visitors up and down with those bright little eyes, until they felt that no detail of their appearance—and perhaps none of their thoughts—had escaped observation. Sir John made Ellery nervous, and, after a few sentences, he found that he had completed his ostensible business, without getting anywhere near the matter he had really come to discuss. He shifted uneasily in his chair.

Sir John Bunnery evidently read his thoughts. "And now, young man, there is something else you want to say to me, isn't there?"

This was not at all the way in which Ellery had expected to conduct the interview. He had hoped to discover what he wanted casually, in the course of conversation, without giving Sir John, who was, after all, a friend of Woodman's, any hint of what he wanted to know. But Sir John was manifestly a man whom it was not easy to pump. Ellery was wondering what to reply when the old lawyer spoke again,—

"I have refused Woodman that advance. Is that what you wanted to know?"

Ellery said that it was not, and then realised that he had admitted wanting to know something.

"Well, what is it then?" said Sir John.

There was nothing for it but either to get out of the room without the information that was needed or to make Sir John Bunnery, at least in part, a confidant. Ellery rapidly chose the latter course, and elected to go to work the most direct way.

"I want to know precisely what Carter Woodman said to you when he asked you to lend him that money. Do you know what he wanted it for?"

"You want to know a lot, young man. And why should I tell you all this?"

"Because Carter Woodman is a murderer."

Those small eyes looked at him very suddenly. "H'm," said Sir John, "and so you think Woodman killed those two fellows at Liskeard House. Is that it, eh? I dare say they were a good riddance."

"I must say you take it very calmly, Sir John."

"In my business, young man, we get used to taking things calmly. Murder is not an uncommon crime."

"But I understood Carter Woodman was a friend of yours."

"If you were my age, young man, and in my profession, you wouldn't be surprised even if one of your friends committed a murder. But, he's no friend of mine—now. Carter Woodman would be a good riddance himself. I could have put him in prison for trying to raise money on false pretences."

"Sir John, you will tell me what you know. I have almost certain proof that Woodman did commit murder; but your evidence may be indispensable."

"In that case, I should naturally give it at the proper time—to the police. Why should I give it to you, young man? I never heard of you before. Who are you?"

"Only a friend of Sir Vernon's and of Miss Cowper's. You probably know my guardian—Mr. Lucas. Miss Cowper and I have been working on the case together."

"Oh, you have, have you? Playing the amateur detective, eh?"

"We've found out any amount the police don't know, anyhow."

"Yes. Amateur detectives always do—in the novels. I prefer to say what I have to say at the proper time to the police. It saves complications."

"But, Sir John, the police are absolutely wrong about this. If you will tell me what you know, I will undertake that the police shall be fully informed within the next few days."

"And why not now, young man? Because you want to do

it all yourself. Is that it?"

"Perhaps it is, and perhaps it isn't, Sir John. But you know best. Let's telephone to the police to send some one round here, and you can tell them and me together."

"And have the police worrying round here all day till heavens knows when. No, thank you, young man." Sir John paused, and then went on suddenly. "I suppose you're going to marry that Cowper girl."

"I don't think that is any business of yours, Sir John. But I have no objection to telling you that we are engaged to be married."

"Tut, tut, don't lose your temper, boy. I'm just going to tell you all about it. Woodman came to see me the other night at my club—no, not the Byron: Foster's, at the corner of Clarges Street. That was at nine o'clock, by my appointment. He was with me for an hour, discussing that loan you seem to know all about. He told me just what I told Sir Vernon in my letter, that Walter Brooklyn had made a will in his favour, and that they were prepared to sign their joint names to a bill. He said that made the loan perfectly safe, on the strength of their expectations from Sir Vernon. That was all he told me."

Sir John stopped.

"Is that all you know?" asked Ellery, with an air of disappointment.

"No, of course, it's not all. You just wait a minute, young man. Don't be impatient." Sir John glared for a few seconds at his visitor and, then continued: "I may say that Woodman already owed me a considerable sum, in connection with a business transaction. So I thought it wise to make a few inquiries about him in the city, and I may tell you, young man, that the fellow's bankrupt—positively bankrupt—a shilling in the pound affair or something like it. Speculation, of course. He can't hold out for more than a few days. There are men on the Stock Exchange who know that for a fact."

"So that Woodman would be very likely to take some desperate step in order to retrieve his fortunes?"

"Such as coming to me and trying to raise money under false pretences. The man's a damned scoundrel," said Sir John.

"Surely murder is worse than raising money on false pretences, Sir John."

"Oh, is it, young man? Of course, you know all about it. I only know that the fellow ought to be locked up. That's enough for me. I might have lent him the money as a friend."

"But surely, Sir John, when you found out all this about him, you wouldn't have considered lending him the money."

"Of course, I did not consider it. Not for a moment, I never meant to lend him another penny. I wrote that letter of mine simply to put Sir Vernon on his guard. I would have gone to the police; but, as I told you, I saw no reason why I should get myself mixed up in the affair. But it would have outraged my legal sense if that man had got Sir Vernon's money by means of some jiggery pokery with that other old scoundrel, Walter Brooklyn. So I wrote to Sir Vernon. You see my position?"

"If that is your position, I don't quite see why you are telling me all this now."

"I am telling you, young man, because I had no suspicion that he had committed murder as well. If that is the case, a man of that sort is too dangerous to be left loose. He might be murdering me next, or Sir Vernon. But now you are going to tell me all about your case against him."

Ellery saw that it was best to tell the whole story, and he did tell most of it. Sir John listened, only interrupting every now and then with a pertinent question. At the end, his only comment was,—

"H'm, not so bad for amateurs. And now, my fine young man, what are you going to do next? If I'm to be the family lawyer, that is a point which concerns me. Is it to be a first-class family scandal, eh?"

"Really, we have been so busy trying to discover the truth, that I don't think we have ever considered what to do afterwards."

"Humph, but you will have to consider it now. Do you think Sir Vernon is anxious to have another scandal in the family? If you do, I don't."

"I suppose the murderer will have to be brought to justice."

"You do, do you? And doubtless you look forward to appearing in court and showing how clever you have been."

"Really, Sir John, I look forward to nothing of the kind. If Carter Woodman could be put out of the way of further mischief without dragging the whole affair into court, I should ask for nothing better."

"How much of what you have found out is known to the police?"

"Nothing at all, I believe. Of course, some other people— the manager at the Avenue, for example—know something of the story."

"They can be dealt with. Well, young man, you think it over, and come back and talk to me before you say a word to the police. Bring your Miss Cowper, too, if you like. I'm told she's a pretty girl." And with those words the old lawyer held out his hand, and bustled his visitor out of the office.

Ellery left Sir John Bunnery's presence feeling as if he had been bruised all over. He had found out what he wanted, but not at all in the way he had intended. And now this masterful old man apparently meant to take full command of the case. He must see Joan, and tell her what had happened.

Chapter XXXIII
On the Tiles

Inspector Blaikie had received very definite instructions from the superintendent as to the course of investigation which he was to follow up. He was to find out all he could about Woodman's financial circumstances, and he was to seek for proof that Woodman had been in possession of Walter Brooklyn's walking-stick. Side by side with this line of investigation, he had intended to look further into his own private suspicions of Ellery; but these, which had been almost removed by his last talk with the superintendent, were finally dispelled by a further talk with William Gloucester. Ellery's alibi was good enough: Carter Woodman was the man whose every concern he must scrutinize if he would find the murderer.

It did not take the inspector long to prove beyond doubt that Woodman was in a state of serious financial embarrassment. Discreet inquiries in the city showed that he had been speculating heavily in oil shares, and that he stood to lose a large sum on the falling prices of the shares which he had contracted to buy. There was nothing to show directly that he had staked his clients', as well as his own, money on the fate of his dealings; but the inspector could make a shrewd guess at the state of his affairs. In all probability, he must either raise money at once, or else face ignominious collapse, and perhaps worse. It was definite that he had been putting off his creditors with promises to pay in the near future, and plunging meanwhile into more serious difficulties in the attempt to extricate himself.

So far, so good; but the other matter gave the inspector far more serious trouble. Try as he would, he could get no clue that would tell him whether Walter Brooklyn had really left his walking-stick in Carter Woodman's office. His first thought had been to see Woodman's confidential clerk, and to find out, if possible without putting Woodman on his guard, what the man might know. He had scraped an acquaintance with Moorman in the course of his investigations, and had several times talked to him about the case. Moorman, he was fairly well convinced, had not the least suspicion of his employer's guilt, and the inspector was sure that he had said nothing to make him suspect. Indeed, he could hardly have done so; for only since he last saw the man had he himself begun to suspect Woodman.

Now, accordingly, Inspector Blaikie, watching for an opportunity when he was certain that Carter Woodman was not in his office, went to see Moorman. He asked for Woodman, and, receiving the answer that he was out, fell easily into conversation with the old clerk. It was quite casually that he asked after a while, "By the way, Walter Brooklyn was here on the day of the murders. You don't happen to remember whether he had his walking-stick with him, do you?"

Moorman looked at him sharply, as if he realised that there was a purpose in the question. "I've no idea," he said. "'Tisn't a thing I should notice, one way or the other. I'm too short-sighted to notice much."

The inspector tried a little to jog his memory, but with no result. Moorman either did not remember, or he would not tell. To ask the young clerk in the vestibule seemed too dangerous; for to do so would almost certainly be to put Woodman on his guard. The inspector could only report to the superintendent that he had failed to trace the stick.

"Look here, Blaikie," said Superintendent Wilson, "this will never do. We know perfectly well who committed these murders, and we're as far off bringing it home to him as ever."

The inspector could only reply that he had done his best.

"Yes; and I'm not blaming you," his superior rejoined. "But it won't do. I see I shall have to take a hand in the game myself. We must find out about that walking-stick, and there's another point I've reasoned out to-day. Where's the weapon with which Prinsep was killed?"

"Why, you've got the club."

"Yes, yes; but you don't tell me that the murderer carried that immense unwieldy thing up two flights of stairs, when he might easily have been seen. No, Prinsep wasn't killed with that club. George Brooklyn was; but it was some other weapon that killed Prinsep."

"There's the knife," suggested the inspector. "But you have that too."

"Really, inspector, you are unusually thick-headed this morning. The man wasn't killed with a knife. He was killed with a blow on the back of the head, delivered with some heavy blunt instrument. Isn't that what the doctors said?"

"Quite. If it wasn't the club, I suppose the murderer carried the weapon away."

"I suppose he may have done, as you did not find it. You are sure there was no object in the room that might have been used as a weapon."

"None at all, I think. The stick belonging to Walter Brooklyn could not have made the wound, I am told—nor any of the other sticks for that matter. It looked much more like a case of sand-bagging, now I think of it in this light."

"Well, inspector, I'm not satisfied, and I feel sure you will not object if I do a bit of investigation on my own."

"Are you taking the case out of my hands, sir?"

"No, no. I want you to carry on, and especially to find out what these young people—Miss Cowper and Ellery—are doing. There are only two or three points on which I want to satisfy myself personally."

"Very well, sir," said the inspector; and he left feeling—and looking—more than a little aggrieved.

Superintendent Wilson, in his rare personal appearances in the work of detection, had one great advantage, he was not known by sight, even to most of the habitual criminal class. He had, therefore, on this occasion at least, no need to disguise himself. He merely went to Carter Woodman's office as a prospective client, who had been strongly recommended to him. He wanted both to have a look at Woodman himself and to see whether anything more could be got out of Moorman on the question of the stick.

Woodman was engaged with a client when he arrived, and he had a favourable chance of making friends with the old clerk before he was shown into the inner office. He used his opportunity for that alone, making no attempt to lead the conversation towards the business on which he had come. In a very few minutes he was shown into Woodman's private office.

Looking his man up and down, he noted, as the inspector had noted before him, the powerful physique, the straining vitality, the false geniality of Woodman's manner. But he could see also that the man was seriously worried. There was, for all his appearance of heartiness, a harried look about him, and he seemed preoccupied as, with an excellent assumption of business incapacity, his visitor began to unfold a long story about a lease and a mortgage which he wished to negotiate. Woodman listened with growing impatience, as the superintendent meant that he should. At length he interrupted, saying that the details could be dealt with later. His visitor was most apologetic—never had a head for business, but positively must get the matter dealt with that day. He lived away in the country—Mr. Amos Porter of Sunderling in Sussex was his description for the nonce—and he would not be in town again for weeks. Woodman finally suggested that, as there was other work he must do, Mr. Porter should settle the details with his clerk—an excellent man of business, who would be able to tell him all he wanted. Mr. Porter, after a perfunctory attempt to go on with his explanation to the principal, agreed; and he was soon back in the other office with Moorman.

Mr. Porter had left his hat, coat, and stick in the outer office when he went in to see Woodman, laying the stick on a chair and covering it with his coat. His business with Moorman was soon done, and he crossed the room to get his things. By a curious accident, while he was struggling into his coat, he dropped his stick at Moorman's feet. Moorman picked it up, but as he was passing it back to its owner, he started violently and almost dropped it.

"A queer old stick, is it not?" said Mr. Porter. "I value it highly for its associations."

Moorman peered at him, oddly. "I beg pardon, sir, but isn't that the stick a gentleman I know used to carry?"

"No, no. I've had this stick for years. I bought it in—let me see, where did I buy it? Never mind. I had no idea there was another like it. That is most interesting. May I ask who uses such a stick?"

"The gentleman's name is Brooklyn—Mr. Walter Brooklyn. He had one very like yours."

"God bless my soul! Not the fellow whose name has been in all the papers? Dear me, what was it about? I know it was in the papers."

"Mr. Brooklyn was suspected—wrongly—of murder."

"Oh, yes, I remember now. And you know Mr. Brooklyn?

How interesting."

Moorman lowered his voice. "He was in the office with that stick on the very day on which the murders were committed."

"Dear, dear. It is coming back to me. There was something about the stick in the papers. How odd it should be like mine."

"It was found in the room where one of the murders took place."

"And you saw Mr. Brooklyn with the stick when he left this office the same day. Dear me, that must have looked very bad for him. But he was released, wasn't he?"

"Yes, the police let him go."

"And did you give evidence, Mr. Moorman? Did you have to say you had seen him leave this office with that stick in his hands? It must be a terrible ordeal to be a witness—terrible."

"I didn't have to give evidence, and in any case I didn't see the stick when Mr. Brooklyn left the office."

"Oh, I see. He hadn't the stick with him when he left. Then, of course, it wouldn't go so much against him, it being found. Why, it might have been my stick"—and Mr. Porter gave a curious high laugh. "Well, Mr.—is it Moorman?—thank you. You've told me just what I wanted to know—about my mortgage. I will write in, sending all the documents. Good-morning."

Safely out of earshot and eyeshot of Woodman's office, Superintendent Wilson had a quiet laugh. "A little diplomacy does it," he said to himself. "Now I know all about the stick. And next for another little exploration."

The superintendent's next visit was paid in his proper person. Driving to Liskeard House, he asked to be shown up to Prinsep's room, where everything was still just as it had been when the murder was discovered. There he made a careful examination of the room and all its contents, seeking for any weapon with which the murder could possibly have been done. His search was fruitless; and, after a while, he passed to the window and gazed out thoughtfully into the garden below. The roof of the antique temple showed over the intervening trees; but the place where the murder of George Brooklyn had taken place was completely hidden by the trees and the bushes growing around them. The superintendent cast back in his mind to discover whether the bushes had been searched for possible clues. He assumed that they had—it was an elementary precaution—but he had best have a hunt round himself. Something might have been overlooked. He went down the private staircase into the garden, and began his search.

Nothing rewarded his efforts, though he spent a good hour searching; and it was with a puzzled expression that he went upstairs again to Prinsep's room, resuming his stand at the window and gazing out. Suddenly something seemed to catch his attention. Leaning as far out of the window as he could, he studied intently what he could see of the roof. "It's just a possibility," he muttered, as he closed the window, and crossed the room.

What Superintendent Wilson had remarked was that almost on the level of Prinsep's window was the roof of that part of the house which projected over the stable-yard. It was not near enough for any entry to the room to be effected by its means; but it was easily within reach of a throw, and an object cast away upon it would be completely invisible and safely disposed of until some day, probably distant, when the roof might need repair. It was an admirable place for the bestowal of any inconvenient piece of property.

By means of the landing window, the superintendent found his way without much difficulty out on to the roof, and was easily able to climb over its gabled side to the flat space in the centre. And there at last his efforts were rewarded; for on the roof lay, clearly just where it had been thrown, a small bag heavily loaded, not with sand, but with small shot—a deadly weapon. Stuffing the thing into his pocket, the superintendent climbed back with more difficulty, and shut the window behind him. He chuckled softly to himself. He had reasoned aright, and here at last was a clue that had not been laid to mislead—a real clue that he must make to point straight at the murderer. He went back to his office to examine his find at leisure.

Chapter XXXIV
The Stable-Yard

While Superintendent Wilson, by his own methods, was thus working towards the solution of the mystery, Joan and Ellery were also pursuing their investigations along their separate line. There was but one thing needed, they felt, to complete their case, and turn their conviction from moral into legal certainty.

How had Woodman got into Liskeard House? That was the question which Joan had set herself to answer. The coach-yard seemed to be the only possible means of access. It was a large square yard opening into Liskeard Street by a pair of massive wooden doors ten feet high, and a small gate let into the wall at the side. Neither the wall nor the doors could be climbed without the aid of a long ladder.

One entering by these doors would find himself in the yard. On his left he would have the side wall of Liskeard House, which had no window looking out on to the yard. On his right would be the large coach-house, now used as a garage, above which lived the chauffeur and his wife, formerly a domestic of Sir Vernon's—both servants of long standing. Their apartment had also a door opening into Liskeard Street, and a way down into the garage.

Immediately opposite any one entering the yard from the street was an extension, built out from the side of Liskeard

House towards the back. The ground floor of this was occupied by store-rooms, accessible only from the yard; but between these a passage led through directly into the garden. Above were rooms belonging to Liskeard House, whose windows looked out only upon the garden.

Joan, as she stood in the yard, noticed first that, if the outer door were open, and the yard itself empty, as at this moment, there was nothing to prevent any one from walking straight through into the garden; for, as she knew, the gate leading to the garden, though it was shut, was never locked save at night. The big front gates of the yard stood open most of the day; and, in any case, the small gate beside them was not locked until the whole place was shut up for the night. A man wishing to get into the garden would only have to watch until the yard itself was empty, and he would then have every chance of getting through without being observed. In the chauffeur's apartments above the garage, only one window looked down on the yard, and this, as Joan knew, was a tiny spare room, seldom occupied. Even if Woodman had come in by this way, there was only a very slender chance that he had been noticed.

The chauffeur came into the yard from the garage, and Joan entered into talk with him. Usually, he locked up, when no one had the car out in the evening, at half-past nine or ten. On this occasion, Lucas's car had been in the garage during dinner, and he had kept the place open after Lucas went in case any one might want a car out. He had locked the whole place up at eleven o'clock, and had then gone straight to bed. Had any one, Joan asked, entered by the yard entrance before he locked up? He had seen no one; but he had not been in the yard all the time. He went away to ask his wife, and came back to assure Joan that, although she had been in the yard part of the time, she, too, had seen no one pass that way. There was no one else, was there, Joan asked, about that night? No one. But then the chauffeur seemed to be plunged into thought. "Yes, miss, there was some one else. Miss Parker—Norah, what used to be the cook, miss—she came in to help with the dinner, and she stayed the night with us. She went to bed early, she did—about half-past ten. She had to leave early next morning—she went away before they found out what had happened in the night."

"Was she sleeping in the little room up there?"

"Yes, miss, and when I looked up at eleven o'clock, she was sitting at the window there. She said she couldn't sleep, and was trying to read herself off."

"Then she might have seen any one come in?"

"Yes, miss, she might."

"Do you know where she is now?"

"She's with my wife this very moment, miss. She's in a job now, away in Essex. That's where she went when she left that morning. But it's her day off, miss, and she's come up to see us."

Joan asked to speak to the woman, and was soon in the parlour with her and the chauffeur's wife.

"Did I see any one come through the coach-yard that night? Yes, I did, miss; but I didn't think nothing of it. It was about a quarter to eleven, and I was looking out of the spare room window when a gentleman came into the yard. It was too dark down in the yard at first to see who it was; but as he passed under the lamp by the gate leading into the garden, I saw his face."

"Who was it? Did you know him?"

"Mr. Woodman, miss. Of course, I thought it was all right, seeing as it was him."

"And he went through into the garden?"

"Yes, miss."

"You didn't see him come out again?"

"No, miss. No one else passed through the yard before Mr.

Purvis here came and locked up."

"Now, Norah, I don't want you to tell any one—or you, Purvis, or your wife—that Norah saw Mr. Woodman come in. It's very important you shouldn't mention it just yet."

Mrs. Purvis curtseyed, and Norah also agreed to say nothing. Purvis himself began by saying, "Certainly, miss, if you wish it," and then he seemed to realise the implication contained in Joan's request. His jaw dropped, and his mouth hung open. Then he said,—

"Beg pardon, miss, but surely you don't mean as Mr. Woodman had aught to do with this terrible affair?"

"Never mind, Purvis, just now, what I mean. I'm not accusing anybody. But I knew some one came in by the yard, and I wanted to make sure who it was."

"Well, miss, you can make sure we won't say nothing about it."

They kept their word, no doubt; and said nothing to any one else. But, when Joan had gone, they said a great deal among themselves. Joan's questions had been enough to make them suspect that Woodman might be concerned in the murders. And, though nothing was said of Joan's discovery, Purvis's dark and unsupported suspicions of Woodman, and Mrs. Purvis's hints of what she could say if she had a mind, were soon all round the servants' hall.

It was not surprising that these rumours soon came to Inspector Blaikie's ears. He was not at first inclined to attach much importance to them; for they appeared to be no more than below-stairs gossip, and the fact of Woodman's unpopularity with the servants, which had not escaped his observation, seemed sufficiently to account for the vague suspicions. Servants, he said to himself, were always ready to suspect any one they disliked; and in this case they were all strong partisans of Winter, and highly indignant at the share of their attentions which the police had bestowed on the men-servants at Liskeard House. All the same, the inspector traced the rumours to the chauffeur's wife, and made up his mind to have a little talk with her.

He began brusquely—it was his way in dealing with women whom he thought he could frighten—by asking her what she meant by concealing information from the police. The woman was plainly embarrassed; but she only said that she did not know what he meant. He accused her of saying, in the servants' hall, that she knew who had committed the murders in Liskeard House, but that she wasn't going to say anything. Her reply was to deny all knowledge, and to inform the inspector that those that said she said such things wasn't fit—not to associate with the decent folks. The more the inspector tried to browbeat her, the less would she say. She grew sulky, and told him to let a poor woman alone, and not go putting into her mouth things she never said.

She didn't know anything, and, if she did, she wouldn't tell him. Inspector Blaikie retired from the contest beaten, but warning her that he would call again.

He did not, however, retire so far as to prevent him from seeing that, as soon as she believed herself to be alone, the chauffeur's wife hurried into Liskeard House by the back way, and went straight up the back stairs. Putting two and two together, he speedily concluded that she had gone to see Joan Cowper, and that Joan probably knew all that she knew, and had told her to keep quiet about it. The inspector made up his mind to see Joan as soon as the woman had gone.

Meanwhile, Mrs. Purvis was telling Joan about the inspector's visit, and begging pardon for having let her tongue wag in the servants' hall. "But I didn't tell him nothing, miss. You can rest assured of that. I sent him away with a flea in his ear, miss."

At this moment Ellery was announced. Joan dismissed Mrs. Purvis with a further caution to say nothing for the present. As soon as she had gone, Ellery told Joan of his visit to Sir John Bunnery, and of the fact that Woodman had been in serious financial straits before the murders took place. "It seems to be true enough, about your stepfather making a will in his favour. It's all very odd: I don't understand it a bit."

"I'm afraid there's almost nothing he wouldn't do for money—except murder," said Joan.

"Old Sir John seemed to think that murder was quite a venial offence in comparison with getting money by false pretences," Ellery answered, laughing.

"Don't be silly, Bob. I've found out how Carter got into the house. And I've got the proof." And then Joan told her story of the coach-house yard—her story which proved beyond doubt that Woodman had been on the scene of the crime.

"Well done, Joan. So that makes it certain he was here."

"I'm really beginning to think, Bob, we're rather clever people."

"My dear, we've done the trick. Do you realise that it practically finishes our case. We've got enough now to be quite sure of a conviction."

"Oh, Bob! How horrible it is when you put it that way. It has really been rather fun finding it all out; but now we've found out, oh, what are we to do about it?"

"The obvious thing would be to tell the police."

"I suppose it would. But think of the trial—the horrible publicity of it. And I don't a bit want to see Carter hanged, though he may deserve it. Think of poor Helen."

"My dear Joan, of course you don't. But it's not so easy to hush up a thing like this."

"Bob, need we tell the police? They don't know what we've been doing. Must we tell them now?"

"Blest if I know, darling. But I forgot to tell you about what the old lawyer chap, Bunnery, said. He wants it hushed up all right."

"Then that means we can hush it up."

"I don't know whether we can or not. But I tell you what I suggest we do. You come down with me and see Carter Woodman. We shall have to tell him what we know, and force him to admit the whole thing. Then we'll see what he means to do—perhaps he might agree to run away to Australia, or something, before the police find out. And then we can see old Bunnery and get his advice, and decide what to do about telling them."

Before Joan could answer this string of proposals, there came a knock at the door, and Inspector Blaikie walked into the room. Joan and Ellery evidently showed their embarrassment, for he stood looking curiously at them for a moment, and then said reassuringly that he had only come in to have a word or two, if he might. Joan asked him to sit down, and offered him a cigarette. The inspector lighted it deliberately, and then he suddenly shot a question at them.

"What is it you have told the chauffeur's wife not to tell me?"

Joan looked quickly at Ellery, and Ellery looked at Joan; but neither of them answered.

"Come, come, Miss Cowper. You really must not try to prevent the police from getting information or you will force us to conclude that you wish to shield the murderer."

Still Joan made no answer.

"I hope, Miss Cowper, that it is only that you and your friend have been doing a little detective work on your own, and wanted to have all the credit for yourselves. But don't you think the time has come for telling me what you know?"

Ellery did not answer the question directly. "Look here, inspector," he said, "you think we know all about these murders, and are trying to keep the truth from you."

"It looks mighty like it."

"Well, in a sense, I don't say we haven't been keeping something back. But I give you my word that we're not in collusion with the murderer or anything of that sort. There is a very special reason why we can't tell you quite everything just now—for what it is worth."

"Does the very special reason apply to Miss Cowper as well?"

"Yes," said Joan; "for the moment it does."

Ellery went on. "Of course, I know you have a grievance. You're going to tell us that we are abetting the criminal, whoever he is, and that we shall be getting into trouble if we're not careful."

"So you will," said the inspector. "Very serious trouble."

"All the same, inspector, I'm afraid we must risk it. Very likely we shall be free to tell you the whole story, or what we know of it, in a day or two. But we won't tell you now. That's flat."

"A day or two is ample time for a criminal to get away."

"Maybe; but I don't think you need worry about that. You've given him enough time to get away if he wants to. In any case, we are not going to tell you. I'm sorry, but——"

"I warn you that you are conspiring to defeat the ends of justice."

"Sorry, and all that. Another time, inspector, we shall look forward to an interesting talk. But for the present—Good-morning."

The inspector took the hint, and left the room in a very bad temper. His parting shot was that he must report their conduct to his official superior.

"What on earth are we to do now?" said Joan.

"Go and see Carter Woodman at once, I think. When we've

done that, we shall know better how to act."

"But suppose he runs away when he hears our story—flies the country, I mean."

"Wouldn't that be the best way out? I don't want to see him hanged any more than you do."

"As the inspector said, we run some risk ourselves that way; but the worst of it is that the whole story is bound to come out."

"I don't see how it can be kept secret in any case—or rather, I only see one possible way."

"What's that?"

"Wait till we've been to Woodman. I want to see if he will be man enough to take it."

"I don't know what you mean. But I suppose we had better see Woodman."

"Yes, and there's no time to lose, if the inspector is on the trail."

Joan and Ellery took a taxi, and ordered the driver to drive to Woodman's office. But they underestimated the inspector's promptness in action. They did not know that behind them followed another taxi, containing Inspector Blaikie and two plain-clothes detectives.

Chapter XXXV
An Order for Bulbs

Superintendent Wilson's examination of his find took him some little time. The bag was of ordinary stout canvas, most unlikely to be capable of identification. The small-shot also was of a kind which can be purchased at any gunsmith's and at most ironmongers. To trace the criminal by means of either of these clues seemed virtually impossible. But this was not the end of the matter. Taking the shot, the superintendent carefully sifted it, and by-and-by he had separated from the pile of shot quite a number of other minute objects which had lain among it. There were several small pieces of cardboard, a few fragments of matches, some wisps of tobacco, a few balls of fluff, two pins, three small nails, and several tiny scraps of paper. Some or all of these might, of course, have got mixed up with the shot before ever it came into the murderer's possession, and most of them were not at all likely in any case to afford a clue. But the chance was worth trying; and the inspector made a minute examination of them all. The scraps of paper alone seemed to hold out any hope of a clue. Two of them were blank: one was an indistinguishable fragment of a newspaper, apparently from the typography The Times: the other two, which fitted together, contained a few words written by hand. The words were unimportant, merely: "12 doz. hyacinths; 15 doz. tulips; 10 doz. sq.——" the last word being cut short by a tear. The paper was evidently part of an order, or of a memorandum for an order, for garden bulbs. But the writing—the superintendent compared it with a note which he had received from Woodman—the writing was very like. He could not say positively that they were the same. He must compare the scrap of paper with other specimens of Woodman's hand. A second visit to Woodman's office, in the guise of Mr. Porter, the unbusinesslike mortgage-maker, would probably afford the opportunity. Superintendent Wilson called a taxi, and drove away in the direction of Lincoln's Inn.

The Fates, watching outside that very ordinary-looking office, had a more than usually amusing time that afternoon. As Joan and Ellery, after dismissing their taxi, entered the outer office, a second taxi drew up a few doors off, just out of view. Inspector Blaikie leapt out, and after him two plain-clothes officers. The inspector rapidly posted his men. "There is no back way out of these premises," he said, "so we have an easy job. I am going right in now, and I want you two to wait outside, and follow any of our people who come out. You know them all by sight. If Carter Woodman comes out, don't lose sight of him on any account. But don't detain him unless it is quite impossible to keep an eye on him. I shall probably keep my eye on the other two myself." So saying, the inspector disappeared into the building. He had no clearly formed plan in his mind; but his suspicions had been thoroughly aroused, and he feared that Joan and Ellery had gone to warn Woodman to fly from the country.

A few minutes after the inspector had entered the office his two subordinates had the surprise of their lives. A third taxi drew up at the door, and out of it stepped no less a person that Superintendent Wilson. While they were debating whether to speak to him, his quick eye caught sight of them, and, rapidly walking a little way along the street in order to be out of view, he beckoned them to come.

"What are you doing here?" he asked.

In a few words the men told him that Inspector Blaikie, and Joan and Ellery as well, were inside, and that they had received instructions to remain on the watch, and to follow Woodman if he came out. The superintendent thought rapidly. If he went in, it would be obviously impossible to maintain his alias of Mr. Porter, and he ran the risk of interrupting a most important conversation. If, on the other hand, he stayed outside, what blunder might not be committed in his absence? Telling the men to remain on guard and follow the inspector's instruction, he entered the building.

He did not, however, go to the door of Woodman's outer office. Instead, he went along the corridor to where, as he remembered, the private door from Woodman's inner sanctum gave on the passage. There he paused and listened. Some one was speaking within; but not a word was audible through the stout door. There was no keyhole, and nothing was to be seen either. The superintendent must fare further, to the back of the building, if he sought to find out what was in progress in Woodman's room. There might be a window, looking on the room, through which he could watch unobserved. He soon found a back-door, leading into a small flagged yard at the rear of the building. It was locked; but the key was in place. Unlocking it he slipped out into the yard, and easily located the window of Woodman's room. By standing on a water-butt, he could see the three people—Joan, Ellery, and Carter Woodman—within. But the window was closed, and he could hear nothing. He remained at his post of vantage, watching.

Chapter XXXVI
An Afternoon Call

Hardly had Joan and Ellery passed from the outer office into Woodman's private room when the inspector entered the room they had left, and asked if Mr. Woodman was in. Moorman, who had met the inspector several times lately, saw nothing strange in the visit, and merely replied that his employer was in, but that he was at the moment engaged. "If you care to wait, sir, I dare say he won't be long."

Blaikie said that he would wait, and Moorman thereupon suggested that he should go in and tell his principal that the inspector was there. But the inspector told him not to bother: he would take his chance when Woodman was free. He sat down, therefore, to wait in the outer office, improving the minutes by conversing with the loquacious old clerk about his employer's affairs.

Meanwhile, Joan and Ellery were seated with Carter Woodman. He had greeted them rather effusively on their entrance; and, in Moorman's presence, they had thought it best to shake hands and behave as if nothing were the matter. Woodman had placed chairs for them, and had again sat down at his desk. While they spoke he continued for a while mechanically opening, and glancing at, the pile of letters before him.

It was Joan who spoke first. "We have come here," she

said, "because it seemed the only thing to do. When we have heard what you have to say we shall know better what our next step must be."

Something in her voice caused Woodman to look up sharply. The tone was hard, and a glance at his two visitors showed him that their errand was not a pleasant one. But he looked down again and went on opening his letters without making any sign.

"We have to tell you," Joan went on, "that we know now who killed John Prinsep and poor George."

Woodman gave a start as she spoke; but all he said was, "Then, my dear Joan, you know a great deal more than I do."

"I will put it in another way," said Joan. "We know that you killed them." She got the words out with an effort, breathing hard and clutching the arm of the chair as she spoke.

Woodman dropped the letter he was holding and looked straight at her.

"My dear Joan," he said, "are you quite mad? And you too, Mr. Ellery?"

"No, we're not mad. We know," said Ellery, with a short, uneasy laugh—a laugh that grated.

Woodman looked from the one to the other.

"I fear you are both mad," said he very quietly. "And now, will one of you please tell me what you mean by this extraordinary accusation?"

"You had better hear what we have to say before you start protesting," said Ellery. "Let me tell you exactly what happened at Liskeard House last Tuesday. Then you will see that we know. You are supposed to have been at your hotel in the small writing-room on the first floor between 10.45 and 11.30, or after."

"So I was, of course."

"But we can produce a gentleman who was in the

writing-room between those hours, and can swear that you were not."

"Oh, I may have slipped out of the room for a while. But it is preposterous——"

"You had better hear me out. This gentleman saw you leave the writing-room and go downstairs at a few minutes to eleven. Shortly after, he went to the room himself and remained there three-quarters of an hour. He saw you return to the writing-room rather before a quarter to twelve."

"This is pure nonsense. But what of it, even if it were true?"

"This. When you left the room you went down to the basement of the hotel, which was deserted, and let yourself out by unbarring the side door leading from the Grill Room into St. John's Street. You also returned that way shortly after half-past eleven."

"Again, I say that you are talking absolute nonsense. But, if it pleases you, pray continue this fairy tale."

Joan took up the story. "You walked across to Liskeard House, and entered the garden through the coach-yard shortly before it was locked for the night. I will pass over what you did next; but at a time shortly before half-past eleven—probably about a quarter-past—you put on John Prinsep's hat and coat and walked up and down the garden, imitating his lameness, in a spot where you could be seen from the back of the theatre. You then went upstairs to John's room, and delivered, imitating my stepfather's voice, a false telephone message purporting to come from him to his club in Pall Mall. Next you put on George's hat and coat, and dressed in them walked out of the front door in such a way that the servants, seeing you at a distance, readily mistook you for George. Am I right, so far?"

"I am listening, my dear Joan, because I had better hear the whole of this wild story that something—or some one"—here he turned and glared at Ellery—"has put into your head. But, of course, the whole thing is monstrous."

"You need not blame Mr. Ellery. He and I have worked it all out together, and we can prove all we say. I should have mentioned that before leaving Liskeard House you arranged the scene of the murders so as to make it seem, first of all, that John and George had killed each other. Under John's body you placed a blood-stained handkerchief belonging to George, and you also left one of George's knives sticking in the body. You killed George with a weapon which, as you well knew, had on it John's finger-marks. Of course you wore gloves, and therefore left no marks which could be identified as your own. The finger-marks on the club with which George was killed were made by John earlier in the day when he showed you the club before dinner. They were defaced, but not obliterated, by the marks made later by your gloved hands. Is that correct?"

"Of course it is not correct. It is a parcel of lies, the whole lot of it."

"Really, Mr. Woodman," said Ellery, "you will find that the whole story is remarkably convincing to others, if not to you. Let me give you an account of the objects you had in view. You knew that it was physically impossible for John and George to have killed each other; but by leaving the signs as you did you hoped to create the impression that either might have killed the other. Your main object, however, was not to create suspicion against either of these two, but to incriminate another person, whom you desired to remove for reasons of your own. You therefore faked the telephone message I have mentioned; and you also left Walter Brooklyn's stick in John Prinsep's room. You also detached the ferrule from the stick with your penknife, and left the ferrule in the garden on the spot where George was murdered. By actual murder you had already, on Tuesday night, removed two of the three persons who stood between you and Sir Vernon's fortune. You hoped that, by means of the clues which you provided, the law would do your work in removing the third. I will not ask you whether this is true. We know it."

Woodman shrugged his shoulders. "Oh, if you know it," he said, "of course there is nothing for me to say."

"You left Liskeard House wearing George's hat and overcoat. These you took back to the hotel, and stowed away in a handbag for the night. You went out the next morning carrying the handbag, which you brought to this office. At lunch-time you took it with you. I do not know where you lunched, but you went into the cloak-room of the Avenue Restaurant, as if you were going to lunch there, and left the hat and coat hanging on a peg. You hoped that it would be impossible to trace them to you. They have been traced."

During Ellery's last speech Woodman's forced calm had first showed some sign of breaking. But he pulled himself together with an effort. "I must say you have laid this plot very carefully," he said.

"Unfortunately, not only have you been traced," Joan went on, "but you were unwise enough not to notice, when you left the coat, that it lacked a button. You left that button deep down in the corner of the bag which is now in that cupboard over there."

With a sudden cry Woodman rose from his chair and sprang towards the cupboard. He tore the bag open and felt wildly in it. Then he flung the bag away.

"No," said Joan, "the button is not there, Mr. Woodman— now. It is safe somewhere else."

"And I think, Mr. Woodman, what you have just done rather disposes of the pose of injured innocence. Don't you?" asked Ellery.

Woodman kicked the bag savagely into a corner and sank into his chair. His face had gone dead white. Shakily he poured out and drank a glass of water.

"Your hopes of removing my stepfather by due process of law," Joan continued, "were unfortunately frustrated.

You were, therefore, in the position of having committed two murders for nothing, unless you could find some fresh means of profiting by them. You found such means. As soon as you heard of my stepfather's release you made your plans. Soon after his release you met him, and somehow or other, persuaded him to make a will in your favour. I do not know how you did it; but I presume there was some agreement between you to share the proceeds of your deal. You then attempted, on the strength of your joint expectations under Sir Vernon's will, to raise a large loan from one who was a friend of yours—Sir John Bunnery. You were in serious financial trouble, and only a considerable immediate supply of money could save you from bankruptcy and disgrace. That, I think, is correct."

Joan paused, but this time Woodman had nothing to say. His face had gone grayer still. He stared at Joan, and his hand strayed towards one of the drawers of the table before him. But he remained silent.

This time, however, Joan pressed him for an answer.

"Do you admit now that what I have said is true?" she asked. And, as he still said nothing, "We can prove it all, you know," Ellery added.

Woodman pulled himself together with an effort. "You have told the police all this?" he asked.

"Not a word as yet," said Joan. "We decided to see you first."

"May I ask why?"

"If it can be helped, we do not want your wife to suffer more than she must for what you have done. Nor do we want a scandal. If you will leave the country, and never come back, we will do what we can to hush the whole thing up."

A light came into Woodman's ashen face. "I see," he said.

"Do you admit that all we have told you is true?"

"It doesn't seem to be much good denying it now."

"You will sign, in our presence, a confession that you committed these murders?"

"I don't know what for. No, I won't sign anything."

"But you admit it."

"Between ourselves, yes. In public, a thousand times no."

Woodman even smiled as he said this.

"You admit it to us."

"Yes, yes. Haven't I said so? But there are some things not even you seem to know."

"Won't you tell us them, Mr. Woodman, just to make our story complete?" said Ellery. "Remember that we are proposing to let you go. We are taking some risks in doing that."

"Not for my sake, I'll be bound. But I don't mind telling you. What do you want to know?"

"How the murders were actually done."

"Oh, I have no objection to telling you. Indeed, I flatter myself the thing was rather prettily arranged."

Woodman had almost regained his outward composure and spoke with some of his accustomed assurance.

"I went into the garden of Liskeard House, just as you said, by the coach-yard. I have no idea how you discovered that. Then I went straight up the back stairs to Prinsep's room. No one saw me go upstairs, I take it, or you would have mentioned the fact. I found Prinsep at his table writing. I laid him out with a big blow on the back of the head."

"With what weapon?"

"With a sand-bag. Then it has not been found? I threw it out afterwards on to the roof of the stables out of sight. Then, as I wasn't sure if he was dead, I made sure with a knife I found lying on the table. It belonged, I knew, to George Brooklyn.

I don't know how it got there. It wasn't part of my plan. I finished him off with that, and went out on to the landing. Just then I heard some one coming upstairs. It was George Brooklyn. Until that moment I had no definite intention of killing George that night. I meant to leave signs which would show that George and Walter had conspired to kill Prinsep. I had put a handkerchief of George's under the body. George's coming just then was deuced awkward. I had no time to clear away the traces, and I had somehow to prevent him from entering the room. So I met him on the landing and told him that Prinsep was in the garden and wanted him to go down. He went down the back stairs with me like a lamb. It was then it occurred to me that, as he had seen me up in Prinsep's room, I should have to kill him too. I led him over towards the temple and let him get a few paces in front. Then I seized the club from the Hercules statue and smashed his head in from behind. After that I had to consider how to cover my tracks. I dragged the body into the temple entrance, fetched Prinsep's coat and hat and walked up and down the garden, as you know. Then I went up again to Prinsep's room, and sent off that telephone message and arranged things there, leaving George's handkerchief under the body and Walter's stick in the room. I had already dropped the ferrule in the garden, and a note in Prinsep's writing, making an appointment for the garden. He had sent it to me the previous day. George had left his hat and overcoat on the landing. I had intended to slip out unobserved somehow; but seeing the coat and hat gave me an idea. I put them on, and walked out as George Brooklyn, thus throwing every one wrong, as I thought, about the time of the murders. All the rest you seem to know."

"H'm," said Ellery. "You are a remarkably cold-blooded scoundrel."

"Perhaps; but we can keep our opinions of each other to ourselves. You would prefer me to go away rather than stay and face your accusation. Isn't that so?"

"I suppose you can put it that way," said Ellery.

"Well, I can't go without money. That's the position. And I want a good lot. I can't lay hands on money at short notice, and you will have to find it. Besides, remember that, if you don't accuse me, I am still Walter Brooklyn's heir, and he is Sir Vernon's. I understand it is most unlikely Sir Vernon will live to make another will. Now, how much can you provide—and how soon? That is the business proposition we have to settle between us. I am prepared to disappear for the present, and I will go further, for a suitable consideration—and promise never to come back to this country. But my condition is that I get half of whatever comes to Joan when Sir Vernon dies. How does that strike you?"

Joan had listened with a feeling of nausea to Woodman's confession. But now she broke in indignantly. "I am afraid," she said, "that you are a little after the fair. It is quite true that, under my stepfather's new will, you appear to be the principal heir. It is also true that my stepfather stood to inherit a large sum of money, until Sir Vernon made a new will." Joan said these words very slowly and distinctly. As Woodman heard them the colour, which had quite come back, faded again from his face, and he stared at her with a consternation that deepened as she went on.

"We had not quite finished our story. After your wicked bargain with my stepfather you attempted to raise money on the strength of being his, and therefore indirectly Sir Vernon's, heir. I know how hard up you were—indeed pressure from creditors will, I hope, provide a good enough reason for your absconding now. If you choose to spread the report that you have died abroad, we shall certainly not object. But you will get no money from us. As I was saying, you went to Sir John Bunnery and tried to raise a large sum from him on the ground of your expectations. But you may not know that Sir John at once wrote privately to Sir Vernon to ask whether you were really the heir, or that yesterday Sir Vernon rallied enough to make a new will. That will, of course, excludes both you and my stepfather altogether."

At these words the colour came suddenly back into Woodman's cheeks. In a second he pulled open a drawer in the desk before him, seized from it a revolver and took aim at Joan. But Ellery was just too quick for him, knocking up his arm so that the bullet embedded itself in the ceiling. Woodman at once turned on Ellery, closing with him, and a fierce struggle began. At this moment there was a sound of breaking glass, and, rapidly opening the window through the hole which he had made, Superintendent Wilson leapt into the room. At the same time, the door leading to the outer office began to rattle as if some one were attempting to open it from without; but it was locked, and resisted all efforts to break it open. Then some one smashed the glass panel above and the head of Inspector Blaikie, with Moorman's terrified face behind, appeared in the gap. At sight of the superintendent, Ellery relaxed his hold for a moment and Woodman broke loose. But this time, instead of aiming at Joan, he turned the weapon upon himself. Putting the barrel of the revolver to his temple he fired. When, a moment later, the inspector forced an entrance, he found Joan, Ellery, and Superintendent Wilson bending over Carter Woodman's body.

Chapter XXXVII
A Happy Ending

Joan, Ellery, and the superintendent faced one another across Woodman's body. Moorman, his nerves gone, crouched in a corner, muttering. The inspector bent down and made a quick inspection of the body.

"H'm," he said, "he's quite dead."

The superintendent turned to Ellery. "And now perhaps it is time for you to give me a little explanation."

"Of this?" asked Ellery, pointing to the body.

"Of everything," was the answer.

"It is straightforward enough," said Ellery. "Mr. Woodman, as you will easily discover if you ask that whimpering object over there, has been for some time in grave financial difficulties. This morning he was disappointed of raising a large sum for which he had hoped; and I am afraid this is the result."

"Is that all you have to tell me?"

"What more should I have?"

"May I ask whether you have any theory as to the murderer of George Brooklyn, or of John Prinsep?"

"I have no theory. And I cannot see what that has to do with this suicide." Ellery emphasised the last word.

"Oh, that's your line, is it? And supposing I suggested that this gentleman here"—he pointed to Woodman's body—"was the murderer."

"I should ask you what evidence you have to support such an extraordinary suggestion."

"Very well, Mr. Ellery. But I had better tell you that I already have full knowledge of the truth. That is why I am here. You and the young lady here had much better make a clean breast of it."

"Don't you think, superintendent, that you had better deal with one thing at a time? Surely, for the moment, this dead man claims your attention. You know where to find us if you want us. I shall take Miss Cowper home."

"By all means, Mr. Ellery. There is work for me here. But I shall have to call on you both later in the day. Could I meet you—say at Liskeard House—about six o'clock?"

"Oh, if that's the attitude you take, I suppose we'd better have it out now."

"That will be best, I think." Then Superintendent Wilson turned to the inspector, who had not recovered from his amazement at the miraculous appearance of his superior. The superintendent pointed to Woodman's body. "Call in your men and have that thing removed. Then we can say what we have to say."

So, when the body had been taken away, Joan and Ellery found themselves face to face with Superintendent Wilson. "I will tell you what I know," he said, "and then I think you will see the wisdom of letting me hear your story. But first there is one thing I must do."

Going to Woodman's desk, he took from his pocket-book the scraps of paper which he had found, and rapidly compared them with other specimens of Woodman's handwriting. "Just as I thought," he said, "and now I am ready."

"Fire away, then," said Ellery.

"Well, it was clear enough to me, from an early stage in the case—even before you confirmed my view with your very convincing alibi, that Mr. Walter Brooklyn was not the murderer. That was the assumption on which I set to work."

"May I ask why?" said Joan. "Of course, I knew he hadn't done it; but what made you——?"

"A quite proper question, Miss Cowper. What made me take that view was a very strong conviction that the clues—the second set of clues, I mean—pointed far too directly to Mr. Brooklyn. They looked as if they had been deliberately laid. I ought to have seen that at once; but I was put off by the other set of clues—the obviously false ones—that the police were meant to see through from the first. It took me a little time to realise that the murderer had been clever enough to lay two separate sets of false clues—one meant to be seen through, and one meant to mislead."

"Yes, we got to that, too, though we didn't put it quite as you do."

"Quite so. Well, as soon as I reached that conclusion, it became clear that the murderer had strong reasons for removing, not only your two cousins, but also your stepfather. My next step, therefore, was to discover who would be most likely to inherit Sir Vernon Brooklyn's money if Mr. Walter Brooklyn was safely out of the way."

"So that brought you to Carter Woodman at once?"

"In a sense, yes. But of course at that stage I had no sort of proof. I set out to prove what was only a theory."

"Yes, that was what we did. Tell us what you found out," said Ellery, half-rising from his chair in his excitement.

"You remember that Mr. Walter Brooklyn's stick was found in Mr. Prinsep's room. Well, I succeeded in proving that Mr. Brooklyn had left that stick in Carter Woodman's office on the day of the murders.”

“Lord, we never thought of that,” said Ellery.

“Moorman, whom you know, admitted that to me, not knowing who I was. I got it out of him when he thought I was merely a client taking an outside interest in the case. He didn’t realise that it was of importance.”

“And that was your proof?” asked Joan, with an air of disappointment.

“Dear me, Miss Cowper, I should be very sorry to try to hang a man on such evidence. That was only a beginning. What puzzled me was that, whereas the weapon with which Mr. George Brooklyn was killed was found on the scene of the murder, there was no sign of any weapon which could have killed Mr. Prinsep. So I made a thorough fresh search, and at last, on the roof of the building which projects over towards the coach-yard, I found the weapon, where the murderer had thrown it out of sight. It was a bag filled with small-shot.”

“But I don’t see how you could prove whose it was.”

“One moment, Mr. Ellery. I took that bag away, and went carefully through its contents. Among them I found two tiny scraps of paper, obviously part of an order, or a memorandum of an order, for garden bulbs. When I went to the desk there just now, it was to confirm my view that the writing was Carter Woodman’s. I was right.”

“So that proved it?” said Joan.

“I would not go so far as to say that,” said Superintendent Wilson. “But it made a case, with certain other points which you probably know as well as I—Woodman’s financial difficulties, and so on. I had not, however, finished my case. In fact, when I came here, I was pursuing my investigations. Your presence and that of the inspector were quite unexpected. Indeed, I may say that you interrupted me.”

“Sorry and all that,” said Ellery. “But, you see, we had

finished our case, and proved Carter Woodman's guilt so that he knew the game was up. Hence the end of the story as you saw it just now."

"I suggest, Mr. Ellery—and Miss Cowper—that, in view of what we both know, the only possible course is to pool our information. I have told you my evidence. Will you be good enough now to tell me yours?"

Joan and Ellery looked at each other, and Joan nodded. They both realised that it was inevitable that they should tell Superintendent Wilson all they knew.

"You tell him, Bob. I'm not up to it," said Joan, smiling faintly. "But, superintendent, you realise, don't you, how anxious we have been that this horrible story should not come to light. It has caused misery enough already: the telling of it will only cause more."

"I understand," said the superintendent.

"Then can't we still keep it to ourselves?" said Joan, with a note of hope in her voice.

The superintendent shook his head. "I suppose you realise," he said, "that you have both committed a very serious offence. But I won't be too hard on you—especially as you have shown yourselves such creditable amateurs in my line of business," he added with a smile. "But I am afraid the whole story must come out now. There is really no question about that."

"But surely," said Joan, "there's no one to try now: so you can't have a trial. I don't see why you should want to drag the whole beastly story to light. It will——"

"Pardon me, Miss Cowper. There will have to be an inquest on Carter Woodman, and you and Mr. Ellery will have to tell what you know."

"But can't we say he committed suicide—it's quite true, he did, and leave it at that," said Joan.

"Yes," Ellery put in, "and give evidence about his

embarrassed financial position as a reason for taking his life."

"Quite impossible," said the superintendent. "I fear the story must come out; but, as there will be no trial, there will not really be very much publicity. You will do best to tell the whole story at the inquest. It will all blow over very soon."

"But what about poor Helen—I mean Mrs. Woodman?" said Joan.

"I am afraid she will have to bear it as best she can."

So it was done. At the inquest the whole story was told, both by Joan and Ellery and by Superintendent Wilson. The papers the next day were full of it, and full, too, of compliments both to the professionals and to the amateurs on the skill shown in unravelling the mystery. But that same day came a parliamentary crisis. The old Prime Minister resigned, and a new one—in the name of conservatism and tranquillity—took his place. Parliament was dissolved, and the drums beat and beacons flared in anticipation of an "appeal to the people." In a few days, the Brooklyn mystery was forgotten, except by those directly concerned and by a few specialists in the records of crime.

Joan and Ellery, of course, are married, and quite disgustingly rich, now that Sir Vernon is dead. They live at Liskeard House when they are in town, and Ellery is managing director of the Brooklyn Corporation. He has made many attempts to get Marian to return to the stage; and perhaps he will yet succeed. For he has just written a play in which, she agrees, the leading part was made for her. Family matters keep Joan rather busy at present; but her first play, produced a year ago by the Brooklyn Corporation, was a great success. She is thinking of collaborating with her husband in another, with a strong detective interest.

Ellery summed up the situation the other day, when he and Joan were talking over the days of the great Brooklyn mystery. "Well, my dear, it was sad about poor old George, but you

must agree that the other two were really a good riddance."
And, although one of them had been in a way her suitor, I
think Joan did agree. But all she said was "Poor Marian!"

THE END